THE

FRENCH COURT AND SOCIETY

REIGN OF LOUIS XVI. AND FIRST EMPIRE

VOL. II.

*REIGN
OF LOUIS XVI. AND FIRST EMPIRE.
BY CATHERINE CHARLOTTE,
LADY JACKSON*

*IN TWO VOLUMES
VOLUME II.*

WILDSIDE PRESS

Large Paper Edition

This edition is limited to one thousand copies, of which this is Number................

CONTENTS OF VOL. II.

CHAPTER I.

PAGE

The Revolution. — Legends of the Revolution. — The 5th of May, 1789. — The Bas Bréton Deputy. — A Day of Hope. — Overruled by M. Necker. — The Assembling of the States. — Royalty, Nobility, and the *Canaille*. — The Entry of Mirabeau. — A Sensation.— A Memorable Day. — The Financial Budget. — The Address of M. de Barentin. — The *Boudoir* Ministry. — Exit of the Grandees. — Exit of the *Canaille* 1

CHAPTER II.

Waiting in Vain. — The Five Weeks' Struggle. — Death of the Dauphin. — Court Etiquette. — The Last Vacant Niche. — The National Assembly. — A Royal *Séance* Announced. — " *Au Jeu de Paume !* " — The Cable Cut; the Vessel Launched. — The Disciples of Beccaria. — Joining the National Assembly. — The Three Orders Assemble. — The Rights of Man.— Open Air Political *Réunions*. — The *Gardes Françaises*. — The Meditated *Coup d'État*. — A Bold Stroke of Policy. — The King of the *Canaille*. — M. Necker Receives His *Congé* . . 15

CHAPTER III.

"By Order of the King." — Sunday in Old Paris. — " *Vive la Liberté !* " — Camille Desmoulins. —Green or Red ? — " *Vive Necker !* " " *Vive d'Orléans !* " — A Deputation to the King. — The Baron de Besenval. — The *Bourgeois* Soldiers. — A Search for Arms. — "Beware! Beware!" — Paris Betrayed. — A Raid on Les Invalides. — " *La Bastille ! La Bastille !* " — A Shout of Triumph ! — Pressed to Surrender. — Surrendered, Not Taken. — A

vi   CONTENTS

PAGE

Hideous Spectacle. — Cagliostro's Prophecy. — A Day
of Doubtful Glory. — " It Is a Revolt, Then ? " — Hasty
Departures. — The Sovereign People. — The *Abbé*, Too,
Must Away. — The King Visits Paris. — The National
Guard. — The *Tricolor*. — Return of the Citizen King . 31

CHAPTER IV.

Recalled. — From Bâle to Paris. — A Triumphant Return.
— "*Au Ministre Adoré.*" — A General Amnesty. — The
Amnesty Revoked. — " The St. Bartholomew of Abuses."
— The Fourth of August. — The Assembly Constituent.
— A Revolutionary Sect. — Defective Pedigrees. — What
is the *Tiers État?* — The Blessings of Freedom. — " *Vive
le Tiers État!* ".   55

CHAPTER V.

Futile Intrigues. — Count Fersen. — Count Fersen's Mission. — Establishing the Constitution. — Rights of Man.
— Trees of Liberty. — A Jest of the Comte d'Artois. —
Cazotte's Prediction. — The Cart and the Scaffold. —
A Warning Note. — Predestined Victims. — Consternation in Paris. — A Mysterious Lady. — A Wearer of
Royal Robes. — Release of the Captive Queen. — The
Roarings of a Tempest. — Mirabeau Destitute. — Apathy
of Mind   67

CHAPTER VI.

The Royal Hunt. — A Prospect of Famine. — A Military
Banquet. — A Fatal Want of Foresight. — Fruitless Projects. — " The King is Lost! " — "*À Mort la Messaline!*"
— Attack on the Hôtel de Ville. — Supplicating the
King. — March of the Patriot Soldiers. — Preparing for
a Defence. — The Pretty Young *Poissarde.* — The Escape Frustrated. — Waiting the Course of Events. — A
Strong-minded Woman. — The *Avant-Coureur*. — Unjustly
Blamed. — Adieu to Versailles   82

CHAPTER VII.

" *Sang de Foulon.*" — Revolutionary Fashions. — Death of
Joseph II. — The Patriotic Fund. — "*Bijoux à la Consti-*

CONTENTS

PAGE

tution." — Madame de Genlis's Brooch. — Louis Philippe. — The New Departments. — The Iron Safe. — A Neglected Royal Dwelling. — The Duc de Liancourt's Dinners. — Pity for Louis XVI. — The *Salon* of 1789 and 1790. — An Eloquent Lesson of Liberty. — Sandals and Togas. — " Charles the Ninth." — An Ardent Patriot. — Slaying Royalty. — Talma. — The Dramatist Chénier. — A Popular Drama 98

CHAPTER VIII.

An Exciting Period. — A Fashionable Mania. — Robespierre's Protest. — A Lively Subject. — Mirabeau and the Queen. — Poetically Ugly. — Saving the Monarchy. — Too Late! Too Late! — "*La Grande Trahison!*" — Proposed Federal *Fête* 116

CHAPTER IX.

Levelling the Champ de Mars. — The Eve of the Federal *Fête*. — Arrival of the Federals. — Marching to Quarters. — Bishop Talleyrand. — The Oriflamme of France. — "*Au Sein de sa Famille.*" — The Constitutional Oath. — An Enviable Privilege. — The People's Thanksgiving. — Frenchmen and Freemen. — Poor Madame Necker! — The Icy Hand of Death. — Retiring into Private Life . 124

CHAPTER X.

The Legislative Assembly. — Mirabeau and Barnave. — " The Heroine of the Gironde." — Roland's Letter to Louis XVI. — Planting a Tree of Liberty. — The King's Great Courage. — Bonaparte and Bourrienne. — A Bold Front. — The Duke's Manifesto. — The Queen's Letters to Fersen. — Comte Roederer and the Queen. — Lodged in the Temple. — Lucile Desmoulins. — The Queen's Sponges and Brushes. — A Grand Turn-out. — Qualms of Conscience 136

CHAPTER XI.

The Convention. — The Year One of the Republic. — Sentence of Death. — Marat and Robespierre. — Charlotte Corday. — The Antechamber of Death. — A Startling

Contrast. — The Witnesses. — Condemned to Death. — The Execution. — Sanson Overworked. — Despatched in Batches. — A *Réunion* of Old Friends. — Cécile Rénault. — Playing the God. — " Perish the Traitor ! the Tyrant ! " 150

CHAPTER XII.

General Paoli. — The Bonaparte Family. — General Cartaux. — The Siege of Toulon. — Serjeant Junot. — Robespierre's *Protégé*. — General Hoche. — Provisionally Suspended. — Bonaparte a Prisoner. — Junot's Defence of His Friend. — The Irony of Fate. — The Future Emperor. — Railing at Fate. — Junot in Love with Pauline. — A Faithful Friend. — A Hand, a Heart, and £48 a Year. — Fréron's "*Jeunesse Dorée*." — The "*Bals des Victimes*." — Marie Antoinette's Laces. — Bonaparte's Star Looms Clearer. — Agitation and Alarm. — Bonaparte Reinstated. — The 13th Vendémiaire. — Bonaparte's Recompense 164

CHAPTER XIII.

Supplying the Army. — A Lucky Fellow. — Bonaparte and His Aide-de-camp. — A Gratifying Change. — First Meeting with Joséphine. — Diane-Hébé. — "*Le Bon Bouilly*." — Offers of Marriage. — Departure for Italy. — Madame Campan. — *Grandes Dames* of the Empire. — The Impetuous Tide of Victory. — A Wife and a Thousand *Louis d'Or*. — " Soldiers of Italy ! " — The Price of an Armistice. — An Independent Conqueror. — Spoken *Rêveries*. — Bonaparte's Views and Aims. — The *Dolce far Niente*. — Joséphine's Victories. — A Portrait of Bonaparte. — An Admiring Contemporary. — " Necker's Intriguing Daughter." — Général Augereau. — The Treaty of Campo-Formio. — Jealous Relatives. — A Present to Joséphine. — The Return to Paris 184

CHAPTER XIV.

Signs of a Change. — The Regency of the Revolution. — The Prince of the Republic. — Enter Aspasia and Pericles. — Fruits of the 18th Fructidor. — An Attempt to Veil Vice. — Barras's Grand Dinners. — A Long Stride Forward. — The Return of Old Friends. — Building a Fortune. — The Contractors' Wives. — Monsieur and

CONTENTS ix

PAGE

Madame Privas. — *Adieu! Ma Bonne Dame.* — Results of the Revolution. — M. de Talleyrand. — The Luxembourg *Fête*. — The Peacemaker. — "*La Grande Nation.*" — The Fraternal Embrace. — Examining the Crown Diamonds. — Rival Beauties. — Imperial Rehearsals. — The *Tricolor* Insulted. — A Hasty Departure. — The Château of La Malmaison 208

CHAPTER XV.

The Scientific Party. — Departure for Egypt. — False Hopes. — The Returned Exiles. — Memories of the Past. — The *Salon* Talleyrand. — Madame Grandt. — A Political Debating Club. — Madame de Staël. — A "*Chevalier des Dames.*" — Joséphine's Thursday *Réunions.* — Joséphine's Extravagance. — Artists and *Littérateurs.* — "L'Abbé de l'Épée." — "*Les Deux Journées.*" — "*La Belle Laitière.*" — Le Château de Mortfontaine. — M. de la Trénise. — The Battle of Aboukir. — The Return from Egypt. — Reproaching the Government. — The Martyr's Prayer. — A Presentiment Fulfilled 229

CHAPTER XVI.

Love and Jealousy. — Madame Récamier. — The Word "Divorce" First Uttered. — Joséphine in Disgrace. — Reconciliation. — Ineligible Visitors. — A Change of Scene. — "Get Up, Little Creole, Get Up." — Taking Possession. — A Forgotten Inscription. — "*Vive le Général Bonaparte!*" — Violets and Snowdrops. — Joséphine's *Coup d'Essai.* — Death of the Trees of Liberty . 249

CHAPTER XVII.

Clearing the Ground. — "*Le Gouvernement, c'est Moi.*" — Fouché and Talleyrand. — The Sociable Fusion. — Proposals for Peace. — Setting Out for the Wars. — Across the Alps to Marengo. — Impelled by Fate. — Celebrating Marengo. — The *Fête* of Flowers. — Hope Deferred. — Bribing M. de Talleyrand. — A National Recompense. — The Offer of St. Cloud Declined. — Bonaparte's Toast. — Général Junot. — In Search of a Wife. — An Ancient Pedigree. — Madame de Permon. — A Midnight Ceremony. — Duroc and Hortense. — The Peace of Lunéville. — The Peace of Amiens. — Carnot's Remonstrances . 261

CHAPTER XVIII.

Fête of the Concordat. — An Old Fashion Revived. — A Fortunate Coincidence. — The Consular Court. — Private Letters from Paris. — *La Politesse* Still Survives. — A Bridal Dress. — Reviving the Old *Régime.* — La Marquise de Montesson. — The Honour of Cousinship. — The Restraints of Etiquette. — The Consular Household. — Improvements in Paris. — Reading the Great Man to Sleep. — Teaching Grand Manners. — Mademoiselle Georges. — Lucien's Second Marriage. — The New Coinage. — A Court Mourning. — A Disconsolate Widow. — Pauline Becomes "a Real Princess." — Pauline's Ears. — Splendour and Simplicity. — M. le Prince and Madame la Princesse. — The Presentation. — Bitter Tears . . 281

CHAPTER XIX.

Lord Whitworth. — English Travellers in France. — Renewal of Hostilities. — The Visit to Belgium. — The Return to Paris. — A Change in Costume. — Madame de Genlis. — The First Consul in Full Dress. — Theatricals at St. Cloud. — The Hereditary Succession. — Napoleon's Vast Ambition. — Joseph's Advice to Napoleon. — "*Aut Cæsar, aut Nihil.*" — The Camp at Arras. — A Proposal to Sleep on. — Surrendering a Pigtail. — Arrest of the Duc d'Enghien. — The Execution. — The Empire Announced. — The Legion of Honour. — Regretting the Republic. — The Tribune Curée. — A Man of Strong Prejudices. — An Old Edition of Virgil. — Singular Coincidence. — Wounded Vanity 303

CHAPTER XX.

The Coronation. — Arrival of Pius VII. — The Nuptial Benediction. — The Eventful 2d of December. — The Pontifical *Cortège.* — The Crown of Charlemagne. — The Crowning of Joséphine. — The Emperor and Empress. — The Presentation of the Eagles. — Madame Decadi's Marriage. — Louis XVIII. and Gustavus IV. — The Iron Crown. — Doing Credit to the Empire. — The Governor of Paris. — The Arch-Chancellor. — *Un Artiste Culinaire.* — Full Dress Dinners. — A More Genial Host. — The France of Other Days. — *Une Altesse Sérénissime.* — The Modern Charlemagne. — The Viceroy. — The Princesse Elisa. — The Princesse Pauline.

— A Chilling Reception. — The Third Coalition. — Trafalgar and Austerlitz. — A Batch of New Kings. — " King Franconi." — Madame Mère. — A Revival . . . 325

CHAPTER XXI.

The Divorce Again on the *Tapis.* — Establishing the Dynasty. — The Imperial Mausoleum. — Following the Headquarters. — Queen Louise at Jena. — Marriage of Jérôme. — A Fresh Crop of Laurels. — Wanted, a Rich Heiress. — Comte Louis de Narbonne. — The Exiles of Coppet. — A Courtier of the Old School. — A Mysterious Story. — Reinforcing the *Noblesse.* — " If Anything Should Happen." — Convention of Cintra. — Count Metternich. — The Blockade. — Plots, Intrigues ; Europe Arming. — A New Campaign. — The Archduchess Maria Louisa. — Prayers for the Emperor. — The Peace of Vienna 351

CHAPTER XXII.

The Zenith of Glory. — The Hour of Trial. — The Guide of Napoleon's Actions. — Poor Joséphine. — La Malmaison. — The Austrian Marriage. — A Dutiful Daughter. — The Imperial Nuptials. — The New Empress. — " From Gay to Grave." — The Old Love and the New. — The King of Rome. — General Count Neipperg. — The Russian Campaign. — Consolation. — His Majesty of Rome. — Death of Joséphine. — Return of Louis XVIII. — Saint Helena 370

LIST OF ILLUSTRATIONS

VOLUME II.

	PAGE
Joséphine	*Frontispiece*
Trianon	60
The Trial	158
Barras	210
Napoleon in 1800	225
Fesch	328
Berthier	348
Battle of Friedland	380

THE FRENCH COURT AND SOCIETY

REIGN OF LOUIS XVI. AND FIRST EMPIRE

CHAPTER I.

The Revolution. — Legends of the Revolution. — The 5th of May, 1789. — The Bas Bréton Deputy. — A Day of Hope. — Overruled by M. Necker. — The Assembling of the States. — Royalty, Nobility, and the *Canaille*. — The Entry of Mirabeau. — A Sensation. — A Memorable Day. — The Financial Budget. — The Address of M. de Barentin. — The *Boudoir* Ministry. — Exit of the Grandees. — Exit of the *Canaille*.

IT forms no part of the plan of the writer of these volumes to attempt to follow in detail the progress of the French Revolution. For abler pens have already told the harrowing tale of a nation's madness, and the wild excesses of a people drunk with blood. But so inexhaustible is the theme, so absorbing and undying the national interest in that great and terrible drama, that again and again its scenes are revived and new episodes introduced, the tender, the romantic, heightening by vivid contrast the horrors of sanguinary deeds; with which sometimes a characteristic touch of grim humour is blended, causing a shudder rather than a smile.

A French critic, writing on the subject in the pages of the "*Revue Suisse,*" says: "The souvenirs of the great Revolution have a tendency to become for us what the semi-fabulous traditions of a Hercules and a Theseus were for the Greeks. Poetry and the drama seek in it their favourite themes, and the history of that great event, not yet a century old, is gradually giving place to legends that each one interprets according to his own feelings or fancy." Doubtless there is truth in this. Imagination has occasionally added some trait of horror to crimes sufficiently revolting in their own naked barbarity. Sinners have been invested with the aureola who had little claim to saintship. Many a mere virago has been put on a pedestal and named a heroine. There can be very few persons, however, who are not familiar with the principal scenes of the great Revolution. It will be therefore sufficient briefly to notice in these pages those only that more immediately concern its outbreak, and relate to the misguided and unfortunate Marie Antoinette; serving also to connect the period when *salons* degenerated into debating clubs, and the court and society of the old French monarchy ended, with that of the renaissance of the social *réunion* under the Consulate, soon to be followed by the splendours of an imperial court.

It was the 5th of May, 1789, — one of the most memorable days in the annals of France. The tapestry displayed on the 4th, on the occasion of the procession of the States General to the Church of St. Louis, still decorated the fronts of the houses in the principal streets of Versailles. The assembling of the States had brought a further large influx of visitors from Paris and the adjacent villages and towns, — each estate of the realm being fully represented, — the people, like their delegates, far outnumbering the rest.

Within the usually quiet precincts of the palace a numerous throng was collected, anxious to catch a glimpse of the aristocratic and high ecclesiastical deputies. Some rolled by in gilded chariots befitting the wearers of mitres and plumes. Others, the poorer clergy and humbler members of the *Tiers État,* — compelled to go to and from Paris since the previous evening, and now travelling together, seemed already inclined to fraternise, — had picked up for their conveyance some very shaky vehicles, which, as well as their horses, had a most tumble-down look. The greater part, however, of the plebeian deputies, being lodged in the neighborhood, made their way to the Grande Salle des Menus on foot, amidst the vociferous cheering of the multitude.

Conspicuous amongst them, though in appearance not of them, — for he wore the ordinary dress of the agricultural class; the vest, belt, and gaiters of the Bas Bréton, — slowly advanced an aged man, with blanched hair flowing over his shoulders, sunburnt face, and deeply furrowed brow. He was a small farmer from Brittany, and his name Gérard. Though one of the deputies of St. Martin de Rennes, a district of that province, he cared not, apparently, to disguise himself in the black woollen garb of a *vilain* of the feudal times, prescribed for the despised *Tiers État* by the queen and her friends, in the *boudoir* council of the Duchesse de Polignac.

The morning of the 5th dawned brightly. Versailles, with its tapestries, its garlands of flowers, its throngs of gaily dressed visitors, wore a festive, smiling air. To many it was indeed a joyous day, a day of hope, the assembling of the States General, in itself a Revolution, having for many months past been looked forward to as the dawn of national liberty.

There may have been hope also, though scarcely mingled with joy at that time, in the heart of the king. But his extraordinary apathy of feeling at least saved him from those acute sensations of fear and trembling which agitated the queen — agitated her almost to fainting when, on the previous day, the sinister cry of " *Vive d'Orléans! Vive d'Orléans!* " met her ear as the royal part of the procession, otherwise unheeded, passed slowly along the crowded streets. The Duc d'Orléans at that cry, affecting an open disregard of the etiquette regulating the march of the procession, chose to separate himself from the princes of the blood and to mingle with the *noblesse*, showing also some indication of a desire to join the deputies of the *Tiers État*.

Again, on this 5th of May, the queen is destined to hear the same applauding cry. It resounds, too, in the midst of the pomp and pageantry intended to overawe the representatives of the people, — to impress them with a sense of their utter insignificance, and the humble part they must expect to play in the national conferences they are so grudgingly summoned to join. Marie Antoinette's hatred of the Duc d'Orléans is the chief cause of his popularity; for the people see in her their enemy, though no hero in him. She would have persuaded the king to run counter to the will of the nation and refuse to convoke the States; probably he would have done so had there not been moments when court surveillance was withdrawn, and he was open to opposite counsels. Being promised, she suggested the assembling of the States at Soissons, or other town not less than fifty or sixty leagues distant from Paris. In this she was overruled by M. Necker. He saw greater danger in adopting a course so likely to exasperate the already excited people than that the queen sought to avoid by it. Ultimately Versailles was fixed on as the most suitable locality both for the installation of the *États Généraux*, and for the holding of their conferences.

This assembling of the Three Estates of the Realm in the great hall of Les Menus of Versailles, this solemn opening of their first session, is a grand and imposing spectacle. The hall is draped with violet satin, woven in gold with the *fleurs-de-lys* and the arms of France. The king presides. He is seated on a throne of violet velvet, with canopy of the same richly embroidered with *fleurs-de-lys* and fringed with gold. The queen is also there, her seat placed a little below the king's. On the left are ranged the princes and princesses of the blood; on the right the dukes and peers. Around them are the great officers of the household. All wear their robes of state.

Towards the further end of the vast hall, and ranging from the centre towards the sides, are the deputies of the *noblesse* and the clergy; forming most effective and picturesque groups. Behind them are eight heralds-at-arms in glittering costume. The Keeper of the Seals, in his robes of office, stands near the steps of the throne, not far from which is placed a table covered with green cloth, with seats around it for the ministers. Ladies and gentlemen in full court dress occupy, as spectators, the seats between the pillars on both sides of the hall. The rows of benches behind the heralds, and at the extreme end of the building, are not yet occupied. But when this grand assemblage of royal and noble personages have taken the places severally assigned them, a door opening on a passage that leads to some stabling in the rear of the palace is suddenly thrown back. A crowd enters, pressing forward with some confusion; for both passage and entrance are narrow, and these five or six hundred men have been massed together and waiting under a shed for the last three hours, with the further humiliation and trial of temper of being then called over severally by name, though possessing each his *billet*, or card of entry.

But the *boudoir* council rates them as *canaille;* such treatment is therefore good enough for them. And, indeed, they are but a homely looking set. Their humble, dingy attire strikingly contrasts with that of the glittering throng into whose august presence they now are graciously admitted, and by whom, as they cross the hall, they are passed, as it were, in review. These men are the deputies of the *Tiers État* or Third Estate of the Realm. Some of them probably have never before witnessed a scene of such dazzling splendour as that which now meets their gaze within the Grande Salle. It has been calculated that the effect of this royal state and magnificence will greatly tend to repress whatever aspiring thoughts those rustic and plebeian breasts may have cherished.

The very names of these men have furnished infinite amusement to the company of triflers forming the queen's and Comte d'Artois's intimate circle. The king himself, taking up the list of deputies, asked, with a derisive smile, as he glanced over it: "What would have been the general opinion concerning him had he formed his council from men obscure in name and birth as these?" He forgot that they were not obscure in the districts they represented; and that, though unknown to him, they were well known to their fellow citizens who had elected them. Few, perhaps, besides Mirabeau — who enters with a haughty, defiant air, that raises murmurs among the *noblesse*, but excites the admiration of Madame de Staël, who says: "He was grand in his ugliness" — could have produced his four quarterings, or his *de* or *de la*, denoting that he was somebody. Yet they were the *élite* of their class. Among them were men of education, distinguished talent, and brilliant oratorical powers. Generally, too, they were animated by a loyal and patriotic spirit. This frankly responded to by the king and the two upper estates, it seems not only possible, but even very probable, that the tottering throne of France might not yet have fallen, but, by united effort, have even been firmly fixed on an enduring basis.

But the deputies are now in their places, and the king, putting on his plumed hat, rises to address the assembled States. A momentary fluttering of feathers ensues, for the *noblesse* cover also at the signal given by the king, and the dignitaries of the Church put on their square-topped caps. Unhesitatingly the commonalty follow the example of their betters, and don their quaint, coarse felt hats. This audacity causes a momentary yet no slight sensation. It is contrary to all precedent; but so much of the old court etiquette has been set aside with impunity by the privileged classes during the last twelve months that this violation of it by the lower strata must pass unnoticed, too. Otherwise the Third Estate of the Realm should not only have remained uncovered, but, according to olden custom, have knelt while listening or replying to the gracious words of their sovereign lord and king.

Louis XVI. speaks with some emotion. Perhaps he is not quite sincere when he declares that it gives him heartfelt happiness to see gathered around him the representatives of the nation of which it is his highest glory to be the ruler. He mentions the public debt and the penury of the state, and announces a diminution in his future household expenditure. He complains of the feverish restlessness of the people, but suggests no measures for allaying it. He recommends union to the Three Estates — trusts that a happy accord may reign in their councils, and this "5th of May be ever memorable as the beginning of an era of happiness and prosperity for France."

With one knee on the steps of the throne, the Keeper of the Seals, M. de Barentin, then delivers a long and tedious discourse in a tremulous, feeble voice. It is little more than a panegyric, setting forth the great virtues of the king and the benefits he has conferred on his subjects; also his extreme indulgence in extending "pardon even to those advocates of false and extravagant maxims, by favour of which they had sought to substitute pernicious chimeras for the unalterable principles of the monarchy." Much impatience is evinced during the delivery of this injudicious harangue. But to the Keeper of the Seals succeeds M. Necker. He is greeted with enthusiasm by the deputies of the *Tiers État*, and also by part of the *noblesse*. For the moment he is the popular minister. What he has to say has been eagerly awaited. He speaks for three hours, and his financial budget is the chief theme of his discourse. It is sufficiently able and lucid, and but slightly dashed with his customary sentimentalism, — M. Necker on this occasion confining himself to the discussion of matters with which he is perhaps more thoroughly acquainted than any other financier of the day.

As he proceeds, a feeling of disappointment comes over the assembly. It is more especially noticeable in the deputies of the Third Estate.

Probably M. Necker becomes conscious of this falling off of interest in his discourse; for, when about to conclude, he seems to remember that he has yet some remarks to offer on the vexed subject of the method of taking the votes of the three orders of the States-General, whether on questions of finance or of proposed reforms in the system of government which may be submitted to them for discussion.

It is of vital importance to the deputies of the people that this question should be promptly and permanently settled. By right it devolves on the king to determine it; as also clearly to define the rules that should govern the conduct of business in the General Assembly of the States. It is so new a thing to both nobles and people to participate in any act of government, that naturally they seek for direction at the outset. The king has expressed a hope that harmony may reign in their councils, but has suggested no regulations for their guidance. He has, however, through the address of M. de Barentin, given them to understand that the subjects he will allow them to discuss are few indeed. Yet the public look to the Assembly of the Three Estates for "the regeneration of France." And Louis XVI. would have done well to associate himself with them, and to have taken the lead in this great national work.* But in fact he rather looks

* Mignet's "*Histoire de la Révolution Française.*"

forward to the dissensions that may arise in the councils of the three orders to furnish him with a pretext for annulling the new power he has so unwillingly called into existence.

Unhappily, too, he is now swayed by the short-sighted and vindictive policy of the queen and her favourites, and the arrogant opinions of the Comte d'Artois and his partisans. No pains have been spared, no flattery or seduction omitted, to gain over the most influential deputies of the two privileged orders to the views of the *boudoir* ministry; that, by systematically opposing the pretensions of the Third Order to interfere in affairs of state, they may the more effectually crush those presumptuous plebeians.

The future of France — the Revolution itself, whether it should be or should not be — depended on the separation or coalition of the three orders, which (as the deputies of the Third very reasonably suggested) formed no general assembly if divided. Convoked not merely to consent to the imposition of certain taxes, and to limit the liberty of the press, but for higher and legislative purposes, unanimity in their views was essential, and more likely to be attained, they conceived, by assembling in one apartment than in three. Their measures would also carry more weight with them, they imagined, voted, *par tête*, as one general assembly than separately as three conflicting orders.

M. Necker had obtained a double representation for the Third Estate, because the whole burden of taxation had hitherto fallen on them. And he is said to have considered the crisis in France more in the light of a financial than a social one. Desiring therefore, while retaining favour with the people, to give no umbrage to the court, he refrained on this occasion from expressing any decided opinion when referring to the question of separate voting. But by this reticence he gave umbrage to both parties. His discourse being ended, the Keeper of the Seals announced the session of the States General opened, the deputies being ordered to assemble on the morrow for the separate verification of their powers.

The king and queen, with the princes and princesses of the blood, then withdrew, followed by the grand officers of the household. The rest of the distinguished company, including the deputies of the *noblesse* and clergy, also dispersed, leaving the *salle* by the porch of the grand avenue.

Those of the Third Order, having witnessed the departure of this brilliant and stately procession, — the last royal pageant the queen appeared in wearing her mantle and robes of state, — made their exit also, but by the back door at which they had entered. However, before they separated — assuming the supremacy on the strength of superior numbers — they determined on forwarding a notice to the deputies of the clergy and *noblesse* requesting their attendance on the following morning in the *Salle des États* (assigned to them as the most numerous of the three orders), there to verify their powers with them in common.

CHAPTER II.

Waiting in Vain. — The Five Weeks' Struggle. — Death of the Dauphin. — Court Etiquette. — The Last Vacant Niche. — The National Assembly. — A Royal *Séance* Announced — "*Au Jeu de Paume!*" — The Cable Cut; the Vessel Launched. — The Disciples of Beccaria. — Joining the National Assembly. — The Three Orders Assemble. — The Rights of Man. — Open Air Political *Réunions.* — The *Gardes Françaises.* — The Meditated *Coup d'État.* — A Bold Stroke of Policy. — The King of the *Canaille.* — M. Necker Receives His *Congé.*

N the morrow of the installation of the States General, the deputies of the Third Order assembled in the *Salle des États*. In vain — as indeed was expected — they awaited the arrival of their colleagues of the clergy and *noblesse*. Their message, when received, was treated with derisive contempt, mingled with surprise at their presumption in sending it. The Third Order, however, were determined that no question of taxation, or of civil and criminal law reform, should be entered upon until the preliminary ceremony of a general verification of powers had taken place. They despatched, therefore, a second message to the two upper orders, again requesting their attendance, and adjourning their sitting in consequence until the following

day. Then began that remarkable five weeks' struggle — on the one hand to compel by persistence, on the other to weary out by inattention — which, on the 17th of June, on the motion of the Abbé Sieyès, resulted in the deputies of the people, after verifying their own powers, constituting themselves a National Assembly.

The first decree of this Assembly was an act of sovereignty which placed the deputies of the clergy and *noblesse* in subjection to them, by the declaration that the legislative power was indivisible, and all taxes illegal that had not received the people's sanction. This memorable sitting was prolonged far into the night, — several provisionary enactments being also made for the avoidance of any temporary inconvenience the previous decrees might occasion the government. The forethought as well as the firmness of the Assembly in these proceedings received the enthusiastic approval of the nation.

In the early days of June, while the unwavering opposition of the Third Order to any separation of the States General was filling the court with amazement, and occupying it with projects for their suppression, the death of the first dauphin occurred at Meudon. It was an event that had long been expected. He had been a weakly child from his birth, afflicted with a spinal disease, causing deformity and a gradual wasting away. At the age of seven and a half years death kindly freed him from suffering, and spared him the further misery of sharing the cruel fate to which the younger child, who now became dauphin, was destined. The Three Estates at this time were alike royalists in their sentiments. The Third, therefore, willingly joined in a deputation to Meudon to sprinkle holy water at the feet of the dauphin, whose body lay there in state in a *chapelle ardente*, or funeral chamber.

They were received by the Duc de Brézé, grand master of the ceremonies, who, leading the way, conducted them to the chapel. Advancing towards the body, after bowing very low, he said in a most lugubrious tone: "Monseigneur, a deputation from the Three Estates of the Realm waits on you." Mirabeau and the Abbé Sieyès formed part of this deputation. They probably may have been acquainted with the court etiquette on such occasions, and have found nothing surprising in it. Some provincial notaries, however, and others of equally rustic notions, were not only amazed at being thus formally announced to a dead child, but were also shocked at it, as "an act of royal pride and presumption, and extreme profanity." It was customary also — but they may not have been aware of that — to place food by the side of the coffin daily, at the hours at which the deceased royal personage had usually dined or taken other repasts. The queen, it was asserted, never cared for this poor child, her affection being wholly lavished on her second son, the Duc de Normandie. The dauphin himself had exhibited a strong aversion to his governess, the Duchesse de Polignac, and even much dislike towards the queen; for rancour and jealousy existed to so great an extent in this intriguing and most depraved court, that favourites, both male and female, did not scruple to play on the feelings of even so young a prince as the dauphin, if their objects, whether to obtain favour or to seek revenge, could in any measure be served by it. He was buried — as were most of the Bourbon kings and princes — with little ceremony and very much haste; his coffin filling the last vacant niche at St. Denis in the tomb of the Kings of France. This was told to the queen, who, regarding it as of sinister augury, shuddered with emotion. She was exceedingly superstitious, and but recently the guttering of two or three candles, causing their flame to be extinguished, had greatly affected her as an ill-omened occurrence.

After the burial of the dauphin, the court went to Marly, — the queen fearing the influence of M. Necker's pacific councils on the wavering mind of the king. He had already suggested a measure for the conciliation and union of the Three Estates. The Third would have acceded to it, but the privileged orders peremptorily rejected it. The deliberations of the former, however, became far more definite and decisive after the 10th of June.

They were joined on that day by the Parisian deputies, of whom the famous Abbé Sieyès was the last elected, and who has the reputation of having both begun and ended the French Revolution.

The queen, the Polignacs, the Comte d'Artois, and generally all who composed the *boudoir* council of Marly, now urged on the king that the moment had arrived when the safety of the throne and the well-being of the nation required him to assert his royal authority, and unflinchingly to crush those factious Commons by one decisive blow. The Cardinal de Rochefoucauld had hurried from Versailles to implore the king to consent to a dissolution of the States, and to delay not an hour in issuing a royal decree suppressing the *soi-disant* National Assembly and annulling its enactments. Even M. Necker was indignant at the course adopted by the Third Estate. He imagined that he held the deputies of that order in leading-strings. But they had broken away from his guidance, upset his calculations, and, instead of yielding a ready obedience to his plans, now sought to impose their own on him. M. Necker was fain to seek consolation in the embraces and sympathetic tears of his worshipping wife and daughter.

The king was undergoing all the misery of halting between two opinions. In this fluctuating state of mind he passed the 19th of June. At last, late in the evening, he was prevailed on by unwise counsellors — who knew not that "of all hazards to which royalty should least be exposed is that of being disobeyed " * — to allow the master of the ceremonies to put up a notice at the entrance of the *Salle des États* informing M. Bailly — whom these presumptuous deputies of the people had elected President of the National Assembly — that their sittings must be suspended. "The king," the notice went on to state, "proposed holding a royal *séance* on the 23d, and in the interval workmen would be employed in preparing the *Salle des États*." Disregarding this notice, which was affixed in the night, M. Bailly proceeded as usual to the hall on the morning of the 20th. He found it surrounded by soldiers, who with crossed bayonets opposed his entrance and that of the deputies, who had begun to arrive in large numbers.

Deprived of their usual place of meeting, where shall their *séance* be held? where find a sufficiently spacious and suitable *locale?* — for they are resolved not to suspend their sittings. "At Marly!" respond some of the deputies; "let us hasten to Marly and assemble under the windows of the palace." "No, no! to Paris!" exclaim others, "where we shall be under the protection of the people." Neither of these suggestions seem to be generally approved. Some consultation en-

* Mignet's "*Histoire de la Révolution Française.*"

sues. During the lull, a calm, firm voice (it is that of Dr. Guillotin, whose name is destined to such fearful renown) proposes the *Jeu de Paume*. "*Au Jeu de Paume! Au Jeu de Paume!*" is echoed on all sides. It is a happy thought, for the *Jeu de Paume*, or Tennis Court, is spacious, is near at hand; and immediately the deputies, headed by their president, and accompanied by an enthusiastic multitude — guarded also by the same soldiers who had barred their entrance to the hall — march thither in procession.

Assembled within the four bare walls of the *Jeu de Paume*, these representatives of the people, standing, bareheaded, their hands raised towards heaven, their hearts full of the sanctity of their mission, solemnly repeating the oath after their president, swear, severally and collectively (one man only of the six hundred present excepted *), "never to separate until France has received from them a Constitution based on firm and solid foundations." By this bold step was the Revolution initiated. By the fatalities of the *séance royale* of the 23d it was rendered irrevocable, or, in the words of the Abbé Sieyès, the cable was cut and

---

* This man, by name Martin d'Auch, added to his signature — each man being required to sign the formula — the word *opposant*, and repeated it aloud. It gave rise to much indignation, and a tumult seeming likely to ensue, a way of egress was pointed out to him. He speedily availed himself of it, — glad, no doubt, to escape from the chance of being very unceremoniously thrust out.

the vessel of the Revolution launched. Able French writers are of opinion that the king might even then have piloted this vessel. But to have done so he must have possessed prudence, have acted with good faith, and, making a merit of necessity, have frankly accepted a position become inevitable, yet, by this wise course, certain of amelioration.

But the king and the queen, with their favourites and counsellors, were of a different opinion. The *séance* of the 23d was held with all the *appareil* and state of the "bed of justice" of the old *régime* — "*Je veux, j'ordonne, je commande*" forming the burden of the king's speech, which was read by the Keeper of the Seals (kneeling on both knees). This was followed up by bringing troops from a distance, surrounding Paris with a *corps d'armée*, and filling Versailles with foreign regiments. Military preparations were being hurried on, trains of artillery arriving from the frontiers, — giving the vicinity of the royal residence the appearance of a camp, and creating alarm in the minds of the people. "What sinister projects were on foot? Against what enemy," it was asked, "was the king about to make war?"

The National Assembly, meanwhile, was diligently engaged in preparing the new Constitution. Several young lawyers from the provinces, students of the works of the Italian political writer, Beccaria, were anxiously endeavouring to replace the old vengeful and cruel criminal code of France by one founded on the theories of their master, — at once more just and humane, and practically more efficacious in deterring from crime. It is singular that almost the first thoughts of the originators of a revolution that was to drench France with blood, and of whose lawless and sanguinary excesses the greater part were themselves to become victims (the Revolution, like Silenus, devouring its own children, as Danton said), should have been of justice and mercy. They desired to abolish the infamous laws that inflicted the penalty of death for the most insignificant offences, and still tolerated, to the disgrace of a civilised country, the horrible torturing of its criminals. The nation therefore looked hopefully forward to the promulgation of the promised Constitution.

The Assembly had acquired also a better claim to the title of National; for on the evening of the 23d, after the famous *séance royale*, forty-seven deputies of the *noblesse* — amongst whom were the Ducs d'Orléans and de Montmorency, the Marquis de La Fayette, the Marquis de Sillery-Genlis, the Vicomte de Beauharnais (husband of the future Empress Joséphine), and other influential persons of their order — appeared in the *Salle des États*, verified their powers, and joined the National Assembly. A large number of the "inferior clergy" had done so on the preceding day, when the deputies were assembled in the Church of

St. Louis, — the Comte d'Artois having deprived them of the tennis-court, by engaging it on pretence of playing tennis there with his friends. On the 24th, Cardinal Juigné, Archbishop of Paris, the Abbé Talleyrand, now Bishop of Autun, with several other prelates, followed the example of the *curés;* and M. Necker, disapproving the measures suggested by court intriguers, and calculated only to foment civil war, tendered his resignation. But the king, embarrassed by the critical state of public affairs, would not accept it. He also wrote to Cardinal de Rochefoucauld, enjoining him to convey his wishes, and, if need were, his commands, to those deputies of his order who still held aloof from the Assembly, that further opposition should cease. For the same object he sent for the Duc de Luxembourg, and on the 27th the three orders of the States General assembled in the same hall as one body, — at first maintaining distinct places; but this rule was gradually relaxed, and they took their seats as they voted, without reference to priority of order.

It, however, soon became evident that both the king's tardy consent to their *réunion,* and his refusal to accept M. Necker's resignation, were mere feints to conceal the real projects of the queen's *camarilla,* from whose pernicious influence, poor man, he could not shake himself free. From the day when the deputies were permitted to resume their sittings in the *Salle des États,* the building had been constantly surrounded by soldiers. The president inquired of the officer in command the object of so very numerous a guard. He replied that it was to prevent the people who flocked in from Paris from entering by the private doors reserved for the deputies. But it was, in fact, to prevent their entrance by any door, as well as to intimidate the Assembly, until the army then encamping round the capital had taken up its positions, and the favourable moment was arrived for dissolving the States General, and bringing rebellious subjects to their senses.

General de La Fayette had laid before the Assembly the declaration of the Rights of Man, as accepted by the United States Congress. He desired that the new French Constitution should be framed after the American pattern; while M. Necker would have had the Assembly take that of England for its model, to which Mirabeau also inclined. His *"Journal des États Généraux,"* afterwards *" Le Courrier de Provence,"* — which, with many others of inferior note, made its appearance at the opening of the States, — gave daily reports of the deliberations of the Assembly. The sale of these *feuilles*, as they were called, was immense. Such, too, the eagerness of the Parisian public to learn what progress the work of reform was making at Versailles, that some Palais Royal orator, possessing himself of a copy of Mirabeau's journal, would mount a table and declaim aloud to an attentively listening audience gathered closely around him, the eloquent harangue of one speaker, the calm reasonings of another, or the violent diatribes some of the deputies occasionally indulged in. This performance would be followed by very unreserved comments on the deputies and their opinions, in language often more forcible than polite; and the questions that had agitated the Assembly would be again debated with much warmth and vehemence at these open air *réunions* and chance gatherings of the people.

Both Paris and Versailles were in a state of great perturbation, and restlessness was spreading to the provinces. In the crowded gardens of the Palais Royal a permanent assembly of the capital seemed to be held — for as one set of revolutionary enthusiasts dispersed another would occupy its place. There too might daily be witnessed the first intoxicating effects of liberty on a people hitherto silent, suffering, and submissive, and scarcely yet free; for the yoke of despotism which had pressed so long and so heavily on them was but loosened, not yet thrown off. For a full release from their burden they looked to the Constitution. They expected it also to provide a remedy for the great widespread distress that prevailed throughout the land.

When, therefore, the constant antagonism of the court towards the National Assembly became known to the people, they assembled tumultuously in the streets and gardens, and a new cry was heard of "*Vive la Nation! Vive le Tiers État! À bas les aristocrates!*" The *Gardes Françaises*, in barracks in Paris, were called out to quell these disturbances. Commanded to fire on the people, they refused; fraternised with them, feasted and drank, and joined in the frantic cries of "*Vive l'Assemblée Nationale!*" Sixteen of these soldiers were put under arrest in the prisons of the Abbaye. The infuriated populace forced the doors and brought forth the prisoners in triumph. At the request of the Assembly, these soldiers were pardoned after, for form's sake, returning for a few hours to close quarters in the Abbaye. But this most effective of the French regiments, both in numbers and training, remained favourable to the popular cause, — the people invariably saluting them as "*Soldats de la patrie.*"

After ten days of tumult and excitement, Paris gradually quieted down and resumed its usual orderly aspect; but it was only in appearance, as when nature is silently assembling her forces in the quietude and calm that precedes the tempest. The king's advisers thought to turn this lull to account, and to hasten the meditated *coup d'état,* by taking the opportunity of more advantageously posting thirty foreign regiments round Paris, and occupying the road between the city and Versailles.* But the Parisians were not un-

* *Mémoires de Marquis de Ferrières.*

observant of these continual military movements. They could not believe them to be wholly objectless. A deputation was therefore sent to Versailles to ask an explanation from the Assembly. Acceding to the proposal of Mirabeau, a respectful address was sent to the king on the 9th of July, informing him that much uneasiness prevailed in the capital in consequence of the massing of large bodies of foreign troops in its immediate vicinity, and praying him to withdraw them. The address was read to the king by M. de Clermont-Tonnerre. He seemed disquieted by the intelligence, and deferred his reply. But the wise *boudoir* council had resolved on a bold stroke of policy that should annihilate the National Assembly, strike terror into the hearts of rebellious citizens, probably fill the Bastille, and restore the good old times of the *ancien régime*.

The next day the king sent word that "the army was assembled round Paris to prevent a recurrence of the shameful scenes and scandalous outrages that had recently taken place there, and had been renewed at Versailles. There also he had quartered troops, but with a view of ensuring the Assembly more freedom of deliberation. He, however," he said, "must be the judge of what military arrangements were or were not necessary in the present agitated state of the public-mind. Yet, if the presence of troops gave umbrage to the Assembly, he was willing to transfer the

States to Noyon or Soissons, and to remove with his court to Compiègne in order to be near at hand to communicate with them."

This was like reviving the old practice of exiling a troublesome Parliament. M. Necker, writing on the events of the Revolution, says that there were so many secrets concealing other secrets in the projects of the court, that he really knew not what was the object of such a proposal, and imagines that the king himself did not know. He thought it probable, however, that the queen and her court, relying on the presence of foreign troops, and expecting further aid, were desirous of urging the king to adopt more arbitrary measures than they dared at once fully disclose to him.

At all events, on the 11th, the entire ministry was changed. There was some hesitation about the dismissal of M. Necker, who had regained his popularity, as Mirabeau said, of "king of the *canaille.*" Maréchal de Broglie opposed it; M. de Bréteuil, though consenting, declared that a hundred thousand troops and a hundred millions in specie would be needed as a counterbalance. The queen replied, unhesitatingly: "And you shall have them." But the king, with tears in his eyes, had just before said to Maréchal de Broglie, who had been summoned from Lorraine to advise with him: "Oh, Marshal, I am indeed unfortunate; I have lost the affection of my subjects, and I have neither army nor finances." * The thoughtless confidence of one speech and the helpless despondency of the other were very characteristic of the speakers.

On the evening of the same day, however, notwithstanding the dread inspired by his great popularity, M. Necker received his *congé*. While at dinner a note from the king desired him to leave the country without delay, and as quietly as possible. So implicitly did he obey the order that, dinner ended, Madame de Staël, whom he left to entertain his guests, was not informed of his dismissal, or made aware that he and Madame Necker were going further than their country house at St. Ouen. There some few preparations for their journey were made, and in less than two hours they again set out, *en route* with all speed, for Switzerland *viâ* Brussels.

* A. Dumas, "*Louis Seize et la Révolution.*"

CHAPTER III.

"By Order of the King." — Sunday in Old Paris. — "*Vive la Liberté!*" — Camille Desmoulins. — Green or Red ? — "*Vive Necker!*" "*Vive d'Orléans!*" — A Deputation to the King. — The Baron de Besenval. — The *Bourgeois* Soldiers. — A Search for Arms. — "Beware! Beware!" — Paris Betrayed. — A Raid on Les Invalides. — "*La Bastille! La Bastille!*" — A Shout of Triumph! — Pressed to Surrender. — Surrendered, Not Taken. — A Hideous Spectacle. — Cagliostro's Prophecy. — A Day of Doubtful Glory. — "It is a Revolt, Then?" — Hasty Departures. — The Sovereign People. — The *Abbé*, Too, Must Away. — The King Visits Paris. — The National Guard. — The *Tricolor*. — Return of the Citizen King.

THE court would seem to have expected that some agitation, if not exactly disturbance, was likely to occur in Paris when M. Necker's dismissal became known. As a precautionary measure, therefore, placards were posted about the city on the night of his departure, exhorting the people, "by order of the king" to remain quietly in their homes on the following day.

The 12th was Sunday, and a remarkably fine summer morning. Consequently, the poorer quarters of the close, stuffy old city were at an early hour nearly emptied of their inhabitants. The

Sunday *fêtes* were then strictly observed; early mass was the rule, outdoor enjoyment afterwards, ending with the theatre in the evening. Notices *de par le roi* meeting them in all directions, took the people by surprise and gave rise to much curiosity, — no special reason being given for them. There had recently been scenes of tumult, and some attacks on the soldiery, yet excitement had greatly calmed down, and Paris was comparatively quiet. Soon the streets were filled with people reading the placards and inquiring of one another of their probable meaning. "Had anything unusual happened, or were they threatened by some unseen danger?" Surprise gradually gave place to indignation; and instead of returning to their homes, they betook themselves to the Palais Royal, the chief revolutionary centre, which speedily became crowded with a noisy, obstreperous mob.

Disdaining the recommendation to keep within doors, the shopkeepers began to put up their shutters, and the citizens, with their families, prepared for their usual weekly excursion to St. Cloud, or to amuse themselves at the Tea Gardens in the neighbourhood of Vincennes, the Bois de Boulogne, or Champs Élysées. The Swiss, Irish, German, and Flemish regiments encamped around the city — and who behaved very well though often attacked — enlivened the usually quiet outskirts by the variety of their uniforms; while disobedience to the royal order to stay at home added the zest of a new pleasure to going out. Citizens whose breasts glowed with the enthusiasm of freedom, hailed each other, as they passed, with the cry of "*Vive la liberté!*" Yet the day would have passed off quietly enough had not the news of M. Necker's dismissal and exile suddenly transpired.

At first none would believe it. It was a ruse, a snare, a device of the enemy. But about four in the afternoon a messenger from the Assembly, escaping the surveillance of the troops posted between Versailles and the capital to cut off communication between them, arrives in breathless haste in the midst of the throng in the Palais Royal, and confirms the startling news.

What is to be done?

The vast crowd, momentarily paralysed, as if by the consciousness of some great and overwhelming calamity coming upon them, eagerly ask what is to be done to avert it. Whoever will point out what measures should be taken, all are prepared to adopt them.

At that moment a young man, of common type of countenance and mean personal appearance,* but very smartly dressed, entered the famous Café de Foy, the small turbulent capital of a small turbulent kingdom — the Palais Royal. The young man was Camille Desmoulins. Soon

* *Mémoires du Comte Miot de Melito.*

after, he appeared in the garden, followed by a number of persons from the *café*. Mounting one of the benches on the side of the Richelieu gallery — a pistol in one hand ; a paper with the account of M. Necker's dismissal in the other — he cried aloud : *"Aux armes!"* then began to harangue the people, who pressed around him, anxious to hear his discourse. What he said was guessed at rather than understood, for excitement increased a natural slight impediment in his speech, and he gesticulated violently. From certain disjointed phrases — " *Necker — son renvoi — le tocsin — St. Barthélemy — Patriotes, Champ de Mars — Égorger — Aux armes! Aux armes !*" etc. — a speech was composed for him ; the intervals being readily filled up by his hearers, who applauded him with extraordinary vehemence. Enthusiasm was easily roused. The few words he had uttered were sufficient. They fell on the ears of the excited mob like sparks on gunpowder. " To arms ! To arms ! Sound the *toscin !*" was the general cry.

But Camille Desmoulins had yet a word or two to address to this frantic assemblage, numbering, it has been computed, not less than ten thousand persons. Plucking a leaf from a branch of the chestnut-tree that waved above, " Shall we take this," he said, "as a sign by which we may recognise and defend one another ? Green is the colour of hope. Or shall we have red, the colour of the Free Order of Cincinnatus ?"

"Green! Green!" is the general response. Immediately the chestnut leaf is placed in the orator's hat; he distributes the novel cockade to those who stand near him; once more he cries, "*Aux armes!*" waves his hat, steps down from his bench, and disappears in the crowd. The people break off branches from the beautiful chestnut-trees of the garden, and scatter their leaves among those who stay to receive them.

But, "To arms! To arms!" is resounding on all sides. The crowd divides; part of them hasten to the Hôtel de Ville. They demand arms, but cannot obtain them, and all are anxious for the honour of sounding the *tocsin*. The other part, after ordering that the theatres be closed, besiege the *atelier* of the sculptor Curtius. They require of him a bust of Necker, which he readily hands to them. "Has he not another of the Duc d'Orléans?" He has a model in wax, which he also allows them to take. (It had been erroneously reported that the duke was also exiled, and at the request of the queen.) These busts are covered with black crape, and a piece of the same material is hung on a pole. Preceded and followed by several hundred persons, both women and men, they are borne through the streets of Paris. The men are uncovered, and insist that the like homage be paid by all spectators and passers-by. "*Chapeaux bas!*" ("Hats off!") they cry; "*Vive Necker!*" "*Vive d'Orléans!*" "*Vive la Nation!*"

Arrived at the Place Vendôme, Necker's bust was thrown down and broken to pieces, during the confusion occasioned by a skirmish between a part of the *Gardes Françaises* and some soldiers of the royal German regiment commanded by Prince Lambesc.

The cause of M. Necker had become the cause of the nation. His dismissal·was no less a surprise to the Assembly at Versailles than to the people of Paris. It excited general indignation, and resulted in a closer *réunion* of the Three Estates. It was seen that no dependence could be placed on the king, and that the queen and her favourites were hurrying both him and themselves to ruin. A deputation was sent to explain to him the dangers menacing the capital, and to urge him to withdraw the troops and confide the safe keeping of Paris to a national militia. Louis's reply was unsatisfactory. The Assembly then unanimously decreed that the king's actual ministry and advisers, of *whatever rank or station* (this was aimed at the queen and the Comte d'Artois), must be held responsible for the unfortunate state of the country. Several other resolutions were agreed to, as necessary in the present position of affairs. Finally, they declared their *séance* permanent until otherwise decreed, the members arranging to relieve each other at stated hours.

Meanwhile, the Bastille had received a reinforcement of Swiss troops, with abundance of ammunition, and the Baron de Besenval had been ordered more closely to invest Paris with his Swiss Guards and chasseurs of Lorraine. The baron disliked the command assigned him, — not that he sympathised with the revolutionary movement, but he did not entirely approve of the measures taken to suppress it. He was second in command of the army, and he and the Duc de Broglie, who commanded in chief, were not entirely agreed on the best mode of distributing their forces. Above all, the baron, a Swiss of ancient family, was immensely rich, and had a splendid hôtel in Paris, which had just undergone redecoration, and was being refurnished in most sumptuous style. He was unwilling that the troops under his command should enter the capital, and it was said that he feared the destruction of his magnificent hôtel.

But it may rather have been, as he said himself, that he feared the seduction of his troops, — the *Gardes Françaises*, who declared for the people, being a full regiment, twelve hundred strong. To risk an encounter between them was to kindle the flames of civil war, and he was averse, he said, to the shedding of blood in such a conflict. He therefore sent to Versailles for further orders. None arriving, after waiting for them until one in the morning, the baron withdrew his troops from the neighbourhood of Paris, and sent them to their quarters. He himself returned to the Invalides and went to bed, leaving the capital to take care of itself.

On the 13th the insurrection assumed a more regular character. Few persons had taken any rest. "None but children slept that night," says a French historian. At four in the morning the people again surrounded the Hôtel de Ville. The *tocsin* was sounded there, and at all the churches; drums were beat through all the streets, calling on the people to assemble in the public places. Bodies of men enrolled themselves under the name of Volunteers of the Palais Royal and of the Tuileries. Each district of Paris also voted two hundred men for its defence. But these battalions of *bourgeois* soldiers were all without arms; Paris echoed on all sides with the cry, "To arms!" and the unarmed citizens respond, "Give us arms!" The gunsmiths' shops are pillaged. A few dozen guns are thus furnished, but many thousands are wanted. The Provost of Paris, M. de Fléssdelles, sends these citizen-soldiers, on the 13th and 14th, to search the monasteries, knowing that no arms will be found there. One, at least, had met with pistol and ball, and the provost's life is the forfeit of the trick he with so much levity has put on them. Again they assail the Hôtel de Ville; but none can give these frantic citizens the powder and guns they are raving for.

There is yet another cry, no less frantically uttered. It is for "flour and bread." A mob of hungry, ragged wretches, from the dark alleys and fever holes of Paris, clamour for food. They fill the Place de Grève, where provisions of all kinds are being brought in from the carts, carriages, and other vehicles that have been stopped at the barriers. The barriers are destroyed, the carriages of Prince Lambesc are burnt, and horrible excesses, and scenes of murder and rapine, occur in various parts of the city. The criminal population of Paris avail themselves of this time of frightful disorder; and the crimes and horrors committed by them on the preceding night determine the authorities of the Hôtel de Ville to illuminate the city as the evening of the 13th draws in.

What a terrible place after dark was the far-famed gay city of Paris in those days, — with its *réverbère* here and there, which, when perchance it was lighted, made nothing visible but the darkness of its cut-throat alleys and its narrow, winding, muddy, unpaved streets! There was light, and luxury, and splendour enough within, for the rich in their sumptuous hôtels. Without, an oasis or two excepted, all was squalor, dirt, and gloom, with that terrible old fortress, the Bastille *par excellence*, frowning menacingly down upon it.

Had the wild dream of taking the Bastille ever entered the mind of any sane person in Paris? Certainly not Camille Desmoulins's, when he mounted a bench and stuttered forth the cry, "To arms!" Voices had then responded: "To arms? — against whom?" "Against an army that is advancing to massacre us," he replied. Another voice, deep-toned and of sinister accent — heard at intervals when the confused mutterings and discordant cries of the mob momentarily subsided — uttered the word: "Beware! Beware!" It was said to proceed from a man of hideous aspect and dwarfish stature — a man who had very recently returned to France after some years of absence in England. "Beware!" exclaimed the people around him. "Of whom? Of what?" "Beware," he cried again, "of the queen and the court!"

This man was Marat, of infamous celebrity. He had once held the post of medical attendant to the stable servants of the Comte d'Artois, and in this capacity learned enough of the arrogance and libertinism of the latter, and the infatuated folly of the queen in those days, to impart the semblance of truth to libellous tales of fearful immorality. But neither did Marat, as yet comparatively unknown, counsel the people to attempt the taking of the Bastille.

On the morning of the 14th of July, even the *bourgeois* militia — who a few days hence, with the consent, willing or otherwise, of the king, were to be organised as the National Guard, having General de La Fayette for their commander and the *tricolor* for their banner — were still unprovided with arms. The arsenal itself contained none. Terror took possession of the public mind, and it was the general feeling that Paris was betrayed. False and insidious reports were spread that the troops quartered in its vicinity were advancing on the city; and it was perceived that the cannon of the Bastille were pointed towards the Rue St. Antoine and the Place de Grève. Never had they thus threatened Paris since the days of La Grande Mademoiselle; when that heroine of the Fronde ascended to the battlements, and, on the refusal of the governor to fire, herself applied the match to them, spreading consternation among the troops of Louis XIV. under Turenne, and causing the gates of Paris to be opened to the grand Condé and his partisans of the Fronde.

A rumour spreads that there are arms at Les Invalides. Troops are encamped in the Champ de Mars, but the citizen-soldiers give a proof of their courage by defiantly passing through them, and, in spite of the governor's remonstrances, taking possession of the two cannon that for many years past had stood at the entrance of the Invalides— but rather for ornament than use. M. de Besenval is there, but calls not on his troops to prevent thirty-eight thousand stand of arms being also taken, with swords, pikes, and sabres, or any weapon the people can lay their hands on. Ammunition, too, is forthcoming, and now for the first time the cry, "*A la Bastille!*" is heard. M. de Launay, the governor of the fortress, at the request of a deputation from the Hôtel de Ville, has drawn back the cannon from their embrasures. Remove them entirely he cannot. They have been there, he says, from all time, — meaning from the fourteenth century. The sentinels are posted; the bridge drawn up, as in time of war. But the governor promises not to molest the people unless the fortress be attacked. Soon, however, the multitude, returning from their successful forage for arms, rush upon the first sentinels, overcome them, kill one, wound the other, and succeed in breaking the chains of the outermost bridge. This brings down a volley of musketry on the assailants. Recovering from this repulse, they return to the charge — maddened, infuriated. Blood has been shed, and they are athirst for more. The Faubourg St. Antoine is one seething mass of human beings — howling, raving: "*Nous voulons la Bastille!*"

For four hours vainly they strive to reach the second drawbridge. At each attempt a volley of musketry drives them back, — wounding many, killing others, inflaming to madness the frantic ardour of all. From thousands of voices rises the unceasing shriek, furious, wild, unearthly — "*La Bastille! La Bastille!*" Hay and straw in cartloads are piled around the frowning old fortress. The smoke and flame drive back the besiegers, but have no effect on the solid masonry of walls, ten feet thick. The aid of the *pompiers* — the firemen of the city — is sought, to raise a stream of water to the battlements and render powerless the charge of the guns. In vain; it reaches not one-third of their height, but it is responded to by a shower of *mitraille*.

Thrice a deputation from the Hôtel de Ville, bearing a white flag, and headed by a drum, strives to obtain a suspension of hostilities. But so great is the tumult, so frenzied the populace, so continuous the firing by both besieged and besiegers, that these efforts are fruitless. The garrison have not perceived them, and the people want the Bastille, not a truce.

But hark! — a shout of triumph! To the cry: "We want the Bastille!" it replies: "You shall have the Bastille! The Bastille shall be taken!" Unexpected aid has arrived. The "soldier patriots," the *Gardes Françaises*, have in large numbers broken from their barracks, defied their officers, and are bringing up the two cannon taken from the Invalides. They demand ammunition from the Hôtel de Ville for charging these two rusty old field-pieces, which once figured with *éclat* at Fontenoy, and were brought thence as trophies of the glory of the "Well-beloved." The moment is a critical one, and would be terrible for the besiegers had the garrison full liberty of action and the governor unlimited power freely to employ the means of defence at his command. The fire of the cannon on the towers of the Bastille, directed on the city, would sweep down the people by hundreds, and speedily clear the Faubourg and the Place de Grève of the insurgent mob.

The people, even with the aid of the *Gardes*, evidently cannot take the Bastille. But its garrison, chiefly soldiers from the Invalides, do not willingly continue to fire on their fellow citizens. They press the governor to surrender. The Swiss are willing to support him, and to hold out to the end. But the governor himself seems to weary of the contest, though resolved not to surrender to the people. He is unpopular. Whether deservedly or not, his office suffices to make him so; and rather than fall into the hands of the infuriated mob, he declares that he will blow up the fortress and perish in it. He descends to the vaults with this object in view. Twenty thousand pounds of powder are stored there; but at the moment he is about to apply the match, it is snatched from his hand, and the man — Béquart, one of the Invalides — who has thus saved half Paris and its inhabitants from destruction, an hour later is hanged with one of his comrades to a *réverbère* on the *quai* by the wretches to whom the fortress was surrendered.

M. de Flue, the officer in command of the Swiss, determines to offer terms of capitulation.

"The governor and the garrison shall march out with the honours of war." "No," reply the people. (The Marquis de Launay is too much an object of hatred to be allowed to march out with flying colours.) "Let down the drawbridges," they cry, "and no harm shall happen to you." Other terms are proposed: "No lives are to be taken, no blood shed." "No harm shall happen to you," again cry the people; "let down your drawbridges." An officer named Élie, of the Queen's Regiment, and commanding the so-called militia, accepts the conditions offered, "on the word of an officer — *foi d'officier.*"

The bridges are let down, gates are opened, doors are forced. In rush the mob, a horde of furies, shouting: "Victory! Victory! Liberty! No quarter! No quarter!" An attempt is made to rescue M. de Launay, by Hullin it is said; but in vain. He is badly wounded himself, thrown down by the mob in their eagerness to wreak their fury on the unfortunate governor. De Launay is cruelly tortured, mutilated, and finally dragged to the Arcade St. Jean, where his head is cut off, and, as it is raised aloft on a pike, spatters with blood the windows of the Salle St. Jean in the Hôtel de Ville, where the electors of Paris are assembled. Shouts of triumph hail the hideous spectacle. Major Sorblay de Lormes of the Invalides, and M. de Miray, the officer next in command, are also killed on the Place de Grève.

The hero of the day, Élie, is borne as a conqueror, crowned with laurel, on the shoulders of an exulting mob. Before him marches one of the seven prisoners found in the Bastille — probably the Comte de Solages — confined there for seven years past, at the instance of his father, who had died without asking for his son's release. This man carries the ancient keys of the fortress. Another walks beside him, with its rules and regulations on the end of a bayonet. These precious relics are to be presented to the National Assembly, that they may be placed in the iron chest of the archives of France. The great key of the outer portal was given to Général de La Fayette, who sent it to America, to his friend, General Washington.

The destruction of the Bastille occupied a large number of workmen for full twelve months. To assist at its demolition appears to have been a fashionable amusement: Chateaubriand* speaks of the most distinguished persons, and among them ladies elegantly dressed, mingling with the workmen who were demolishing the walls amidst the acclamations of the surrounding crowd. Every huge mass of masonry was removed with a triumphant shout; for there was an anxious desire to realise Cagliostro's prophecy. He had said in 1786 that within five years from that time the people should dance on the site of the Bastille.

* *Mémoires d'Outre Tombe.*

And dance they did, and with frightful glee, the new dance of the Carmagnole to the tune of "*Ça ira.*" Courtiers, ambassadors, and illustrious foreign visitors, came to gaze on the dungeons, as gradually they were opened to view, and to shudder at the horrible ingenuity revealed in some modes of torture once practised within those massive walls. Old France and young France assembled together to watch the destruction of the "trophy of servitude," whose taking, or rather surrender, was to mark the epoch of emancipation and liberty in France.

Pity that the 14th of July, a day deemed so glorious by the French, should have been so deeply stained with infamy and crime, — should have been but the beginning of a series of days and years crowded with horrors that excite the painfullest emotions, that make the blood run cold, and are too appalling for the mind to dwell upon. And yet, so firm a foot had despotism set on the neck of its subjects, that this wild, determined, furious bursting of their bonds could alone free them from it.

By a singular coincidence, the king, who with his usual weakness and obstinacy now yielded to, now resisted, the wishes of his advisers, had at last been prevailed on to fix the night of the 14th and 15th for carrying into effect the meditated *coup d'état* that was to dissolve the Assembly and terrify turbulent Paris into submissiveness. But at about nine o'clock that evening the news of the insurrection and its astounding result reached the Assembly. The news had been carefully kept from the king; and, as was usual with him, whatever might happen, he had gone early to bed. But M. de Liancourt, one of the deputies of the *noblesse*, being Grand Master of the Wardrobe, and having, therefore, access to the king at all hours, required that he should be awakened. Still half asleep, he drowsily raised himself on his elbow to learn why he had been thus unseasonably disturbed. M. de Liancourt then informed him that the Bastille had been attacked, had surrendered, and was in the hands of the people. It was considered too wild a tale to give credence to; but other arrivals confirming it, the king exclaimed: "It is a revolt, then?" "Sire, it is a revolution," replied the duke. This changed the face of things. But it was late; the king wished to sleep on the matter. M. de Liancourt was therefore thanked and dismissed, and Louis lay down and resumed his snooze.

On the morrow the king, accompanied by his two brothers, but without his usual escort, went to the Assembly; spoke uncovered; promised to withdraw the troops, and to recall M. Necker. He expressed also full confidence in the Assembly. This gratified the deputies. They rose *en masse* and escorted the king, who was on foot, back to the palace. A deputation of fishwomen and *dames de la halle* waited on him later in the day to urge him to visit Paris. These ladies, always so prominent on public occasions, were gaily decked out with tricoloured ribands; the green cockade had given place to the red and blue of the arms of the city of Paris, placed on the national white flag, and henceforth to form the patriot banner. On the 15th a full family council was also held, the ministers attending. The troops departed on the 16th, and with them the Comte d'Artois, his wife, and two sons; the Polignacs, Gramonts, and Vaudreuils; the Princes de Condé and de Conti; the Ducs de Bourbon and d'Enghien, Maréchal de Broglie, and others of lesser note who were alarmed at the progress of the Revolution. It was proposed that the king and queen should also leave, escorted by a body of troops to Metz or some other strong frontier fortress.

The queen, who was in favour of this scheme, packed up her diamonds in a single case for the greater convenience of carrying them; destroyed many papers, and arranged that Madame Campan should accompany the children as governess. But the king unfortunately could not decide for himself. Those who were consulted on the subject, and who were for the most part about to emigrate that night themselves, counselled him to remain. The French troops could not be relied on; and the sovereign people, annoyed that he did not hasten to Paris to grace their triumph and confirm their appointment of M. Bailly as Mayor of Paris, La Fayette as commandant of the newly organised National Guard, and tell them in person that M. Necker was on his way back, threatened to go to Versailles and fetch him. To prevent further disturbances — and, what he dreaded still more, the possibility of the Duc d'Orléans being named lieutenant-general of the kingdom, should he absent himself — the king determined to stay, and sent word that he would go to Paris on the 17th. Unfortunate decision! But so little did he appreciate the danger of his position, or understand the state of the public mind, that he, as well as the queen, on taking leave of the Polignac family, bade them reckon on the continuance of his friendship, and assured them that their various offices, pensions, and places should be strictly reserved for them. A six weeks' or two months' absence, while the *émeute* was put down, was the extent of the exile expected.

Monsieur and Madame de Provence determined also to remain at Versailles. The chapter of accidents might, perhaps, bring about the opportunity Monsieur still longed for, — that of supplanting his brother; while Madame, no less wily and *spirituelle* than he, but more refined and dignified, would have been glad to show that the second place on the throne might be also more worthily filled.

The queen had thought to retain the Abbé

Vermond at Versailles, to accompany her and the king in their flight; but on the night of the 16th, after the Polignac party had set out, it was decided, with her unwilling consent, that, in consequence of rumours abroad of a menacing nature, the *abbé* must lose no time in decamping, too. Nor could he go cheered, like the rest, with the hope — false though it proved — of speedily returning to France to find his wealthy *abbayes* and other rich benefices reserved for him, with their revenues intact. Of all men in France, the Abbé Vermond was, perhaps, the most generally and deservedly detested. None had done such real harm to the nation as he. His pernicious influence over the queen had been ruinous to her; and since the death of M. de Vergennes, the *abbé's* views on state affairs, secretly enforced on the queen, had chiefly prevailed in the cabinet coun cil where the queen presided. Opposed to the reform of abuses, or to that revision of the laws which the changed circumstances of the nation demanded, and which, readily yielded, would have removed all excuse for violence on the part of the people, the Abbé Vermond was certainly chargeable with much of the trouble afflicting the country. Yet it may truly enough be replied that only under a ruler weak and incompetent as Louis XVI. could such a man have been allowed to exercise any influence, direct or otherwise, in state affairs at all.

But Monsieur l'Abbé, early on the morning of the 17th, was journeying towards Valenciennes. He was *en route* for Vienna, and was in humble guise; but more for personal safety than from humility. The king, too, no less sorely against his will, left Versailles on the 17th to visit Paris at the command of the people. He was escorted by a company of the National Guard of Versailles, — men of all sorts and sizes, variously attired, without uniform, and carrying old guns, pistols, and pikes, but all gaily sporting a cockade and streamer of the *tricolor*. At Sèvres a party from the city, similarly conditioned, replaced the Versailles troop,* and accompanied the king to Paris; which he only reached after being six hours on the road. He had a weary, anxious look; everywhere he was received in silence; none cried "God bless him!" and not the faintest *viva* met his ear.

A singular procession was drawn up at the Cours la Reine to accompany him to the Hôtel de Ville. There were the rebellious *Gardes Françaises*, and the cannon brought from the

---

* Not for some time did these citizen-soldiers get into decent trim, — sorted into sizes, drilled a little, and trusted with a musket. The uniform was a longer affair still. At first only the officers could succeed in getting their uniforms made; for when, all at once, all France became soldiers, a heavy burden was thrown on the hands of the tailors. Like the rest of the world, they were far too much engrossed by revolutionary revels to tie themselves long to their shopboards, or very diligently to ply the needle even in the cause of *la patrie*.

Bastille; a company of the self-constituted National Guard, headed by Général de La Fayette, their commandant; also, the new Mayor of Paris, — all new and strange to the poor king. The mayor, M. Bailly, handed him on a silver salver the keys of his good city of Paris. "Sire," he said, "these same keys were presented to your ancestor, Henri IV., of glorious memory, when, after besieging Paris in person, he conquered his people; but the people who now present them have conquered their king." The king appears to have made no reply, or if he murmured a few words they were lost amidst the vociferous cries of "*Vive la Nation!*"

The *cortège* then moved on to the Hôtel de Ville, where the king was received with loud acclamations. A tricoloured cockade was offered by M. Bailly. The king accepted it and placed it in his hat. Then, for the first time that day, burst forth one general cry of "Long live the king, our friend, our father, the citizen king!" Louis XVI., with the *tricolor* in his hat, was supposed to be reconciled to his people. They had "conquered their king," and a proposal was made to erect a statue to him — the victors to the vanquished — a proposal containing so poignant an epigram that all France laughed at the *naïveté* of the committee of the Hôtel de Ville and the new Mayor of Paris.

After having confirmed the appointments of

the new magistrates, approved everything the people by their deputies had decreed, and promised the recall of "exiled virtue" (M. Necker), the king left Paris for Versailles. His long absence had caused much disquietude at the palace. The temper of the people was so uncertain that it was doubted whether he would be permitted to return. It was a great relief, therefore, to the anxious fears of the queen and Mesdames, and other members of his family, when, late at night, a courier sent on before him announced the "citizen king's" speedy arrival.

CHAPTER IV.

Recalled. — From Bâle to Paris. — A Triumphant Return. — "*Au Ministre Adoré.*" — A General Amnesty. — The Amnesty Revoked. — "The St. Bartholomew of Abuses." — The Fourth of August. — The Assembly Constituent. — A Revolutionary Sect. — Defective Pedigrees. — What is the *Tiers État?* — The Blessings of Freedom. — "*Vive le Tiers État!*"

THE king's letter of recall reached M. Necker at Bâle. But though flattered by its humble and apologetic tone, he doubted whether it would be prudent or politic to obey it. As was customary with him in any perplexity, he referred the question to his wife. Madame Necker decided that it was his duty to obey. She was suffering greatly from a nervous affection, but thought it better that both she and her husband should be exposed to the chance of some personal peril than to the greater evil of remorse. The horses' heads were immediately turned towards Paris; and such was the enthusiasm of the people throughout his journey that they were disposed to deprive M. Necker of his horses and draw him from town to town themselves. But he pleaded haste; preferring greater speed and less enthusiasm. The post-masters, however, would not consent to forego the honour of being his postilions.

Flags and banners lined the road, and from Bâle to Paris the air resounded with frantic cries of " *Vive Necker! Vive la Nation!* " He arrived within a league of the Porte St. Antoine on the 30th July, and there found an escort awaiting him, — a detachment of the National Guard with tricoloured banners. Both were novelties to him. An officer in smart new uniform, with glittering epaulets, stepped forth and presented the minister with a tricoloured cockade. Of course he placed it in his hat; then, with colours flying, and a band playing " *Vive Henri IV.*," varied by " *Charmante Gabrielle,*" in compliment probably to Madame Necker, the journey was continued to the gates of Paris. The Parisians had given up the day to festivity, and stood crowded together by thousands to witness the triumphal entry of the lately disgraced minister. The theatres — which had been closed as a sign of mourning at his departure — were that evening illuminated, and gave special recitations in honour of his return. A shower of bouquets, forming the *tricolor*, fell from the balconies, which were filled with ladies in elegant *toilettes*. A carriage-full of flowers was presented by the inevitable *dames de la halle*. A deputation of the electors of Paris from the Hôtel de Ville, and another of deputies from the National Assembly, were also there to greet him in the name of the nation. Congratulatory addresses were read aloud, though not a word was heard amidst the din of voices and the delirious shouts of joy of so vast a multitude.

Madame Necker had often expatiated on the godlike attributes of her husband. She may be pardoned if, on this day of his great triumph, she believed, for a brief space, that the hero of such an ovation was more than an ordinary mortal. But amongst the assembled throng none welcomed him with greater enthusiasm than his daughter. Madame de Staël was there in her carriage, accompanied by several friends; but the density of the crowd prevented any near approach to the hero of the scene. Much excited by the rapturous joy of the people, she extended her arms towards her father, and could scarcely be restrained, in that most ecstatic, perhaps, of the many ecstatic moments of her life, from leaving her carriage and crushing through the crowd to embrace him.

But the mob took possession of M. Necker and his wife, and with gleeful shouts drew them in their carriage to their hôtel. Posted up at the entrance were some complimentary verses, beneath which was inscribed in large letters, "*Au ministre adoré.*" M. Necker had reached the height of popular favour. There were probably none in France that day, with the exception of the king and queen, who did not regard him, more or less, as one of the safeguards of the nation. He alone, it was believed, could avert national bankruptcy, could restore prosperity to France by his skilful financial operations, and aid the Assembly, who, day after day, were discussing "the Rights of Man," in placing liberty and equality on a firm basis.

But how evanescent is popular favour. It was especially so in France at that moment. The people passed in the course of a few hours from one extreme of opinion to another, at the bidding of any Palais Royal demagogue with a loud voice and abundance of scurrilous language at command. A great change had taken place in the temper of the people during M. Necker's short absence. The lawlessness which had so largely prevailed among them; the cold-blooded murders they had been guilty of, and still gloated over; the barbarous deaths to which M. Foulon — his successor in the ministry — and M. Berthier, his son-in-law, had been put — shocked M. Necker exceedingly. His own popularity had in a great measure been the cause of these deplorable excesses. He therefore proposed, on visiting the Hôtel de Ville on this day of national rejoicing, the proclaiming of a general amnesty.

It was instantly acceded to by the electors, and received with loud acclamations when communicated to the mass of people outside surrounding the building. That there was pardon and grace for all was soon made known from one end of Paris to the other. Not an hour elapsed before a messenger was despatched to Villenauxe with an order to conduct M. de Besenval in safety to the frontiers of Switzerland. He had resigned his command, and received permission to return to his country. Passing through Villenauxe, he was arrested. The Swiss Cantons demanded his release. But M. Necker, fearing that the baron, who was advanced in years, might be as summarily and barbarously dealt with as others had been, seized the moment of his highest favour to save the life of his countryman.

The next day, however, it was perceived that by this general amnesty the populace would be likely to lose several of their intended victims — "enemies of *la patrie*," as they were termed, "deserving death for their crimes." The leaders of the mob and Palais Royal orators therefore protested against it, and declared it illegal, — the assembly of electors having, they said, no power to issue such decrees. The consequence was that the amnesty proclaimed with so much enthusiasm on the 30th of July was revoked on the 2d of August. The baron was the only man who profited by it; and M. Necker, who fancied he could control the Revolution because he had been for a moment its hero,* began from this time to struggle with and resist it.

* M. Mignet.

But the Revolution was now marching on with rapid strides towards completion, — towards that 4th of August when, worn out by prolonged sitting and endless discussion, seigniorial rights, from very weariness of the subject, were recklessly abandoned, and the last sighs of feudality exhaled. The *noblesse* vied with one another in completing this total abnegation of feudal rights. Singularly enough, the proposition so eagerly taken up originated with the Vicomte de Noailles, the younger son of the younger branch of his family, who had neither property nor rights of his own to renounce. At Versailles, and by the emigrants of the 16th of July — now at Turin and Vienna — this 4th of August was named the "night of dupes" — "the St. Bartholomew of property." Others regarded it as the "St. Bartholomew of abuses;" while the people called it the consecration of their deliverance from oppression and servitude. In the space of five hours a thousand years of feudality and its prerogatives, privileges, and rights of fortune, were abolished; the clergy also — some of them not too willingly — acquiescing in the various sacrifices required of them. Cities and provinces followed the example of individuals, — the deputies renouncing in their name all charters that gave preëminence over other cities, though enjoyed by them — as many had been — from time immemorial.

This renunciation of privileges, promulgated that evening as decrees of the Assembly, and pre-

Trianon.

Photo-etching from a Photograph.

ceded by a declaration of the Rights of Man, changed the face of the kingdom. It made all Frenchmen equals; opened to ambition all offices of state, also promotion and command in the army and navy; gave to all freedom to exercise any trade or profession — guilds being abolished — and the hope of acquiring property. It was the passing from an order of things in which all had belonged to individuals, to another in which all was to belong to the nation. The 4th of August was a revolution as important as the rising of the people of Paris on the 14th of July, of which it, in fact, was the result. A medal was struck commemorative of this great event. A deputation announced it to the king; and he was further informed that the Assembly had decreed him the title of the "Restorer of liberty to France." A *Te Deum* was also sung at Versailles, in the presence of the king and the deputies, to the sound of all the church bells and discharges of artillery.

It is likely, however, that the work of reform would have been less promptly effected, and also have been less complete, if, instead of opposition and attack, it had been met by conciliation and a disposition to yield to reasonable demands. But every refusal became for it an occasion of success. Authority was resisted; intrigue defeated; force overcome. At the period now arrived at the entire structure of absolute monarchy had perished, and by the fault of its chiefs.* The Assembly of the States, having completed this work of destruction, entered on a new phase of their mission as an Assembly Constituent.

Socially, as well as politically, the France of the old *régime* disappears from this time. The court and the *salons* will soon know it no longer. That of the new *régime* supplants it. To a society elegant, *spirituel*, and refined — though doubtless frivolous and depraved — succeed clamorous, vulgar assemblages, whence politeness and gallantry are banished. For women now rant and rave there, and political harangues take the place of conversation. Foremost among these female politicians is Madame de Staël. Unfeminine in feature, unwieldy in figure, she declaims, in a loud, harsh voice, on the questions of the day, with a vehemence of gesture and hardihood of expression that excite the envy of many a weak-voiced orator, anxious, but unable, to obtain a hearing in the vast hall of the Assembly.

As the Revolution advances, the *salon* of the Swedish ambassadress is transformed into a Jacobin club; her society into a revolutionary sect; and she and her lovers (she exacts much love) engage in political plots and intrigues. The lady's husband meanwhile — a reckless, middle-aged spendthrift, whose pocket-money his wife has reduced — " presides, like the Venetian ambas-

---

* Mignet, "*Révolution Française.*"

sador, at a gambling-table, hoping, though always a loser, to pay a few of his debts with his gains and to have something left for his *menus plaisirs*. Perhaps at the particular moment in question things had not quite arrived at this pass in Madame de Staël's *ménage*. But they were well on the way to it, and the enthusiasm of the eloquent ambassadress for freedom was more energetically proclaimed at that period than by the rest of the female politico-fashionable world.

Society in general, however, gave indications of a readiness to embrace the "new ideas." To many there was a pleasurable feeling in the thought of putting off certain social shackles — of being released from the vexing and humiliating necessity of giving precedence to the Duchesse de this, and the Comtesse de that. For very recently the king, who was fated to be always in the wrong, had requested Chérin, the *juge d'armes*, to examine the pedigrees of the ladies who claimed the privilege of appearing in the royal carriages. Proofs of their ancestors' nobility of birth from the year 1400, without any trace of ennobling having occurred, were required from those who aspired to that honour. In one or other of those essentials the pedigrees of several *grandes dames* were found to be at fault; and the distinction they coveted, or had already enjoyed, was consequently refused or withdrawn. This gave rise, of course, to much malevolent feeling towards the queen and the court. It was remarked, too, as a singular coincidence, that the ladies of defective lineage were precisely those towards whom the queen, in her caprice, exhibited marks of her disfavour.

The destruction then, at one fell swoop, of the cherished rights and privileges of the *noblesse*, both *haute* and *petite*, was an act of heroism that greatly commended itself to those ladies. It was balm to their wounded *amour propre;* it smoothed their ruffled dignity. For if one set of privileges ceased to exist, the rest, as a natural consequence, must follow; and to sit in a *fiacre* with a deputy of the *Tiers État* would soon be as proud a distinction as filling a seat in the king's or queen's own carriage — and even a prouder one. For what says l'Abbé Sieyès, in his pamphlet, "*Qu'est ce que le Tiers État?*" — a pamphlet which on every *toilette* table now usurps the place so long filled by the "*Nouvelle Héloïse.*" "What is the *Tiers État?*" — It is nothing. What does it desire to be? — Something. And what will it eventually be? — Everything." And soon this prediction will be verified, and to an extent that but few then dreamed.

Among the people, says a contemporary writer (Dussaulx), all is already changed. "The very gait and dress of our Parisians are changed. The aspect of the streets is not the same — the signboards are all freshly painted. 'Le grand Necker' has effaced Saint Antoine and his pig; the *bonne femme* without a head has given place to the *Tiers État* or *l'Assemblée Nationale*, and so forth." Where, so lately, all was peace and quietude, now a thousand discordant voices, a thousand cries are heard. Every street corner has its open-air orator, expounding the Rights of Man, or declaiming on the affairs of the nation, with his opinion on the veto, suspensory or absolute. A gaping crowd is collected, who listen with a serious or jesting air, while around a brisk sale of newspapers goes on, — the vendors loudly vociferating their numerous names. Along the walls, in flaming red and blue, mingled with white, are papers that have been put up at night, being either too libellous or infamous to be openly sold, even in those glorious days of liberty — or rather dawn of liberty. For this is but the beginning of things, and men whose deeds of blood and infamy will yet astonish the world are scarcely yet aware whether there be limits or end to villainy and licentiousness among the blessings of the reign of Freedom.

Messengers are hurrying to and fro with news from the Assembly to the Hôtel de Ville or Palais Royal. It is a great condescension on their part. Men and women, girls and boys, come trooping after them, all eager for the news; for nothing is secret in these good new times, when everything belongs to everybody, and all like to hear that M. and Madame Veto have not yet taken flight.

Then there are parties of visitors, come from afar, on a pilgrimage to the fallen Bastille; and what movement and animation are given to the usually quiet streets by the marching and counter-marching of the newly organised National Guard. One would think that a city of the dead had been suddenly quickened into life. Convents are filled with soldiers, shops and sheds turned into guard-houses. Everywhere young men are being drilled, or are practising with firearms, and none willing to serve but as officers. Children look on for awhile, then try to imitate them, — falling into line and stepping together in a quick march. Octogenarians mount guard with their grandsons. "Who would have believed it?" they cry; "who would have believed that we should live to see the happy day that assures us of the blessing of dying free? *Vive la liberté! Vive le Tiers État!*"

CHAPTER V.

Futile Intrigues. — Count Fersen. — Count Fersen's Mission. — Establishing the Constitution. — Rights of Man. — Trees of Liberty. — A Jest of the Comte d'Artois. — Cazotte's Prediction. — The Cart and the Scaffold. — A Warning Note. — Predestined Victims. — Consternation in Paris. — A Mysterious Lady. — A Wearer of Royal Robes. — Release of the Captive Queen. — The Roarings of a Tempest. — Mirabeau Destitute. — Apathy of Mind.

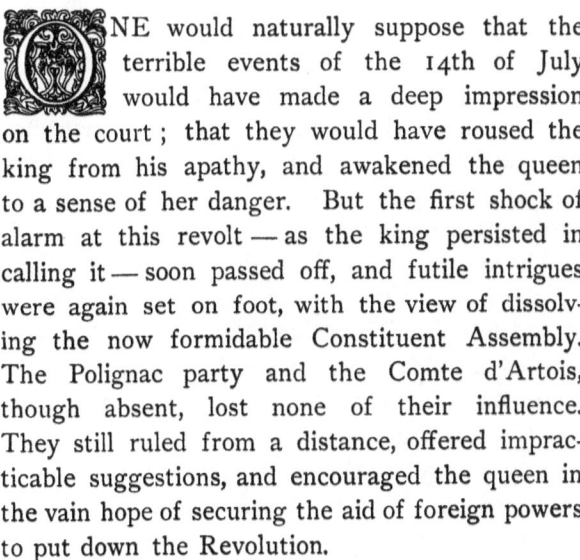NE would naturally suppose that the terrible events of the 14th of July would have made a deep impression on the court; that they would have roused the king from his apathy, and awakened the queen to a sense of her danger. But the first shock of alarm at this revolt — as the king persisted in calling it — soon passed off, and futile intrigues were again set on foot, with the view of dissolving the now formidable Constituent Assembly. The Polignac party and the Comte d'Artois, though absent, lost none of their influence. They still ruled from a distance, offered impracticable suggestions, and encouraged the queen in the vain hope of securing the aid of foreign powers to put down the Revolution.

Versailles was sombre, but apparently tranquil. The king had resumed his usual occupations. The queen and M. de Bréteuil (he succeeded the *abbé* as confidential counsellor) were regarded by the people as the real king and first minister, — Louis XVI. and M. Necker being merely their masks. Silently the former were endeavouring to carry out their ill-digested plans, aided by the Swedish Count Fersen, between whom and the queen a strong mutual attachment had long existed. Fersen, however, was a man of honourable principles, and some ten years before, as already observed, had put restraint on his own feelings, and shown respect for the queen when she, in her heedlessness, forgot self-respect. He was still her devoted friend, and had considerable influence over her. But his aristocratic leanings, which were extreme, made that influence, under the menacing and revolutionary aspect of French affairs, prejudicial both to her and the king, anxious though he was to serve them.

The queen too readily adopted his prejudices, opinions, and views. She judged M. Necker as Count Fersen, who disliked him, did; and he considered the able Genevese banker a mere financial charlatan. He had a great aversion to Général de La Fayette, whom he looked on (perhaps rightly) as playing the demagogue more from pure vanity and love of notoriety than from any sincere or settled principles.

In the course of the next two or three years from this time, Count Fersen visited several foreign courts, secretly seeking sympathy for the queen, and endeavouring to induce the European powers to coalesce in an invasion of France, — passing undiscovered in and out of Paris, in pursuit of his mission, in various disguises, even entering the palaces, to communicate with the king or queen, by secret doors and passages apparently familiar to him.

Unfortunately, he was not so well acquainted with the intricacies of that maze of winding streets that formed so large a part of old Paris, when he undertook to act as coachman, and to drive a lumbering vehicle out of the city, on the fatal night when the royal family began their unsuccessful flight to Varennes. Every moment was then precious; and the time gained which the queen lost in joining the rest of the fugitives, and Count Fersen in reaching the Barrière St. Martin, might have placed the ill-fated royal party beyond the reach of harm. With very slight precaution on their part, chance appeared likely to work out for them their imperfectly understood plan of escape — partly divulged to many, but fully confided to none.

But to return to Versailles, where royalty yet dwells, now weaving schemes of revenge, now forming projects of flight; and where the Assembly, aware of these secret intrigues, and that their own existence is menaced, urge on too rapidly the work of establishing the Constitution. The most important questions of social order are hastily discussed, and are determined without due forethought. The passions of the people are flattered ; their lawlessness too readily excused ; and thus, inconsiderately, the Constituent Assembly lay the foundation of that terrible power, so terribly used, and so soon to dominate their own.* The tide of emigration, though its flow was not yet rapid, had already begun to set in. Some far-seeing people had accepted the 4th of August as a warning to leave the land of liberty while yet there was time to make provision for their exile.

Hitherto, the owners of large estates had been regarded with a sort of reverential awe by the peasantry on and around their domains. But now, wherever the "Rights of Man" had proclaimed to the peasant his own heaven-given dignity, he refused to make "the sign of servitude" (removing his hat) in the presence of his former lord. Yet from lifelong habit it was almost second nature with him to do so, and often his hand would involuntarily fly to his head, and his hat be partly raised, at the sight of an aristocrat. But presently dignity nudged him, and being stung to the quick by the consciousness of having nearly been guilty of degrading himself by this act of baseness, he would mutter a curse, deep if not

* *Mémoires du Comte de Miot de Melito.*

loud, — deeper and deeper still, perhaps, because
not on himself, but on the tyrant who had so long
loaded him with the debasing chains of servitude
that he could not shake them off at once and forever at his will.

In the towns, the people, both men and
women — the latter always the more violent and
savage of the two — would spring to the door of
any passing carriage,* shake their fists at the
occupants, and threaten them with a day of retribution and vengeance near at hand. Everywhere
bands of citizen-patriots were planting their trees
of liberty. No wonder that there were many who
cared not to wait for the results of their taking
root, — preferring such freedom as they could
find under the vine and fig-tree of a foreign soil,
to the full development of liberty and the rights
of man under the shade of the poplars of France.
Numerous were the letters, counselling this or
that line of conduct, received by the king and
queen at that time, entreating them to fly while
yet there was time, or submitting projects for
successful evasion. They were chiefly from persons who themselves were emigrating, and were
in most instances disinterested.

The tumultuous scenes of daily occurrence in
Paris gave to those who resided near the capital a
more alarming idea of the lengths to which turbulence and license would carry the populace than

* *Souvenirs de Madame Vigée Lebrun.*

was conceivable by residents at a distance. There was, however, no lack of movement at Versailles, but it was not of so lawless a character. The château was even more quiet than usual, owing to the departure of several of its habitual residents. The king is said to have expected the fate of Charles I. He certainly gave himself no trouble to avoid it, or to avert a similar catastrophe from his family. A portrait of that monarch was placed in his apartment by the Comte d'Artois — *in jest*, it is said — a few days before he left Versailles.

There were ladies of the court, too, who, on hearing of the sanguinary scenes that had followed the insurrection of the 14th of July, remembered with a shudder Cazotte's extraordinary prediction, two or three years back, in the *salon* of Madame de Coigny. A charming poet and agreeable writer, Cazotte was an immense favourite in Parisian society before political discussion supplanted epigrammatic and *spirituelle* conversation. He was a man of much dreamy religious sentiment, partaking of the nature of mysticism, and highly imaginative. Occasionally, he fell into a meditative, trance-like mood, — unconscious, apparently, of the presence of those around him. When observed to be in this state, he was eagerly questioned, being supposed to be endowed at such moments with second sight. Cagliostro and Mesmer were then the fashion, and Cazotte in some sort divided honours with them. Not that he professed to make gold and diamonds, to heal the sick, and to perform the many other wonders of Cagliostro; nor did he give *soirées*, like Mesmer, and astonish and amuse the *beau monde* with feats of mingled science and quackery. Cazotte professed none of these things. He was simply a dreamer of dreams, and society attached importance to them.

His most memorable semi-unconscious utterances were those referred to above.

"Cazotte," exclaimed two or three ladies, speaking together, "What do you see?"

He heaved a deep sigh, but replied not.

"Speak, Cazotte!"

"Ah! no."

"Why not?"

"Ah! do not ask me. It is too sad."

"You must tell us what it is."

"Fearful events, then; fearful things coming on France, coming upon you all, — even upon you who speak to me."

"But what is it you see?"

Cazotte shuddered. "I see a prison," he said, "a cart, a large open place, a strange kind of machine, resembling a scaffold, and the public executioner standing near it."

"And these things — the scaffold and the executioner — are for me?" asked Madame de Montmorency.

"For you, madame."

"Do you see me there, Cazotte?" asked Madame de Chabot, laughingly.

"I see you there," he replied.

"You are mad to-night, Cazotte," cried Madame de Chévreuse, "or you are trying to frighten us."

"Would to heaven, for your sake, madame, that I were," he exclaimed.

"You say you see a cart; is it not a carriage, Cazotte?" inquires Madame de Montmorency.

"It is a cart," he answers. "To none after the king will the favour of a carriage be allowed."

"To the king!" exclaimed several of the company, who had not hitherto joined in questioning the dreamer, among them Madame de Polignac. "To the king?" she said, addressing Cazotte.

"To the king," he muttered, despondingly.

"But the queen?—myself?" she asks, speaking eagerly.

"The queen, too, is there. Madame de Polignac stands in the distance, and a mist envelops her."

"You are mad to-night; you are surely mad," they cry, trying to laugh. But in spite of the wild improbability of such a prediction being realised, the laugh is a forced one. They have been accustomed to strain his prophecies to fit passing events, and to believe them verified.

The prediction in question must have been strained to a very considerable extent, and words have been subsequently thrown in, as touches of light, before it became so literal a prophecy of the scenes of the Terror. To a reflective mind, however, and to a dreamy imagination such as Cazotte possessed, it was not difficult to foresee that much evil was looming on France, and that at no distant future, retribution — terrible, sanguinary — would be visited by the oppressed on the oppressors. Even Louis XV., in his oft-repeated "After us the deluge," had sounded a warning note to the court and society of his successor, — a court and society no less heedless and extravagant, and even more depraved, than his own.

But as a conclusion to the famous prediction, Cazotte was asked if, having sent so many of his friends to the scaffold, no revelation was vouchsafed him concerning his own fate.

"As regards myself," he is said to have replied, "I am as the man who for three days went round the city of Jerusalem crying aloud, 'Woe! woe!' to the inhabitants thereof; but who on the fourth day cried 'Woe! woe!' to himself, — 'Woe to me!' A stone from a sling was aimed at him, struck him on his temples, and he died." As was usual when his visions were ended, Cazotte heaved a deep sigh or sob, and a few minutes after, silently, and as if still suffering from some oppressive thoughts, took up his hat and cane and departed.

Cazotte was guillotined in 1792, — the rest of

the predestined victims at about the same time. Madame de Polignac, with her husband and her lover, was certainly anxious to lose no time in placing a safe distance — signified probably by the mist in which she was seen enveloped — between her and the court of Versailles.* It does not appear that the queen was aware of Cazotte's prediction, or, like the king, she probably would have thought any attempt to fly from her fate utterly useless. But the king was not more firmly bound to his fate by his apathy than the queen by her vindictive temper and prejudices. She would

---

* The Duchesse de Polignac died at Vienna in December, 1793. It was inscribed on her tomb that her death resulted from grief for the fate of the unfortunate Marie Antoinette; but the letters of Count Fersen seem to say that the loss of the estates, places, and pensions so lavishly heaped on her and her friends and relatives was a deeper grief still. All hope of reinstatement died in this grasping, worthless family when the king was beheaded. The Duc de Polignac remained at Vienna as a sort of political agent to the Comtes de Provence and d'Artois. The boy born in M. de Vaudreuil's apartments, and who was afterwards known as Duc de Polignac, and minister of Charles X., was then about ten years of age. It was customary to wake him up twice in the night, and to ask him: "*À quoi penses-tu, Jules?*" to which the sleepy boy would reply: "*À venger mon roi.*" It was expected that a day would come when this lesson, so strangely impressed on the boy's mind as a mission to be fulfilled by him, could be put into practice; and doubtless when the Comte d'Artois, as Charles X., was in his old age inflicted on France as her king, the minister did his best to aid his master in avenging the fall of the old *régime*, and in his futile attempt to resume the sceptre of a despotic monarch, and to rule the nation according to his *bon plaisir*.

be saved only by favourites, and was so unfortunate as to be unable to believe in fidelity and disinterestedness outside her own circle, though she had met with so little within it. Yet she was narrowly watched at this time, and one morning Paris was thrown into a state of extreme consternation by the news received at the Hôtel de Ville from Franche-Comté, that "the Autrichienne had fled!"

"But luckily," said the official statement, "her mysterious mode of travelling had roused suspicion in the intelligent and active minds of the municipal officers of Jougnes, and they instantly arrested her." It was further announced that the lady ("*une grande et belle personne*") travelled in a large and luxuriously furnished carriage, without armorial bearings, — in itself suspicious, they thought. She was accompanied only by a supposed *femme de chambre* and a single lackey, the former insolent in manners and speech, and remarkably well dressed, — probably a princess in disguise; the latter, a man of strangely impertinent countenance, affected to treat the matter as a mere laughable *contretemps*, though he evidently was much alarmed.

The mysterious lady was stated to be of very majestic appearance, but disdainful manners, her replies to the questions put to her by the authorities being given with much haughtiness, but in language that confirmed their suspicions; for it struck them as queenly. She was unwilling to allow her carriage to be searched, and objected, she said, to any disarrangement of her wardrobe. This, of course, did not prevent the authorities from doing their duty. They searched the carriage, but found little to excite suspicion, except a sum of 14,000 *francs* in double *louis d'or*, and, locked up in a case, a sort of gold wand, the use of which neither the lady nor her companions would explain, but, on the contrary, laughed derisively at the question. On opening the portmanteaux they became immediately aware that the supposed wand was a sceptre, for the first thing that met their astonished gaze was a dazzling jewelled crown, further search revealing royal robes and mantles of state.

The lady then condescended, they said, to invent a ridiculous tale to account for possession of these articles, and pressed the chief of the zealous officials to allow her to continue her journey. But so sumptuous a carriage, so swaggering a lackey, and a maid of such airs and graces, they were convinced, could belong only to a wearer of royal robes, — to the queen in fact, the " Autrichienne " of Versailles. Forthwith, under strict surveillance, the lady and her companions were removed to the house of a shoemaker, the head of the municipality of Jougnes, there to await orders from the Hôtel de Ville for their safe removal to Paris.

The news of the queen's capture was transmitted to Paris by a courier who reached the Hôtel de Ville three or four hours before the arrival of a second messenger bringing a letter which the captive lady had obtained permission to send on her own account. It had been ascertained that the queen had not left Versailles, and the letter last received explained that the haughty owner of the luxurious travelling-carriage, the sceptre, jewelled crown, and royal robes, was Mdlle. Sainval, the great tragic actress. She was going to fulfil an engagement at Besançon, and thither "the authorities of Jougnes" were immediately ordered to use all diligence in forwarding the captive queen, and were informed that, should any fine be imposed on her for a breach of engagement, — which, as she explained to them, was likely to happen, — they would be held responsible for the reimbursement of the amount, as well as for any further loss their lack of intelligence and overmuch zeal had occasioned her. So, with many apologies, the majestic Mdlle. Sainval was released and went on her way — rejoicing, probably, at her fortunate escape.

To be mistaken for the queen was a dangerous honour; for so inveterate was the hatred of the people towards Marie Antoinette, that in a more populous place than the little town or village of Jougnes, Mdlle. Sainval would have stood a fair chance of losing her head, and having it carried in triumph to Paris before there had been time to prove that she was only a tragedy queen. The populace generally were becoming exceedingly lawless, and gave a very wide interpretation to the principles of freedom as laid down in the declaration of the rights of men and citizens. Versailles was soon to have a striking example of it.

The court had a party in the Assembly represented by those eloquent orators, the Marquis de Cazalès and the famous Abbé Maury. It is said that the *abbé's* enormous voice overpowered even the thunder of Mirabeau's, but that when contending against each other, as sometimes happened, their united voices were as the roarings of a tempest, threatening the safety of the roof of the great hall. Mirabeau's father, the marquis, died in 1789. This great economist, general philanthropist, and family persecutor, had subsisted for the last few years on an allowance from his younger brother. Fruitless speculations, lawsuits with Madame de Mirabeau, the purchase of innumerable *lettres de cachet* for locking up his wife, his son, and other near relatives, had, together with neglect of his property, utterly ruined him. His death, therefore, brought no increase of income to his eldest son, who seems to have been in great straits at this time. The Assembly had just voted an allowance of eighteen *francs* a day to each deputy for his expenses. This was but a poor revenue for the extravagant and dissipated Mirabeau, who had little to supplement it beyond the precarious produce of his journal.

"I am destitute, even to wanting an *écu* — lend me something," he writes to his friend, the Comte de la Marck. The count sent Mirabeau fifty *louis d'or*, and thinking his services in the Assembly might be useful to the king, and that they might without difficulty be bought, requested the Duchesse d'Ossun to name the circumstance to the queen. She indignantly rejected the idea of treating with Mirabeau. "We shall never," she said, "be reduced to the ignominy of seeking his services." Poor Mirabeau! the disorderly part of his life was better known than the persecution and suffering he had been subjected to, and to which so much that was censurable in his conduct was attributable. The queen's Austrian friends endeavoured also to enlist the sympathies of Bishop Talleyrand in the cause of royalty. He, however, was unwilling to "incur risk, — the Revolution being destined," he said, "to prove stronger than the court." The king, it seems, had no voice in this matter, and indeed it was useless to appeal to him. He was satisfied with being able to eat and sleep in peace, and daily to enjoy his favourite diversion of the chase.

CHAPTER VI.

The Royal Hunt. — A Prospect of Famine. — A Military Banquet. — A Fatal Want of Foresight. — Fruitless Projects. — "The King is Lost!" — "*À Mort la Messaline!*" — Attack on the Hôtel de Ville. — Supplicating the King. — March of the Patriot Soldiers. — Preparing for a Defence. — The Pretty Young *Poissarde*. — The Escape Frustrated. — Waiting the Course of Events. — A Strong-minded Woman. — The *Avant-Coureur*. — Unjustly Blamed. — Adieu to Versailles.

HE hunting season had again come round, consequently Louis XVI. felt relieved of most of his troubles. Nothing could detain him from the chase. Everything yielded to it. Business of state, the tumult and agitation in Paris and the provinces, all the recent vexing decrees of the Assembly, were alike forgotten. Unfortunately, there was no similar relief for the people. The poorer part of the population of Paris were again becoming clamorous. "Bread! bread!" that cry which preceded all the earlier revolutionary scenes, was once more heard. There had been a partial failure of the crops — an oft-returning evil in France. The system of agriculture was bad, and this year, owing to the agitated state of the country, there had

been great neglect in gathering in the grain. Much of it that promised well in the early part of the year had been cut down while green, to serve for forage for the horses of the foreign cavalry. So said the demagogue orators of the Palais Royal, while others declared that it was done by the revolutionary agents themselves. At all events, the prospect of famine was now added to the many miseries that afflicted the frenzied people.

This was at the beginning of October, when the famous dinner was given by the household troops to the newly arrived Flemish regiment and some officers of the National Guard stationed at Versailles. The theatre of the palace was converted into a banqueting-hall for that special occasion. The king's private band attended. Wine was liberally supplied from the royal cellars, and was so liberally partaken of that the banquet became a scene of riot and disorder. The king, returning from the chase, entered the hall in his hunting dress, accompanied by the queen and dauphin. Passing round the tables they spoke to many of the officers in flattering and gracious terms. All were standing; suddenly the officers drew their swords, and, holding them aloft, glasses were filled, and the health of the royal party was drunk with enthusiasm. When they retired, the band played Grétry's air, "*O Richard! O mon roi, l'univers t'abandonne!*" The exciting "March of the Uhlans" followed, and roused these half-intoxicated soldiers to a pitch of frenzy.

The march ended, the charge was sounded, and the reeling guests, imitating a military assault, began clambering up the boxes of the theatre. The king, with the queen and some of her ladies, again appeared in an upper box, looking down with approval on these drunken revels, and sanctioning them by their presence. The national cockades were torn from their hats, trodden under foot, and replaced by the white cockade of France and the black cockade of Austria, distributed to them by the ladies of the household. The remains of the feast, with four hundred bottles of wine, were served up the following day for a breakfast to the same party. Not yet quite recovered from the effects of the excesses of the previous night, they became even more wildly hilarious than before, shouting tumultuously *vivas* for the king and queen, and *à bas* for the Assembly, — the queen, who presented the National Guard with colours, making known to them that she had been highly gratified — enchanted, in fact — with the manifestations of their loyalty at the banquet.

The queen's sincerest friends were those who most deeply deplored the fatal want of foresight shown by the court.

"What can one say to such people?" said the Emperor Joseph, replying to the French ambassador, who had asked for orders for his court on leaving Vienna. "What can one say to people who allow banquets to be given by their household troops to secure the fidelity of a few officers and soldiery of the National Guard, without being sure of the army?"

The object of provoking so noisy a display of attachment to the royal cause was to deter a turbulent assemblage of Palais Royal "patriots" from invading Versailles, as they threatened to do, in order to "liberate the king and take him to Paris," — the king being supposed to be prevented by the queen from sanctioning the Assembly's decrees of the 4th of August. Owing to his dilatoriness in this matter, Paris had been in a constant state of fermentation. At Versailles, though less impetuous, the agitation was no less real. The Assembly desired the king's acceptance of the "Rights of Man," simply and purely. But he delayed, temporized, hoping, though with no clearly defined purpose in view, to gain time and to evade it.

It was a misfortune for the royal family that whatever plans, whether for flight, or for their personal safety at Versailles, were at this time suggested to them by attached friends, willing even to risk their lives in accomplishing them, were always frustrated by the fault of either the king or queen. The latter was too eager; seeing only the result, she overlooked the details and the precautions necessary to secure it. The king, on the other hand, often approving and even desiring what was proposed, could not bring his sluggish mind to consent to act alone, or to let others act for him, until the opportunity for acting at all was past.

As in the case of the military banquet, which led to such sad results, the steps which at any time were taken by the court were always those least calculated to further their own views, while they further inflamed the minds of the people.

"In their projects," said the old Comte de Narbonne-Fritzler to the Marquise de Donnissan, "they have neither plan, precaution, nor unity; and it is the same with their opinions. Had Paris made a sudden attack on Versailles on the night of the banquet, there would have been some fighting and a good defence, though without any order. Now, it is different. Officers and men are sobered down, and some of them are rather ashamed of the antics they played. Indifference has succeeded enthusiasm, and the king is lost!"

This was said on the evening of the 4th of October, when a report arrived that Paris was in a state of tumult, and that threats had been uttered of marching on Versailles.

The newspapers had given flaming accounts of the banquet, — the reception of the guests in the great Hall of Hercules; the theatre converted into a banqueting-saloon, which had never been done but on one previous occasion, the *fête* given to the Emperor Joseph II. All these particulars, read in the Café de Foy and repeated in the Palais Royal Garden, excited the strongest indignation. Further details were supplied the next morning. "The *tricolor* had been trampled under foot!" Have the gods permitted this desecration! The guests of the famous *café*, usually so uproarious, are suddenly struck dumb by excess of indignation. Their patriotic breasts swell to bursting with feelings that find no adequate utterance in words. But they listen. What comes next? "The white cockade of absolutism and the black cockade of the 'Autrichienne' have supplanted the *tricolor* of freedom at Versailles." "It is civil war!" they cry. "Let us to Versailles!" "We will exterminate the Regiment de Flandre, and bring the king to Paris. *À mort la Messaline*."

The infamous Danton is said to have been among the guests of the *café* that morning, and, if silent then, to have found a voice in the evening to utter his fearful oaths and imprecations at the Cordeliers. The insurrection, as all know, took an unexpected turn, and a troop of hungry women formed the vanguard in the march on Versailles. A crowd of them, worn and haggard, many with children in their arms and their clothing in rags, had surrounded a baker's shop on that chill, damp October morning, crying for bread. But no flour had arrived from Corbeil, and bread was not to be had. "*À Versailles, bonnes femmes!*" cried a man passing by. "*À Versailles!* there is bread enough there and to spare. *À Versailles!* the land of plenty, feasting, and revelry. *À Versailles!*"

Instantly a young girl separates herself from the crowd, and rushes into a neighbouring guard-house; she seizes a small drum, and running swiftly through the streets, cries aloud, "Bread! bread!" beating the *tambour* as she runs. Soon a mob is collected, — three or four hundred women, presently increased to as many thousands. They follow their leader, echoing her cry, "Bread! bread!" She leads them to the Hôtel de Ville. The guard is thrust aside (they cannot fire on women). The doors fly open, yielding to the impetuous attack. The hôtel is entered. There is no bread there; but these women now demand arms, and such as they find — about 500 guns, two small cannon, and sundry pikes and staffs — they take. They sound the *tocsin*, and their cry is now, "*À Versailles!*" "We will give the men," they exclaim, "a lesson in courage. If they cannot support and protect us we will do it for ourselves."

Stanislaus Maillard, one of the foremost assailants of the Bastille, undertook to conduct these women to Versailles. As nothing could prevail on them to change their purpose of going there, he thought to keep them in some sort of order and prevent depredations on the road. The mob of viragoes accepted his guidance, and the strange *cortège* set out, two of the most prominent of the party riding in front, astride of the cannon. Twelve of the number had been detached to precede and announce the rest, and "to supplicate the king, in the name of the main body, for bread and flour, and for his promise to consent to the declaration of the "Rights of Man."

The populace, by this time, had assembled in thousands on the Place de Grève. Large numbers of them, together with the National Guard, who were there in force, also the *Gardes Françaises*, determined to follow the women, to avenge, they said, the insult offered by the "Autrichienne" and the "Flamands" to the national cockade. Général de La Fayette and the mayor were early on the scene, eloquently haranguing the Amazon army, and vainly entreating them to disperse. With as little success the popular general now declaimed to his troops. They listened impatiently, and finally told him that if he would not go with them, as was his duty, they would march to Versailles without him. This was decisive. The signal was given, and at seven in the evening, headed by the general on his famous white charger (often suspected of being an aristocrat, notwithstanding his *tricolor* decorations), and followed by some hundreds of the noisy ragamuffins of Paris, some of them carrying pikes and old pistols, the patriot soldiers began their march.

Meanwhile the twelve women who formed the advanced guard arrived at Versailles, drenched with rain, weary, footsore, and fainting with hunger. Their wants were relieved at the hôtel of the Minister of War, M. de la Tour-du-Pin, whom they informed of the mob that was following. A message was sent to the king, who was hunting in the forest of Meudon. "The Grand Master of the Household, M. de Saint-Priest," says M. de Melito, "appeared to be in a very bad humour. He declared that the imbecile weakness of the king and the folly and imprudence of the court were alone to blame for all that happened." He, however, despatched some of his people to Rambouillet to get the château in order to receive the royal family that night. Eight carriages were prepared for their departure in the dusk of the evening, luggage packed in them, and a troop of cavalry ordered to be in readiness as an escort.

Presently the king, who had dismounted in the forest, returned in a carriage; the gates of the Court of the Ministers were then closed, and eight hundred of the household cavalry mounted guard before them. The doors of the palace were also closed, and a picket of Swiss soldiers placed before each. Everything was in the greatest confusion; china and glass were thrown out of the windows; men and women running hither and thither in the galleries as if demented, says Madame de la Rochejacquelein. An attack on the palace was expected; but in what form to look for it they knew not. M. de Saint-Priest could tell them only what he had heard, — that a mob of infuriated drunken women and tatterdemalions of Paris was advancing under the pretext of asking for bread. About seven hundred gentlemen were then at the palace, — all in full dress, *chapeau sous le bras*, and armed only with dress swords. Some few had found pistols or swords, and in that unmilitary fashion they declared themselves determined to defend the château if attacked.

Five minutes after the king's return, Maillard and his band arrive, singing " *Vive Henri IV.*," and more like furies than suppliants. All shops are instantly closed; drums beat to arms, the *tocsin* is sounded, and the troops are drawn up in order of battle on the Place d'Armes. Entrance to the courts of the palace is refused, and Maillard then introduces fifteen of the women to the Assembly. The president, M. Monnier, accompanies them to the palace. "The king cannot be seen," they are told. "He is closeted with M. Necker and the rest of his ministers." Much confusion ensues. They are disappointed and angry; but they stir not. Another minute and they would have forced their way in. But, advised probably by his ministers, a message from the king orders that those fishwomen, or women disguised as such, be immediately brought in. The youngest and prettiest among them is put forward to address the king — to implore him for bread. Of course he is much moved, and under the strong pressure of this emotion, Louis XVI. both gives his sanction to the declaration of the "Rights of Man," and promises that Paris shall be amply supplied with flour, and bread be abundant. Singular, if he had power to regulate the supply, that he did not sooner relieve the wants of the people.

Evening was closing in; it was six o'clock. The weather was misty and rainy, and the queen very anxious to depart; but, unluckily, it was not yet so dark but that some twenty or thirty men of the National Guard espied the royal carriages, leaving the palace stables to pass round to the gate of the Orangery to take up the king and queen and their suite. Instantly, and in spite of the remonstrances of their officers, these men, taking a near cut by a narrow passage, reached the gate of the Orangery before the carriage came up, closed it, and compelled the drivers to turn back. "The king," they said, "is trying to escape; we will not allow him to leave. *Vive le roi!*" This unlooked-for event deranged all the plans of the château. But it was the king's fault that it did so.

At nine, news was brought in that Général de La Fayette was on the road to Versailles at the head of his National Guards and the *Gardes Françaises*, followed by a crowd of the Parisian people. M. de Saint-Priest immediately sought the king and prayed him to leave before their arrival. "The road is open," he said; "a picket of the household troops at the gate of the Orangery will prevent any recurrence of the *contretemps* of this evening, and your majesty, on horseback, at the head of the escort, can freely pass whithersoever you please." Poor Louis! He would wait the course of events. "The men had turned back his carriages, but they had cried at the same time, *Vive le roi!*" M. Necker smiled; he knew the value of such cries. His voice was therefore, like M. de Saint-Priest's, for departure. The king merely shook his head. He would remain. But it was not from courage to face whatever might happen, but from want of resolution to depart. Alas! poor Marie Antoinette! As she had found in earlier days no sincere friend to arrest her in her headlong course of folly, so now in that hour of menacing danger she finds no protector in her poor, miserably weak husband and king. Truly, she rightly named him "*le pauvre homme.*"

The nature of this new invasion, led on by La Fayette (some persons whispered Cromwell), was the subject of much conversation in the "*Œil de Bœuf.*" He was disliked by many simply because of his popularity, and unfortunately neither the queen nor the king had any confidence in him. A general feeling of uneasiness prevailed, — a fear that the troubles of the day were not ended. There were, however, among the company in the "*Œil de Bœuf*" certain persons who evinced neither fear nor affliction; conspicuous among them was Madame de Staël, decorated with an enormous bouquet, and indulging in loud bursts of laughter.*

The women received by the king appear to have been content with his promise for the immediate provisioning of Paris with flour, and soon after to have been on their way back with the news. The more audacious and dangerous portion of their companions remained. Mingled with them were men wearing the dress of the *poissardes* and women of the *halle*, — wretches who were more athirst for blood than hungering for bread. But as night advanced comparative quietude seemed to be restored, broken only by occasional hoarse shouts and wild laughter. They proceeded from a number of men and women seated round a large fire, regaling themselves with slices from a horse that had been shot in the course of some random firing in the afternoon, and which they were roasting or broiling, — the cookery being considerably impeded by the rain.

At near midnight M. de La Fayette arrived at the château, pale as death, wet through, and much splashed with mud. He had ridden hard for some distance in advance of his troops. His purpose

* *Mémoires de la Marquise de la Rochejacquelein.*

was to check any alarm that might be felt by the royal family at the sudden incursion of the mixed multitude of National Guards, *Gardes Françaises*, and volunteers of all sorts, whom he had unwillingly been made to lead. Little credence was given to this statement. But as M. de La Fayette answered for the good conduct and fidelity of his Parisian Guards, and begged that the honour of guarding the château might be granted them, the queen and the court were in some measure reassured. He prevailed also on her majesty and her agitated ladies to retire to their apartments, and to seek sleep without fear.

At two in the morning the council ended its sitting and the ministers also sought rest; the Assembly, too, broke up. The guard was then set, and the remaining troops lodged in the churches of the two parochial districts of Versailles. Tranquillity reigned within the palace; order, apparently, was restored without. Maillard's women and their companions had sought shelter from the rain in outhouses and sheds, and in such houses as would receive them. Some found their way into the great hall of the Assembly and slept on the deputies' benches. La Fayette at five in the morning, being assured that all was quieted, retired to the Hôtel de Noailles, disposed to seek rest for an hour or two himself. He had been twelve hours in the saddle and two nights without sleep, and as daybreak was at hand, might well suppose that he incurred no risk by doing so.

Yet M. de La Fayette has been blamed for the horrors that followed; even for indirect complicity in them. But so closely did they follow on that moment of calm and repose, which seemed, for that night at least, to be fully secured, that ere he could have retired to rest — if he retired to rest at all, for at seven o'clock he was at the head of his troops in the Place d'Armes — evil-doers must have been on the watch for the opportunity of working revenge on the *Gardes du Corps* and on the queen, for the insult to the national cockade on the night of the banquet. This appears to have been the real motive of the outbreak. The minds of the people had been inflamed by the reports which had reached Paris of that scene; and if distress sent the women to Versailles, vengeance prompted the men to follow.

The accounts of that terrible night of the 5th and 6th of October vary greatly; probably very few knew precisely what did take place, beyond the fact of the fighting and bloodshed, so sudden was the attack, so great the confusion, and the anxiety to save the queen from the fury of the assassins. Madame Campan was absent; her account of what passed was received from her sister. That of the Comte de Melito, an eye-witness of the events of those few days of agitation and terror, being given with less exaggeration, is probably more trustworthy than many others. He was indeed not so much a participator in those scenes as an interested spectator of them. Their result is well known. The king and queen, at the demand of the people, left the royal residence of Versailles, which they were to see no more, to take up their abode in the capital of the Revolution, whither the Assembly soon followed. They were deprived of their household guards and placed under the surveillance of the citizen-soldiers. There were no more presentations, and the last vestiges of the old court *régime* and the monarchy of the superb Louis Quatorze disappeared. Royalty was vanquished; and Louis XVI. and Marie Antoinette at the Tuileries were but the captive slaves of their subjects.

CHAPTER VII.

"*Sang de Foulon.*" — Revolutionary Fashions. — Death of Joseph II. — The Patriotic Fund. — "*Bijoux à la Constitution.*" — **Madame** de Genlis's Brooch. — Louis Philippe. — The New Departments. — The Iron Safe. — A Neglected Royal Dwelling. — The Duc de Liancourt's Dinners. — Pity for Louis XVI. — The *Salon* of 1789 and 1790. — An Eloquent Lesson of Liberty. — Sandals and Togas. — "Charles the Ninth." — An Ardent Patriot. — Slaying Royalty. — Talma. — The Dramatist Chénier. — A Popular Drama.

THE queen and the Duchesse d'Orléans were no longer the leaders and arbiters of fashion. The Revolution had already usurped even the sovereignty of *la mode*, and had brought into favour a peculiar shade of crimson, which was displayed in the windows of the Palais Royal shops, attractively ticketed, " *Sang de Foulon.*" * Scarcely does the period of the Terror afford an incident, not in itself a deed of blood, more revoltingly suggestive of the sort of sanguinary ferocity that already, in 1789, pervaded the nation. One shrinks from the thought of women — women of whatever grade — complacently arraying themselves in colours symbolising the barbarous murder of a victim of revolutionary

* E. and J. Goncourt, "*Société Française,*" etc.

fury. Yet "*Sang de Foulon*" rivalled for a time even the national *tricolor*. It was never combined with it, being a red of a different shade.

The three colours were arranged in the *toilettes* of the day in every possible variety, but always avoiding too large a proportion of white. Even in the *demi-converti costume* — denoting that the wearer was halting between two opinions — no white material, except lace ruffles and cravat, appeared, the rest being black and scarlet. This dress, later on, would have surely conducted the wearer to the scaffold. But while the Constitution was framing, it was permitted, if royalist leanings were not too openly professed, that the *demi-convertis* — chiefly the younger nobles — who were inclined to adhere to the Revolutionary movement, but could not, without a pang, at once divest themselves of aristocratic associations, should, unmolested, make up their minds.

Costume was indeed generally intended at that time to be a sort of pictorial profession of faith, — whether "*Mise à la Constitution,*" "*Négligé à la Patriote,*" "*Déshabillé à la Democrate,*" or other significative name were given to it. The *Democrate* was distinguished from the rest by a fourth colour,* the satin skirt of this dress being of the dull yellowish brown called "dead-leaf." It signified that the monarchy of the old *régime* had passed away, of course with the approval of

* *Journal de la Mode*, 1789-90.

the fair wearer of the *Democrate*. While the broad border of bright, tricoloured velvet, the cuffs, collar, sash, and other trimmings of the same, with the "*bouquet à la nation*" (flowers of the three colours surrounded with sprays of myrtle) worn in the "*bonnet à la citoyenne*" and at the waist, denoted the joyous new order of things which had succeeded it.

The "decided aristocrats" wore black, taking advantage of the death of an archduchess, for whom the queen and her court were in mourning when the events of the 5th and 6th of October occurred. Shortly after, the Emperor Joseph II. died, — but little regretted, Madame Campan says, by the queen. He did not yield her the sympathy she had looked for from him in her troubles. Years before he had very solemnly warned her that she was running headlong to ruin. Louis XVI. he held in great contempt, and he was something of a revolutionist himself in his desire to initiate reforms in his own dominions. However, his death served as an excuse to the queen's friends for continuing to wear black. The tricoloured cockade they could not escape. All were required to wear it. It was to be had in varnished leather, even in stiffened tapes, to suit all tastes and fancies; and "*Ruban national! Ruban national!*" was cried through the streets from morn till night.

Jewels were now no longer worn. Those who

had any concealed them. To provide temporarily for the needs of the state, and save *la patrie* from bankruptcy, noble ladies, ladies of the upper *bourgeoisie*, popular actresses, — all, in short, who had pearls and diamonds, or precious gems of any kind, had recently brought them as offerings to swell the amount of the patriotic fund. All classes, from the owner of a pair of shoe-buckles, to the possessor of a service of plate, threw their gold and silver into the refining pot of the nation, to be converted into specie. The king and queen gave up their plate, even to the silver handles of their knives; and like the superb Louis XIV., when in similar straits, were reduced, as Madame de Maintenon said, to eat their dinner off china, with china handles to their knives and forks. The superb service of ancient gold plate, used at St. Cloud, and of inestimable value, from the beauty and elaborateness of its chasing and engraving, went with the rest to the mint. "There was a real epidemic of offerings on the altar of national bankruptcy." And not only were jewel-cases and plate-chests emptied, but society, from the lowest to the highest grade, turned out its pockets to transfer their contents to the empty treasury.

To supply the place of the sacrificed jewels, for the ladies must have ornaments of some kind, "*bijoux à la constitution*," and "*à l'égalité*" were invented, — plaques of china or metal, enamelled in the three colours, earrings of white glass bearing the inscription "*La patrie*," also "*souvenirs de la Bastille*," pieces of the stones of that edifice polished and set as rings, brooches, etc. The man Palloy, to whom the demolition of the fortress was entrusted, made a fortune by selling large portions of the stone piecemeal, and in making them into models of the celebrated state prison. Though this "constitutional jewelry," from its simplicity and inexpensiveness, was supposed to be within reach of the means of all "*citoyennes*" who cared to adorn themselves with it, there were yet specimens in the possession of some ladies that must have been of considerable value.

The brooch worn by Madame de Sillery-Genlis when, owing to the abolition of titles, she became for a time "*la citoyenne Brulart*," is described as a medallion of the polished Bastille stone, having in the centre the word *Liberté*, in small diamonds. Above this a single diamond of larger size represented the planet that shone on the evening of the 14th of July, and near it, in small diamonds, the moon, as she appeared on that memorable night. Beneath the word *Liberté* was a branch of laurel in emeralds, fastened to the stone, as it seemed, by a tricoloured cockade composed of rubies, diamonds, and sapphires. Here was a superb *liberté* and *égalité* trinket! — excellent in workmanship and of artistic design as well as intrinsic value.

The lady who describes it * was visiting Ma-

* Helen Maria Williams, "*Souvenirs de la Révolution.*"

dame de Genlis, then staying at the Duc d'Orléans's Château de St. Leu, in the Valley of Montmorency, with the duke's children. She says they were a charming family. The Princesse Adélaïde was then about thirteen, M. de Chartres (Louis Philippe) seventeen, and the very cream of politeness. He declared himself a sincere friend of the Constitution, and not only willing, but anxious to renounce splendour and titles, and rejoicing greatly that his father's immense estates would be shared by his brothers Montpensier and Beaujolais. Madame de Genlis, also, we learn, expressed herself in the same spirit of philosophy in her allusions to the division of property and the distinctions of rank. The Duc d'Orléans, though one of the wealthiest subjects in Europe, was extremely avaricious. For gain he had surrounded the gardens of the Palais Royal with shops. The palace itself was scantily and meanly furnished, having nothing noteworthy in it but the fine gallery of paintings collected by the regent.

The Duc d'Orléans was at this time in England, ostensibly charged with an important diplomatic mission. His presence in Paris was thought dangerous, and a pretext being afforded him, he consented to absent himself for a while. Some writers on the Revolution have thought that he was credited with far more influence and popularity than he really possessed; that he rather followed than led the multitude; and that in the

Assembly, though he always voted with the majority, the majority never voted with him.

After the events of the 5th and 6th of October, and the transfer of the seat of government from Versailles to Paris, — the king and the queen being safely caged, — though it cannot be said that the capital was quiet, yet, comparatively with the past, there was a lull in the storm. The nation paused, as it were, in its work of destruction, to look back on what had been done. It looked forward, too, while contemplating the Assembly — whose sittings had become more attractive to the ladies and the Parisians generally than either opera or play — completing the constitutional labours of national regeneration, from which results so immense were expected. They had already rearranged the division of the kingdom, shuffled the provinces together like a pack of cards, and dealt them out, to their great disgust, into eighty-three departments. They had abolished all titles, but had created a new one for the king — "*pouvoir exécutif*" — without power to execute anything.

Armorial bearings had disappeared with the titles, as well as livery, the badge of servitude. Only the public or hackney carriages were to be used. The Duchesse d'Orléans had been compelled to alight from hers in the Champs Elysées, when going to visit her children, and to take a *fiacre*. The patriotic gifts, large as they were, had availed little for replenishing the immense void in the coffers of state. The forced circulation of the monetary paper called "assignats" was therefore decreed until the value of the Church lands could be realised.

These measures had so fully occupied the minds of the Assembly in their discussion, and the time of the Parisian Guard in rigorously carrying into effect the defacement of the carriages and fronts of the hôtels of the *noblesse*, that poor Louis XVI., though the chase was denied him, had had leisure to follow undisturbed his favourite occupation as a blacksmith. It seems almost incredible that he should have been able to forge the famous iron safe in the apartments of the Tuileries, — undiscovered, too, — as he is said to have done, at this time. It is more probable that it was secretly brought in, and that the man Gamain, who had worked with Louis XVI. at Versailles, was then summoned to fix and complete it. Unfortunate, indeed, that he did so, and that the king, on his trial, condescended to deny all knowledge of it.

The Tuileries had so long been abandoned by royalty that some weeks elapsed ere the king and queen with their family could be established there with any degree of comfort. Many articles of furniture, linen, etc., were sent for from Versailles, where much damage had been done on the 6th, — the servants of the royal household in their wild terror having thrown plate, china, and glass, dressing-cases, and many small articles of valuable furniture, out of the windows. The mob did not pillage; their object was destruction, and that chiefly of human life. The apartments of the Tuileries had been given to various official persons and their families, who, being now obliged to vacate them, sold their furniture for the use of the unexpected royal inmates. Monsieur and Madame occupied a part of the Luxembourg.

The Princesse de Lamballe was allowed a suite of apartments in the Tuileries. To gain partisans in the Assembly she held receptions there three times a week. They were numerously attended, but of course by a more mixed assemblage than had hitherto frequented her *salons*. The queen had thought of attending these *soirées* as a distraction, and with the idea also of ascertaining the state of public feeling towards her; but after appearing a second time she was prevailed on to see the inexpediency of doing so. Six thousand passports were issued in the course of the first fortnight after the king left Versailles, and chiefly to persons of distinction, and of the wealthy class, who carried away with them all they could realise by the hasty disposal of their property.

But although so many were leaving, and many more were anxious to follow, — remaining only with the hope of being useful to the king and queen, — yet in 1790 Mr. Arthur Young* mentions the grand dinners given by the Duc de Liancourt at the Tuileries during his term of service in attendance on the king. He was particularly struck, however, by the negligence of the guests in the matter of *toilette* compared with what he had observed on his first visit, three years before. "Several," he says, "were in mourning costume; others without powder; and many wore boots, with even traces of Paris mud on them. Instead of the witty, sparkling conversation of other days," he continues, "we had now long dissertations on politics, or details of plots and conspiracies, and this to the exclusion of all other subjects." From his conversation with these royalists, he learned that they flattered themselves there was a wondrous change in public opinion, — the result of some arbitrary acts of the Constituent Assembly. The people, they believed, were "beginning to pity the painful situation of their king," and a counter-revolution of course, for a while, was looked for.

But such pity as could be felt for Louis XVI., or any one, content, as he was, to sit down apathetically under his troubles, and refuse to move a finger either to save himself or those unfortunately connected with him, was far more likely to inspire contempt than to kindle enthusiasm. The queen

* "Journeys in France during the years 1787, 1788, 1789, and 1790."

and her children were truly to be pitied, and it was greatly to be lamented that her prejudices, like the king's apathy, were ever an obstacle to the success of those efforts which loyal and devoted friends were anxious to make for their rescue.

The state of public feeling was more clearly seen in the subjects which popular artists chose for their pictures, in that and the succeeding year, for exhibition in the *Salon* of the Academy of Painting. It was even more noticeable in the kind of pieces that filled the theatres to overflowing, and excited the enthusiasm of the audience to the highest pitch. The *Salon*, in which, for the most part, the ideas of the day were represented, in 1789 and 1790, displayed on its walls every phase of the Revolution. "The opening of the States General of France" was an effective sketch of an impressive scene by Darameau. The same subject, but more elaborately treated, with the companion picture of the "Constitution of the National Assembly of June 17," was contributed by Moreau. "The Oath"—the scene at the tennis-court; "The taking of the Bastille;" "The Hôtel de Ville on the 5th of October," with others by various artists, formed a perfect panorama of the revolutionary riots of the last two years.

The "*Milice Parisienne*," or National Guard, figured largely in these pictures. Portraits of La

Fayette, M. Necker, and other heroes of the hour, abounded, and drew around them crowds of admirers. But the picture that all were eager to see — the picture of the year — was David's "*Les deux fils de Brutus.*" As it addressed itself to the passions of the people as the glorification of the punishment of traitors, its bleeding heads and headless bodies created a sensation far beyond that of any picture in the *Salon*. Artists saluted it as a *chef-d' œuvre* of art: the public as an eloquent lesson of liberty. David, who became one of the most furious Jacobins of the Robespierre faction, was proclaimed "the harbinger of freedom;" whose fearless patriotism, displayed in his previous picture, "*Les Horaces*," had directed the ideas of the Revolution even before the Revolution was openly declared.

But David, though a powerful painter, had so thoroughly carried out the emphatic lessons of Joseph Marie Vien, his master, on the necessity of a close imitation of the antique, that "his pictures were mere representations of groups of marble statues, of wonderful physical proportions and extravagant attitudes, draped in Greek monumental heroic costume." His earlier manner appears to have been less offensive. By the side of his horrible picture, "*Les fils de Brutus*," was hung the "*Amours de Pâris et d'Hélène*," — the repetition of a picture painted for the Comte d'Artois, and which has been called "David's

Adieu to the Graces." In his "Death of Socrates," an alteration is said to have been suggested by his friend, the poet André Chénier. Socrates was represented with the poisoned cup in his hand, and as if addressing those around him. To Chénier it seemed that Socrates would not have taken the cup until his discourse was ended, and he was prepared to drink its contents. After a moment's reflection David admitted that Chénier was right. The cup was transferred to the slave, and some details altered, — denoting that the sage whose hand was extended to take the fatal draught had uttered his final *adieux*, and was about to drink the hemlock.

David was preëminently the painter of the Revolution, and with François Vincent, and Girodet (David's favourite pupil), greatly contributed towards introducing that taste for sham classicism which prevailed to so great an extent in France during the Revolution, in dress, furniture, etc. David and his pupils flaunted about Paris in sandals and togas, and otherwise scantily and uncomfortably attired, — setting an example of civic virtue in its glory, almost as great as that of many of Plutarch's heroes, whose lofty republicanism all true citizens were ambitious of imitating; while the "citizenesses" of this modern Rome took for their model the severely virtuous matrons of the ancient republic.

It was Joseph Chénier, the brother of the unfortunate André (guillotined only two days before the monster Robespierre met his well-deserved fate), who introduced national tragedy to the French stage, in his revolutionary play of "*Charles IX., ou l'École des Rois.*" * It was performed at the Théâtre Français on the 4th of November, 1789, and met with enthusiastic success. A twelvemonth before, its author had read his tragedy at a *soirée* given for the occasion by the Vicomte de Ségur. The play was long, and the numerous and distinguished company found its many tirades against the altar and the throne rather wearisome. "It created no emotion," wrote one who was present; "many of us could not repress a yawn, but all cried, 'Admirable! admirable!'" and most fervently so when the reading ended. Chénier had already produced two or three unsuccessful plays, preaching politics and philosophy.

* Chénier, in the "*discours préliminaire*" of his published play, claimed "the glory" of having written the first really national French tragedy. Yet the famous President Hénault, more than forty years before, had composed a tragedy in prose, and in five acts, entitled "*François II., Roi de France.*" He, too, had desired — encouraged, he said, by the example of Shakespeare and the English stage — to introduce the national drama in France. "Cannot we find," he wrote, "in our own historic annals, events as interesting, and passions as powerful, to depict as in those of Greece and Rome? Are not Cardinal de Lorraine and the Duc de Guise plotting the ruin of the Prince de Condé, as interesting as the confidants of Ptolemy deliberating on the death of Pompey? or is the career of Catherine de' Medici less dramatic than that of Dido or Agrippina?"

But between January and November the revolutionary feeling of the country had made extraordinary progress; and to this "Charles IX." owed its success. The new ideas of the period found in it vigorous expression, with force and boldness in their application. In vain the critics declared that it was bombastic in tone, that its versification left much to be desired, and that historical truth was violated in order to heighten the effect of the more sombre scenes of the play. One ardent patriot who witnessed its first representation, stood up on his seat in the pit, as he once stood on a bench in the Palais Royal gardens, and, after the tumultuous applause raised by the line —

"Les attentats des rois ne sont pas impunis!"

had subsided, exclaimed aloud: "This play will advance our affair far beyond even the October days." The speaker was Camille Desmoulins. Vociferous cheers followed, and "*Ça ira! ça ira!*" shouted in chorus in all parts of the house, proved that he had but spoken the thought or the wish of the greater part of the audience. Danton, too, was heard to say, that "if 'Figaro' had given the death-blow to the aristocracy, 'Charles IX.' was destined to slay royalty." It was, therefore, as a means of accelerating the fall of the monarchy that the play gained popularity, and not any merit that was seen in it.

It, however, developed the great powers of Talma in the principal part, rejected by another actor. Talma had latterly been studying his art under Molé and Dugazon, — contrary indeed to the advice of friends, who had failed to recognise in his earlier efforts any indication of that latent fire of genius without which his aspirations for distinction in the career he was bent on pursuing were vain. From his extreme nervous sensibility he became speedily imbued with the sentiments of the character he was to personate. But until this excessive emotion was fully under control, the power of effectively depicting absorbing passions before an audience was in a great measure denied him. His natural gifts, therefore, were for a time an obstacle to the full recognition of his merits. Talent and genius united could not, however, ultimately fail of attaining that high position in his chosen profession to which his ambition pointed.

"Charles IX.," by introducing a new kind of national drama, opened a new path to Talma. The character of the hero of the piece was also especially suited to his powers of portrayal. His voice, always a little hollow, was more adapted to the expression of rage and profound emotion, than of pathos and tenderness. Naturally he was of a gloomy, melancholy temperament; yet he would sometimes be carried away by the vehemence of his feelings, but without losing dignity. Though not tall, his bearing gave him the appearance of height, and his portraits show that he had a splendid head and expressive face.

The reform in stage costume, begun by Le Kain and Mdlle. Clairon, was rigidly continued by Talma. The historical costume of Charles IX. is said to have been extremely becoming to the young tragedian, who was at this time about twenty-three years of age; and, with that of Catherine de' Medici and the rest of the characters, to have lent an attraction to the piece. Madame de Genlis was present, with the sons of the Duc d'Orléans, — young gentlemen who wore the uniform of the National Guard, and also made a present to their tutor of the uniform of that distinguished corps, which numbered more officers than men. All good patriots indeed made a point of attending "The School of Kings," and gave it with voice and hand an enthusiastic reception. Civic crowns were voted to Chénier, who was proclaimed the Corneille of the Revolution; and to have spoken against his tragedy was a new crime often laid to the charge of aristocrats. The unfortunate Marquis de Favars — who was hanged about this time, and towards whose unjust condemnation the Comte de Provence is said to have secretly and basely contributed — was asked on "his trial" whether he had not joined in a project for securing the failure of the tragedy of "Charles IX."

The king was urged to prohibit the performance of this play. He refused. He had in fact, no power to do so, and the pretension of the "*pouvoir exécutif*" to exercise such an act of authority would have been met only with derision and contempt. Some priests did threaten to withhold absolution from their penitents if they attended any representation of the play, or bought a copy of it. But this had no effect, probably, either on the attendance at the theatre, or the sale of the book. For many successive months every place in the house was always secured a fortnight in advance, and of several editions of the play — which was published with historical notes, a preliminary discourse, and a dedicatory epistle to the nation — scarcely was one printed before another was required.

CHAPTER VIII.

An Exciting Period. — A Fashionable Mania. — Robespierre's Protest. — A Lively Subject. — Mirabeau and the Queen. — Poetically Ugly. — Saving the Monarchy. — Too Late! Too Late! — "*La Grande Trahison!*" — Proposed Federal *Fête*.

O exciting were the events of the period — exasperating many to frenzy, exalting others to the height of insane joy — that the coolest and calmest of temperaments often yielded to their agitating influence. This irritable state of public feeling led to innumerable duels, until duelling became so general that society seemed to have entered on a war of self-extermination. Its battle-field was the Bois de Boulogne. The fashionable weapon was the pistol, an innovation from England rapidly supplanting the sword, and which daily drew large numbers of spectators to the Bois, curious to see its merits tested. There was always a plentiful sprinkling of the gentler sex amongst the throng, who, with evident enjoyment, witnessed these combats, and, as at a tournament, incited the ardour of the combatants by their presence, their smiles, and their plaudits.

Offensive words uttered in the heat of debate often brought the more ardent, younger, and impetuous of the deputies to these morning *ré-unions*, to give and take satisfaction, as was now *de rigueur*, in the passage of arms. Barnave, Cazalès, and the two Lameths had many duels, both with pistols and swords, — a bullet in the shoulder, a shot or two in the arm, a grazed head, and a few deep flesh wounds being the slight result in their case. Actors were especially prone to duelling, and Talma, an excellent fencer, was often *en scène* in that way. It was a sort of mania, peculiarly fierce at that time, and chiefly determined duelling *à mort*. No efforts could put it down. Men claimed it as one of the rights of citizens, to risk their lives if they liked; nor did the practice greatly abate until the guillotine came into full play.

Strangely enough, the Assembly were then in lively debate whether to accept or reject Doctor Guillotin's invention for cutting off heads rapidly and painlessly, having already decreed that the manner of inflicting capital punishment should in all cases be by beheading.* When this decision was come to, one of the deputies, a young law-

---

* Louis XVI. is said to have requested a description of Doctor Guillotin's machine, and its mode of action, which appears to have been sometimes uncertain when first submitted to the Assembly. As he had some mechanical skill, he perceived where the defect lay, suggested the remedy, and gave a sketch of it. It was adopted, — his own head, within a year after, falling by the machine he had been interested in, and had made more effective. — A. DUMAS, "*Le Drame de '93.*"

yer, rose and protested against the infliction of capital punishment in any form or for any crime. "Society," he said, "had no right to take the life of one of its members, though he should be a dangerous person or even a guilty one."

The name of this deputy was Maximilien Robespierre! His protest was supported by his colleague, Duport, whom he afterwards sent to the scaffold. What sanguinary projects that protest concealed! Who, among the Assembly to whom it was addressed, would have believed, could the fact have then been suggested to them, that all present, with but few exceptions, were destined to fall victims to this deputy, with a face, in form and expression, so strongly resembling a tiger's, — to this Robespierre, in his efforts to wade through blood to power; or that the horrible machine whose merits they had heard set forth with so much earnestness by its humane inventor, amidst the laughter of the Assembly, was ere long to be so closely put to the test by themselves?

Perhaps some of them really were suspicious of evil lurking under the enjoyment of the " Rights of Man," for among the applicants for passports — averaging now two hundred daily — were several of the representatives of the people, who had given in their resignation, and, under the plea of ill health or pressing affairs, were seeking repose for themselves and families in the more congenial climate of Italy, Switzerland, or elsewhere. Many stanch royalists also emigrated at this time, disheartened by the inactivity of the king. One of them, in a letter addressed to him on leaving France, speaking the feeling of many, said: "As you will not be my king, I will no longer be your subject."

But the spring was advancing, and the queen, becoming anxious for a less confined and more pleasant residence at that season than the Tuileries, — then hemmed in on two sides by narrow streets and unwholesome dwellings, — the removal of the royal family to St. Cloud was not opposed by the Assembly; but to prevent any attempt at flight a strong detachment of the Parisian National Guard was ordered to accompany them. Aides-de-camp were also appointed to attend the king, queen, and dauphin in their walks and drives.

It was, however, at St. Cloud, in a summerhouse in a shady part of the gardens, distant from the château, that the Comte de la Marck contrived the interview between Mirabeau and the queen. It was the month of May, 1790, and Mirabeau, under the pretext of visiting his friend, Clavières, who had a residence in that direction, rode out early in the morning towards St. Cloud, and was met at a short distance from the château by the count, who admitted him to the park by a private entrance, and presented him to the queen, who was waiting in the summer-house to receive him.

Mirabeau was then suffering in health, his naturally robust constitution being completely undermined by a long course of profligacy and persecution, to which had latterly been added the exhaustion of his stormy political career. The queen had nerved herself, as it were, for this interview, as for a much dreaded ordeal, and had resolved to make an effort to be gracious. From the accounts she had received of his overbearing manners in the Assembly, the arrogance of the messages he had sent to the king, his reported hideousness of person, the rolling thunder of his voice, and the infamy of his past life, she was prepared to find in this all-powerful but degenerate Mirabeau a man of repulsive exterior, rough and bearish, if not actually discourteous.

M. de Chateaubriand says of Mirabeau's countenance that "its ugliness was placed on the foundation of beauty peculiar to his Florentine race, and that it produced the effect of a sort of powerful figure of Michael Angelo's 'Last Judgment.'" His father said more plainly, if less poetically, that he was "as ugly as Satan." There was, however, fascination in this ugliness, and, when he chose, a seductive charm in his manners, that was attractive to most persons who came under its influence. A thrill, almost of terror, would pass through the minds of others, "when," to quote

Chateaubriand again, "he shook his long, thick masses of hair, and gazed on the people." There was the spell of the basilisk in his eye, and many in the Assembly had felt it.

The impression he made on the queen was by no means unfavourable. He could be as courtly in his demeanour as, when it suited him, he could be uncouth. Then he had a winning tongue, and could control the tones of his deep bass voice, so that a lady's ear need not be appalled by it, even in a tiny *kiosque* or summer-house. The interview is said to have lasted an hour, and that Mirabeau ended it with the exclamation: "Madame, the monarchy is saved!" The queen condescended to extend her fair hand. Mirabeau touched it with his lips, and with a smile, which has been compared, with more romance, perhaps, than truth, to a momentary gleam of glory illumining his scarred and livid satanic face, took his leave.

Doubtless, he left the royal presence in a well-satisfied frame of mind. His terms for "saving the monarchy," previously arranged with the Comtes de Mercy-Argenteau and de la Marck, were accepted. They have been variously stated. The following are thought to be the most correct: "A sum, once paid, of 500,000 *francs*, or £20,000, to free him from debt, and 50,000 *francs*, or £2,000, monthly for such expenses as he might find it needful to incur for the realisation of his promise. Had he lived, it was probably then too late to save the monarchy, or with a new Constitution embodying many desirable reforms (which was part of his plan) to have restored order and tranquillity in France.

With Monsieur and Madame, who could have understood his views and aided him in the carrying of them out, success might possibly have ensued. But it was not in the power of any one of the many who so sincerely desired it, either to serve or to save poor Louis XVI. and Marie Antoinette. "I am making use of Mirabeau," wrote the queen to Count Flashslanden, the Emperor Leopold's minister. Yet Mirabeau's plan for escaping to the frontier was used only when Mirabeau was no longer there to subdue the Assembly and prevent pursuit.

As for Mirabeau himself, it was soon perceived that a golden shower had fallen on him from some quarter, and suspicion pointed to the right one. He had been very short of cash during the absence of the Duc d'Orléans, whose interests he had hitherto promoted. And now the duke had returned he was far less intimately linked with him than before; for Mirabeau had his own hôtel in the Chaussée d'Antin — then called Rue de l'Hôtel Dieu. It had belonged to Mdlle. Julie Soubise, Talma's much injured first wife, whose suppers and *soirées d'artistes* had been famous before her marriage.

The same *salons* now resounded with the noisy

mirth of Mirabeau's dissipated companions, and expensive habits succeeded to the moderate style of living which straitened means and the pressure of debt had hitherto forced on him. Such a change was not likely to pass unnoticed. Mirabeau had already supported the pretensions of the king to declare war, should the necessity arise, against the claim of the Assembly to take the initiative in such a case. Great, then, was the outcry. From one end of Paris to the other the journals proclaimed, *"la grande trahison du Comte de Mirabeau."*

This defection, as it was called, raised a storm against him. But his speech, in answer to the attack of Barnave and others, silenced all. None found a word to utter in reply. Admiration alone was expressed at the conclusion of this powerful display of eloquence. It was his apparent sacrifice of popularity, on this occasion, to the upholding of the royal prerogative, that is said to have overcome the queen's unwillingness to consent to a personal interview with him.

However, the proposal of M. Sylvain Bailly, the Mayor of Paris, to celebrate the first anniversary of the taking of the Bastille by a *fête* in the Champ de Mars, at which all France should be invited to assist, was so enthusiastically responded to that, for a time, all else was forgotten — even to *"la grande conspiration du Comte de Mirabeau."*

CHAPTER IX.

Levelling the Champ de Mars. — The Eve of the Federal *Fête*. — Arrival of the Federals. — Marching to Quarters. — Bishop Talleyrand. — The Oriflamme of France. — "*Au Sein de sa Famille.*" — The Constitutional Oath. — An Enviable Privilege. — The People's Thanksgiving. — Frenchmen and Freemen. — Poor Madame Necker! — The Icy Hand of Death. — Retiring into Private Life.

ALL Paris was assisting in the patriotic work of levelling the Champ de Mars, to prepare it for the grandest *fête* and the most important ceremony that occurred during the period of the Revolution, — the anniversary of the surrender of the Bastille, and the confederation of the Communes of the whole kingdom, on the 14th of July, 1790. To the requisition that all France should attend, the eighty-three departments sent each its representatives. Whatever had been hitherto overlooked of privileges and distinctions, titles or orders of chivalry, the Assembly now finally abolishes. All are to meet on an equality at this great scene of fraternisation, to take the oath of fidelity to "the Nation, the Law, and the King."

The *Te Deum* at Notre-Dame, on the evening of the 13th, with the solemn chant following it, which was composed for the occasion, and appears to have been grandly dramatic, was an impressive preparation for the great event of the morrow. A very large number of musicians and choristers assembled to give due effect to the music, which — as described by one who was present * — "was so highly expressive that it caused the intensest excitement in the hearers. Discords, skilfully placed, produced melancholy emotions, and suggested ideas of trouble and disquietude; preparing the mind for a recitative, that powerfully affected the audience, by vividly recalling those scenes of consternation and horror which prevailed in Paris on the 13th of July, 1789" — heralding the greater horrors of the 14th. The words were: "People, your enemies advance with hostile sentiments and menacing looks. They come to bathe their hands in your blood. Already they encompass the walls of your city. Rise! rise from the inaction in which you are plunged. Seize your arms! Fly to the combat! God will fight for you!"

A chorus followed, deep and solemn, of instruments and voices, with which was mingled the tolling of a loud, heavy bell, in imitation of the *tocsin*, when, during the attack on the Bastille, the bells of every church and convent in Paris sounded an alarm. This confusion of sounds was inexpressibly awful. It chilled the blood: every

* Helen Maria Williams, "Souvenirs of the Revolution."

heart seemed frozen with terror. But at length the bell ceased. The music changed its tone, and the audience breathed more freely. Another recitative announced the complete defeat of the enemy. This was succeeded by a grand flourish of trumpets and the rolling of drums; the whole terminating with a song of triumph, and a hymn of thanksgiving to the "Supreme Being."

There had been heavy rain for some days, and on the 13th there was every appearance of its continuance. Yet from all parts of France the Federals were arriving by hundreds, and from some departments by thousands. Patriotism, or curiosity, it was observable, had been more powerfully stimulated by recent events in some remote districts than in others. Many of these patriots had trudged the whole distance, and were weary, wet, and footsore; for they were of every class. Most of them saw Paris for the first time in their lives, and found all things new and surprising. The greater number brought with them only poorly filled purses; many had exhausted their contents on the journey, and reached the capital fainting with hunger and fatigue. There was also among them a large proportion of the well-to-do agricultural class, with others of superior grade.

In every house were quartered as many of this vast influx of visitors as the inhabitants were able or willing to receive. As they were marched to the quarters assigned them, baskets filled with bread, fruit, wine, and cooked provisions, were brought by the people to the doors, or were let down from the windows of the houses on the route. The theatres, all exhibitions and public buildings, were open to the Federals gratis; and, generally, they were well lodged and provided for. The costumes of every province, or new department — all quaint, and many picturesque — would have made a pretty sight of themselves. But the 14th dawned frowningly. Dark masses of cloud swept over the sky, and soon the drenching downpour began, — as though the heavens were weeping for the deeds of blood that marked with infamy the day so strangely fêted in the name of liberty. Nothing daunted, however, the Federals, with the banners of their respective departments, assemble, to the number of a hundred and fifty thousand, on the site of the Bastille, to march to the Champ de Mars.

There, in the centre, erected for the occasion, rises the grand altar, — "*L'autel de la Patrie.*" And, arrayed in full canonicals, with a broad tricoloured scarf passed over the right shoulder and falling under the left arm to the very edge of his violet robes, M. de Talleyrand-Périgord appears on the scene. He is now Bishop of Autun, as well as a deputy of the National Assembly. With halting gait, and the same equivocal smile that hovered on his face from youth to old age, he ascends the steps of the altar, which is raised twenty feet above the ground. M. de Talleyrand is charged with what are termed the religious functions of the *fête*, — no other bishop having been willing to undertake them. He will celebrate high mass, assisted by sixty almoners of the National Guard, wearing white robes and tricoloured scarfs.

Seats, rising one above another, in the manner of an amphitheatre, surround the vast arena of the Champ de Mars. Two hundred thousand persons are seated there as spectators. Half of them, at least, are women, in white dresses and tricoloured scarfs. Not less than from two to two hundred and fifty thousand others, men and women, spectators also, are compelled to be satisfied with standing-room. All are provided with umbrellas, and, to those who, from upper windows, and the roofs of adjacent houses, look down on this multitude, the scene presents the appearance of an immense parti-coloured tent.

But, hark ! — a salvo of artillery ! The Federal host arrives, escorted by fourteen thousand of the cavalry and infantry of the French army. On they come — tramp, tramp ! Banners are raised aloft, but not flying. Bands are playing, and soon the ear is greeted by the well-known strains, " *Vive Henri Quatre*," and " *Charmante Gabrielle*." The oriflamme heads the march; that ancient royal standard of the Kings of France becomes to-day the national standard of the people. Soaked with wet, it hangs heavily down, or clings round its staff with a sudden gust of wind. The people are dripping wet, too, but their ardour is not even damped.

What a shout of welcome rends the air as the newcomers take up the position assigned them! Would that it could rend the clouds and bring forth the bright beams of the July sun to dry the ground, that resembles a sea of mud, bespattering the wet garments of this mighty host, as they jostle each other, wade to and fro, dance where they can find any space, or play other wild antics in it!

Twelve hundred musicians, in four separate orchestras, play popular airs at intervals; but at about three o'clock, when the efforts of the multitude to be gay under difficulties had begun to flag, the whole of the orchestras, at some signal given, suddenly struck up the air, "*Où peut-on être mieux qu'au sein de sa famille?*" It heralds (rather ironically, circumstances and weather considered) the arrival of the king, *alias* "*Pouvoir Exécutif.*" He and the royal family have come from St. Cloud, unwillingly enough, no doubt, to take part in the ceremony of the day. Shortly after, the clanging of bells, the firing of cannon, and a *grande fanfare* of trumpets, announces that mass is about to be said.

This is a solemn farce indeed. The officiating bishop "begs La Fayette not to look at him lest he should laugh." The country cousins of the vast congregation are disposed to be silent and serious; but their Parisian friends show some impatience, and a greater desire for "*Ça ira*" than for a *Te Deum*. The pious bishop, however, soon brings the service to an end,* and the great event of the day — taking the oath — is proceeded with. It devolves on Général de La Fayette to be first to pronounce it.

He mounts the steps of the altar with his drawn sword in his hand. Resting the point on the tabernacle containing the Holy Host, he, in a loud voice, says, speaking in the name of the people: "We swear to be ever faithful to the nation, the law, and the king; to maintain the Constitution decreed by the National Assembly and accepted by the king, by every means in our power; and to dwell in amity with all Frenchmen, united by the indissoluble bonds of fraternity." The tricoloured banner is then waved over the altar as "the sign of universal confederation being accomplished." Salvos of artillery, and frantic cries of "*Vive la Nation! Vive le Roi!*" respond to it. The king's turn then comes.

In a small pavilion near the grand altar, a seat called a throne has been prepared for him. There he has, at least, the enviable privilege of being sheltered from the implacably descending torrents

---

* This is said to have been the last time that Bishop Talleyrand officiated in any ceremony of the Church.

of rain. For some unexplained reason the king takes the oath in his pavilion. Rumour said that it was a side door opened to him as a way of escape from the fulfilment of his oath, should he find it desirable to avail himself of it. But an altar served by Bishop Talleyrand is, to the mind of Louis XVI., an altar profaned. This may account for his not approaching it. The people, however, are not satisfied. They have seen nothing; they have heard nothing, and they cry vehemently, "*Bis! Bis!*"

M. de La Fayette steps forward. He draws his sword, waves it above his head, and silence ensues for the distance of a few yards around him. "My friends," he says, "the king has taken the oath, and an oath cannot be asked for a second time, like an opera air." Few, of course, hear his words; but La Fayette is the popular man of the hour, and as he seems satisfied, the multitude cannot be otherwise. The queen, at the same time, holds up the dauphin. Does the haughty, vindictive Marie Antoinette really deign to make an effort to conciliate the people, or does she mentally bid them behold the avenger? Whatever feeling prompted the act, it is a great success. Vociferous acclamations follow: "*Vive le dauphin!*" but, alas, no "*Vive le reine!*" though a ray of sunshine suddenly gleams through a rift in a cloud and momentarily rests on the head of the dauphin and on the oriflamme of France.

It is accepted by all as a favourable omen, but interpreted according to each one's wishes. By way, however, of the people's thanksgiving, twenty thousand of the Federals join hands and dance round the altar, singing "*Ça ira! Ça ira!*" With this performance, and with plenty of coarse jesting, peals of laughter, snatches of military songs, and renewed torrents of rain, this grand national, farcical *religious* and rainy *fête* concludes. The king leaves his throne in the pavilion. La Fayette is at last able to sheathe his sword. The constitutional bishop limps down from the altar. His eyelids droop lower than usual, and a smile more expressive of mockery than pleasure plays on his fair, effeminate face.

It was remarked that the king exhibited no emotion at any part of the ceremony; that he gazed with perfect indifference on that surging mass of upwards of half a million of his subjects assembled around him, and that he took his departure hastily, speaking to none who were present, being anxious, no doubt, to get back to St. Cloud to dinner.

The people prolonged the *fête* of the Federation from the 14th to the 17th, dancing being kept up unceasingly during those three days on the Place de la Bastille. Then the Federals began to return to their homes, duly impressed with the proud feeling that now they were Frenchmen, freemen, and their several departments integral parts of "*la grande Nation.*" The *fête* of the Federation doubtless did serve to nationalise France; for, hitherto, "all France" meant "all Paris;" and the provincials were more prone to pride themselves on their separate denominations of Brétons, Provençals, Burgundians, etc., than on the national one of Frenchmen.

Soon after this event M. Necker tendered his resignation. Thwarted in all his financial measures by Mirabeau, whom, when power was in his hands, he had neglected; and his popularity as well as his occupation being gone, he proposed to retire to his native Switzerland. But a twelvemonth since his dismissal had caused a Revolution. The Bastille might still have been standing had he not received his *congé*. Now, his departure is almost a flight; and the Assembly — for it is not to the king that his resignation was sent — scarcely deign to notice it. Through the towns where so lately the post-masters contended for the honour of being his postilions, or even serving him as horses, on his return he was frequently hissed and hooted. At best, none deemed it worth while to show him any attention. At Bar-sur-Aube he was arrested, and had to wait the arrival of an order from the Assembly before he was allowed to continue his journey. Poor Madame Necker! How acutely she must have suffered when her divine husband was subjected to this humiliation.

Mesdames, the king's aunts, alarmed at the decrees against the Church, also determined on flight, and selected Rome for their city of refuge, looking to receive consolation for themselves from the sovereign pontiff, and to obtain from him indulgences for the French nation. They, too, were twice stopped on their journey, though armed with two passports. But Mirabeau, favouring the court, and having also arranged a plan for the departure of the king, vigorously opposed any decree that forbade emigration. In anticipation of such a decree, families were hastening to leave the kingdom. Nor could the ridicule and contempt with which it was attempted to check the general disposition to seek the blessings of freedom beyond the limits of fair France, deter any who had the means, or could raise them, from beating a hasty retreat.

The revolutionary torrent continues to roll on, gathering strength as it proceeds; and the only man of a calibre capable of stemming it, of snatching the king and his family from the fate too surely awaiting them, or of saving France from the domination of sanguinary ruffians, is suddenly smitten down by the icy hand of death. On the 2d of April, 1791, a painful illness of three days ended the mighty Mirabeau's career of suffering, turmoil, and strife. The whole nation mourned him; and to provide a fitting receptacle for his remains, the new church of St. Geneviève was then transformed into "*Le Panthéon*," with the dedication, "*Aux grands hommes, la patrie reconnaissante.*"

The flight of the royal family from Paris shortly followed the death of Mirabeau. Monsieur and Madame, who took different routes, and carried out their plans with secrecy and prudence, reached Brussels without misadventure. But unhappily, from the king's want of caution, he and his family were recognised at Varennes, arrested, and brought back to the capital, and placed under the strict surveillance of the National Guard. The people were greatly exasperated. The Assembly assumed the functions of royalty, and declared the king provisionally suspended. But on the 13th of September, when Louis XVI. accepted and swore to maintain the "*Acte Constitutionnel*," the "*pouvoir exécutif*" was again placed in his hands.

Soon after, the Assembly announced that their mission was ended, and that, leaving France in the hands of a constitutional king and a legislative assembly, the deputies would resign office and retire into private life. On the close of the session, the populace greeted the deputies generally with *vivas*, loud and reiterated; but to the "virtuous Pétion," and the "incorruptible Robespierre," a sort of ovation was accorded. This was a sign of sinister augury.

CHAPTER X.

The Legislative Assembly. — Mirabeau and Barnave. — "The Heroine of the Gironde." — Roland's Letter to Louis XVI. — Planting a Tree of Liberty. — The King's Great Courage. — Bonaparte and Bourrienne. — A Bold Front. — The Duke's Manifesto. — The Queen's Letters to Fersen. — Comte Roederer and the Queen. — Lodged in the Temple. — Lucile Desmoulins. — The Queen's Sponges and Brushes. — A Grand Turn-out. — Qualms of Conscience.

THE "National Legislative Assembly" opened their first session on the 1st of October. The king had now an opportunity afforded him, had he known how to use it, of recovering much of his lost prestige; also of averting many of the evils of the Revolution by a judicious employment of the power that remained to him. But neither king nor queen would accept the position of constitutional sovereign, though the former had taken the oath to do so, nor would they be guided in the matter by the advice of friends.

Barnave, who, with Pétion, had been sent to Varennes to bring back the royal family, had become sincerely devoted to the queen and princesses. Frequently he saw the queen in private. Unlike Mirabeau, who had sold himself to the court, Barnave was disinterested. Yet Marie

Antoinette would not listen to his urgent entreaty that, if only to avoid the many personal annoyances a refusal might lead to, she would appoint her household herself, as the Assembly requested she would do. She pleaded against it that, selecting the members of her household from the constitutional party, she would offend those who composed her former one. She would, therefore, be obliged to dismiss the new household as soon as the old order of things was restored, or not a single noble of their court would then remain with them. The king had the same scruples, both with regard to his household and his ministers.

Yet the queen's correspondence at this time (1791-2) with Count Fersen, carried on through the agency of M. Goguenot, would seem to bear witness to a keener appreciation, on her part, of the dangers then threatening her. But only by Fersen and an invasion of foreign troops would she consent to be saved. Fersen, however, could do nothing more than tell her of a hiding-place in the Louvre, where, as a last resource, she might conceal herself until help could reach her. M. de Mercy-Argenteau, who still lingered in France, to serve her if possible, told the Comte de Lescure that Austria was making no preparations for war; and that none of the European powers, unless forced to do so, were disposed to entertain the project of an invasion.

Meanwhile, the Revolution was marching on

with giant strides. During the early part of the twelvemonth in which the Legislative Assembly held sway, that phalanx of young and eloquent orator's of the Gironde, who, unhappily, were not statesmen, came prominently into notice. The king, having still the power of forming his own Cabinet, in March, 1792, chose his ministers from among them, the queen contemptuously naming them the *sans-culotte* ministry. The gifted Madame Roland, the "heroine of the Gironde," who, with her husband, looked forward to the realisation of their dream of a republic, whose citizens should be submissive to the laws and fertile in virtues, then began the short but brilliant career that was to end on the scaffold.

The intense dissimulation and feebleness of the character of Louis XVI. were fully exhibited in the petty ruses he employed to evade sanctioning the measures of these Girondins, without actually rejecting them. The state of suspense and inaction this imposed on them produced Roland's celebrated letter to the king on his constitutional duties. It was, in fact, written by the minister's wife; but its sentiments were so entirely approved by him, that he found nothing to add to or to alter in it. The result was the king's dismissal of the Girondin ministry on the 11th June, — and probably the sealing of his own doom. For the Girondins were not of the men of blood, or of those who then desired the king's dethronement.

A movement was also on foot at that time to stay the Revolution, headed by such men as La Fayette, Lally-Tollendal, and others, who still called themselves "constitutional monarchists." They strove to put down the Jacobin and other revolutionary clubs, hoping thus to stem the torrent to which they had been among the first to open the floodgates. Vain hope! Such possible alleviation as might, perhaps, have been brought to the king and family on those fatal days of June and August, so near at hand, had Général de La Fayette been Mayor of Paris, as proposed, was frustrated by the blind infatuation of the queen. "La Fayette," she said, "wishes to be Mayor of Paris that he may become Mayor of the Palace." Whatever influence the court could command was therefore exerted to raise Pétion to that office, and he accordingly succeeded M. Bailly.

The 20th of June was the anniversary of the taking of the oath in the tennis-court. It was a famous pretext for a civic *fête*, and the planting of a tree of liberty. Thirty thousand men, women, and children, — filthy, ragged, disreputable; the *sans-culottes*, as the Abbé Maury named them, — assembled and paraded the city, chanting the famous "*Ça ira!*" under the windows of the Tuileries. Strangely enough, the king ordered the outer gates and doors to be opened, and the wretched rabble of course flocked in. The National Guards on duty pushed a table into a deep embrasure, placed a chair upon it, and, with their assistance, Louis XVI. mounted and took his seat in that dignified fashion — the guards forming the barrier between him and the *canaille*. Where the doors were not found open, hatchets, hammers, pikes, blunderbusses, etc., with which the mob was armed, were used to force an entrance.

"Never," say some French historians, "did Louis XVI. display greater courage than on this deplorable occasion." But surely, never did he show himself less fit to be the ruler of his people. At no time was he dignified; and his fat, unwieldy, commonplace person, seated in a chair on a table, must have been little calculated to impress with any feelings of respect the drunken, ruffian mob he had admitted to his palace. And it did not. They insulted and menaced him. The odour of their dirty garments, the heat of the day, and the crowded state of the room having, it appears, created thirst, the king readily drank a glass of wine, which one of the men handed to him from a bottle he carried. Some accounts say that he drank from the bottle itself. But whichever it was, it produced a shout of applause. A still louder one hailed his acceptance of the *bonnet rouge*, presented to him on a pike, and which he placed on his head.

The guards then threw open the window where the king was sitting, that the outside mob might understand the shout of the mob within, and see the "*Pouvoir Exécutif*" crowned with a greasy cap of liberty.

Two young men — one seeking military employment, the other some subordinate post in a government office — were then standing on the terrace of the Tuileries, spectators of the disgraceful scene. The military aspirant raised his eyes, when the window was thrown open that all might see the degradation of the king. A movement, as if of impatience, escaped him: "How came they to suffer this *canaille* to enter?" he said. "They should have blown four or five hundred of them into the air, and the rest would have taken to their heels." This is pretty much what he did himself three years later, on the 13th Vendémiaire (5th October), 1795. The speaker was Bonaparte, his companion Bourrienne.

Meanwhile, Pétion arrived. The Mayor of Paris had been rather tardy in his movements; for his sympathies were more with the mob than with the king. He, however, mounted a table and "invited" the tumultuous assemblage to take leave. Obedient to the voice of this demagogue, the *sans-culotte* rabble began to disperse, — but not without many insulting expressions, and threats of further violence if the king did not sanction certain decrees of the Assembly.

The Duc de Liancourt, who commanded a division of the army at Rouen, and whose troops were devoted to him, prayed the king to allow him to escort him to that town. He declined; and rejected also the proposal of La Fayette, seconded by numerous officers of the National Guard, to conduct him to Compiègne, and to place him at the head of his army. But, like the queen, he now looked for his deliverance from a coalition of the European powers. Until that deliverance came, he believed himself safe from further intrusion, — having, as he fancied, received the insurgent mob with so bold a front that they would shrink from again encountering him.

But in spite of ungrateful rebuffs, Général de La Fayette did not abandon his purpose of serving the king and queen, if possible; or, failing in that, of saving them by some means from the fate which menaced them. Yet his efforts were constantly thwarted — paralysed by the queen's hatred of the man who sought to serve her. Their only results, therefore, were La Fayette's loss of popularity, and the breaking up of the constitutional party. The first attempt of the corps of emigrants to march on France, aided by Prussian and Austrian troops, together with the publication of the Duke of Brunswick's threatening and contemptuous manifesto, raised throughout the length and breadth of the land the frantic cry: "Citizens, the country is in danger!" Revolutionary ardour, already at fever heat, responded: "Vengeance! Down with the throne! Down with the traitor king!"

The people demanded that the Assembly should within twenty-four hours pronounce the king's deposition. An attack on the Tuileries was openly organised and prepared for. It had, unfortunately, been provoked by the impolitic threat of the duke's manifesto to sack Paris, if any insult were offered to the king or attempt made on the château. He menaced with all the horrors of an invasion, such towns as should dare to defend themselves. Their houses were to be burnt or razed to the ground, their inhabitants treated as rebels. This was the aid — the supreme revenge — that poor Marie Antoinette had been looking forward to, and which was to restore the old order of things.

As far as means within reach permitted, the château was prepared for defence against the threatened attack on the 12th of August, as reported. It was thought that it could hold out until the invading army arrived. But on the 29th July the queen writes to Count Fersen that "it is most important to gain twenty-four hours." Again, on the 1st of August, she writes, and it is her last letter to him, more urgently deprecating delay, for "unless help," she says, "arrives promptly, Providence alone can save the king and his family." Yet another opportunity of flight was offered. But the queen still feared to compromise the interests of the throne by accepting other help than that on its march from Coblentz. That help, as all know, never came.

The *tocsin* sounded and drums beat to arms at midnight on the 9th. The attack on the Tuileries was made on the 10th. The Assembly were powerless to prevent it; for it was an insurrection of the populace, the sovereign *sans-culottes*. They were incited and encouraged by the chiefs of the Commune of Paris, — the red-handed monsters under whose sanguinary domination France was about to fall, and whose crimes were to impress on the French Revolution a character of bloodthirstiness more insatiable than any that history records. The 10th was a day of massacre; thousands lay dead in the Place de Carrousel, around the Tuileries, and in the Champs Élysées. This carnage was the work of some bands of men from different parts of France, but chiefly from Marseilles. At the cry of "*La patrie en danger!*" they had enrolled themselves as volunteers, and singing the famous but sombre "Marseillaise," — composed by an officer of the army of the Rhine for his own battalion, — marched to Paris, and were put into barracks as "Federal troops."

As related in Comte Roederer's "*Chronique des 50 jours*" — considered a scrupulously exact narrative of what took place — the queen's conduct and language on that terrible occasion awakened a reminiscence of Maria Theresa in her early days. Until then Marie Antoinette had seemed to have inherited only the thoughtlessness and the dissipated and extravagant tastes of her father, Leopold the First. But her conversation with Roederer, and her whole bearing, while her poor, miserably helpless husband, "*le pauvre homme,*" even then indifferent, inert, impassive, stood by without proffering a word, showed that she possessed the qualities of a heroine. United to a man of more energetic and dignified character, her career might have been a far different one. Folly and frivolity subdued, the instincts of a noble nature might have been developed and have shed lustre on the throne she shared, — instead of awakening only tardy sympathy for a misguided, unhappy woman in the day of her trouble and humiliation.

The calmness and firmness of M. Roederer doubtless protected the king and his family from personal violence, when, at his urgent advice, they sought refuge with the Assembly from the fury of the mob and the Marseillais. Their removal to an apartment in the former convent of the Feuillants, and thence to the Temple, are events too well known to need noting in detail in this brief sketch of that terrible drama, the French Revolution.

It was difficult, no doubt, to live in the midst of ardent patriots without in some degree sharing in their enthusiasm for *la liberté régénératrice,*— that wonder-working principle which was to inaugurate the reign of wisdom, virtue, and justice in

France, and eventually to regenerate the world. But it seems incredible that women, at least, should not have lost faith in it, when they perceived that the desired end could be reached only through scenes of anarchy and bloodshed. Yet there were women, young and lovely, as some writers would have us believe, who revelled in those scenes of horror, and gloated over them no less frantically than the men. The wife of the miserable enthusiast, Camille Desmoulins, appears to have been of that number.

"The charming Lucile" has been usually represented as the type of gentleness, *naïveté*, grace, and simplicity, as well as of beauty. A letter given by M. de Beaumont Vassy in his "*Mémoires sécrets, etc.,*" throws a very different light on her character. The original letter was in M. de Beaumont's possession. It had been placed at his disposal by M. Motton de Vervins, who was related to the Desmoulins family. It is from Lucile to her mother, and was written on the evening of the 10th of August. As Lucile has been credited also with the advantages of education, and of course *esprit*, it is surprising to find that this letter is a wonderful specimen of French phonetic spelling and the absence of punctuation. But M. de Beaumont attributes that partly to excitement.

The letter is too long to give *in extenso;* a few extracts will, however, furnish an idea of the whole.

The gentle Lucile informs her dear mother that "since yesterday at midnight until past one this afternoon the *tocsin* has not ceased sounding. We are victors, the château is burning, the blood of the Swiss is flowing in rivulets; Suleau's head has been cut off and is being carried through Paris.* The monsters had surrounded the dome of the château with cannon, and our unfortunate Marseillais received the first discharge; the king is at the Assembly; he is to be deposed; La Fayette is in Paris; his house is to be razed to the ground; a good many people are wounded, but, thank God, none of our patriots; C. [Camille] cannot leave the Commune or the Section; the patriots and the people are now going to encamp in the Tuileries; I am writing at Danton's; no women are allowed to go out; but risk it and come here — ask only, if you pass the barriers, whether you can repass them, for the people are still killing, and will show no favour; they are breaking the mirrors in the château, and have brought me and Mme. Danton the sponges and brushes from the queen's *toilette;* the silver they would not touch, but trod it under foot. They are now coming triumphant, crying '*Vive la Nation!*' and carry-

* Suleau, the witty journalist of the monarchist party. He was stabbed by the furious revolutionary woman, Théroigne de Méricourt, while waiting for his pass to be examined. With the dagger drawn from the wound he strove to defend himself, but was cut down and massacred, and his head paraded through the streets as the first trophy of victory, on the morning of the 10th.

ing on pikes the torn clothing covered with the blood of those scoundrels. Oh, what a ferment! C. and all the patriots are going to embrace those generous Marseillais."

Thus wrote the "charming Lucile," the worthy helpmate of Camille Desmoulins, "the first apostle of liberty," the active promoter of all those atrocious insurrections. Yet, like the brutal Danton, he was sentimental and maudlin, when, by and by, becoming slightly nauseated by the sight of the ever-flowing, sanguinary torrent, he was regarded as a doubtful patriot, and required to submit his own worthless head to the action of the guillotine. He violently resisted all efforts to force him to mount the scaffold until his clothing was nearly torn off him.

To the sack of the Tuileries succeeded the revolting massacres of the September days, when the poor Princesse de Lamballe was so barbarously murdered, and when Madame de Staël, who had remained in Paris until the *tocsin* sounded as a signal for the butchery to begin, thought to awe the frenzied *sans-culotte* mob by the *éclat* of her equipage. In the ambassador's state carriage, with its six gaily caparisoned horses, and a retinue of servants, and friends disguised as such, in state liveries, she expected to pass out of the city unmolested. Neither as Necker's daughter nor as Swedish ambassadress did the mob respect her or the pomp and parade of her grand turn-out.

They took her to the Section, where Manuel, the syndic of the Commune, shielded her from further violence, and probably saved her life. She passed the day alone in his apartment while he was urging on the slaughter. Sometimes an emotion of pity or a qualm of conscience stayed his hand, and instead of striking down his victim he opened the prison door and bade him escape for his life. When night came on Madame de Staël was conducted to her hôtel, and early on the following morning, ere the work of carnage again began, Pétion escorted her beyond the barriers, closing his eyes to the fact that among her servants were men denounced as traitors to *la patrie*, and for whose heads the guillotine was waiting.

CHAPTER XI.

The Convention. — The Year One of the Republic. — Sentence of Death. — Marat and Robespierre. — Charlotte Corday. — The Antechamber of Death. — A Startling Contrast. — The Witnesses. — Condemned to Death. — The Execution. — Sanson Overworked. — Despatched in Batches. — A *Réunion* of Old Friends. — Cécile Rénault. — Playing the God. — "Perish the Traitor! the Tyrant!"

N the 21st of September the National Convention, superseding the Legislative Assembly, took possession of the theatre of the Tuileries for their place of meeting, and immediately declared royalty abolished. On the 22d, at eighteen minutes thirty seconds past nine — the hour at which the sun on entering the sign of the balance arrived at the true autumnal equinox, and *Egalité* was proclaimed in the heavens by equal days and nights, the Republic, "one and indivisible," was proclaimed throughout France. "*Liberté, Egalité, Fraternité*" was the motto adopted. A bitterly satirical one under the circumstances; for in this model republic tumult and disorder everywhere prevailed, and frightful crimes were committed.

With the new era, the year one of the Republic, the months were renamed according to a method suggested by Fabre d'Églantine, by which the name of each month should represent its ordinary temperature and the rural occupations peculiar to it. As the sun could not be prevailed on to favour the decimal system, the year perforce continued to consist of twelve months, but of thirty days each, divided into three decades of days. The ancient Pagan names of the days were abolished, and *primodi*, *duodi*, etc., substituted for them. The five days left at the end of each year were called the *sans-culottides*, when from all parts of the republic the French people were to assemble and fraternise in Paris for the celebration of the *fête* of liberty and equality. When leap year occurred the extra day was to be devoted to a "*grande fête à la Révolution.*" The day was divided into twenty hours, and clocks and watches were adjusted accordingly.

The republican calendar being arranged and published and the Gregorian abolished, and the destruction of all that in any way recalled the idea of royalty being strictly commanded, the Convention proceeded on the 21st Frimaire (11th of December) to condemn and pass sentence on the king. The appeal to the people to confirm the sentence was refused. It was suggested by the Girondins with the hope that his life might be spared; for, if in that assembly pity yet dwelt in any breast, none had courage otherwise to express it.

France crouched in abject terror at the feet of the sanguinary Robespierre and his satellites.

Louis XVI. was condemned to death by a majority of votes that would in ordinary cases have been deemed insufficient. He was beheaded on the morning of the 21st of January, 1793.

Early in May the defection of Général Dumouriez became known. Robespierre availed himself of it to denounce the Girondins as his accomplices. Their arrest was ordered. Some of them fled to Caen, and it was then that Charlotte Corday, a native of Calvados, determined on ridding the earth of the monster Marat. She imagined that he was the denouncer of the Girondin deputies and the cause of all the misery and bloodshed then desolating France. Two or three numbers of his infamous journal, *L'Ami du Peuple*, had fallen in her way and misled her as to the extent of his influence. But she accomplished her purpose unflinchingly, and at a moment more favourable for it than probably often occurred. For this leader of the rags and dirt — otherwise *sans-culottes* — of Paris was playing the Sybarite, actually taking a bath. This was indeed a strange luxury for an ardent patriot, so careful to identify himself as one, in all respects, with the *canaille*. Unlike his powdered and scented and well-dressed friend, Robespierre, who made his home in a mean, scantily furnished garret, Marat, in his *sabots* and Carmagnole costume, dwelt in an apartment consisting of two or three rooms, with a *salon* whose sofas, chairs, and hangings were of blue satin. The only object out of harmony with the general arrangements of this comfortable and even elegant abode was Marat himself.

The revolting ceremony of the apotheosis of Marat was arranged by the furious Jacobin painter, David, who, two years before, had designed the funeral car and superintended the absurd procession that accompanied the body of Voltaire to the Pantheon. The remains of the wretched Marat were some few months later placed beside those of the great poet and philosopher. They occupied the place of Mirabeau, now rejected as unworthy of such honour, — his connection with the court having been discovered. The following year Marat was removed from the Pantheon to the public sewer, and Jean Jacques was torn from his chosen grave to replace him.

Charlotte Corday suffered for her deed (it was surely no crime) on the scaffold, and met her fate heroically. But she sacrificed her life without benefiting her country; for a greater monster even than Marat survived, and blood flowed on in an ever increasing torrent. The guillotine was permanently set up in Paris in the Place de la Révolution (Place de la Concorde), and every town in the kingdom had its auxiliary machine.

On the 2d of August poor Marie Antoinette was removed in the dead of the night to a cell in the Conciergerie, there to await her trial. She and her children, with the Princesse Elisabeth, had been subjected to every indignity and privation that could render their imprisonment in that dreary Temple Tower more wearisome, humiliating, and painful. Yet sympathising, devoted friends had unweariedly sought opportunities of alleviating the sorrows of the unhappy captives, if only by a word of hope or consolation furtively addressed to them. There had even been plans arranged for their escape. But the rigour with which the poor prisoners were guarded, and generally the brutal character of the guardians, frustrated the willing efforts of the more humane and well-intentioned among them to give effect to those plans.

The dauphin had been taken from her and placed with the infamous Simon, the cobbler. Now there was the further anguish to be endured of a last parting with her daughter and sister-in-law, with lonely confinement for upwards of two months in that "antechamber of death," the Conciergerie. For it was not until the 14th of October that Marie Antoinette was summoned to appear before the judges, who were also her accusers, and had already condemned her to the scaffold. There were wretches present who cried as she entered, "À bas l'Autrichienne! À bas Madame Véto!" Yet even the fear of the guillotine failed wholly to check the visible signs of pity and deep-felt sympathy her appearance elicited in others. Adversity had awakened in Marie Antoinette the dignity of character and elevation of sentiment which lay dormant during those earlier years, given up to dissipation, levity, and frivolity.

How startlingly the sorrowful present contrasts with the gay, thoughtless, yet brilliant past; when, in her bridal dress of satin, and pearls, and diamonds, the Duc de Cossé-Brissac led her to the balcony of the Tuileries to gratify the eager desire of the dense multitude to see her, and bade her behold in them 200,000 adorers. Shouts of "*Vive la dauphine!*" rent the air; "*Vive le dauphin!*" also, but he did not show himself. Marie Antoinette was then a very youthful bride — but, alas! what a bridegroom! Twenty-three years have passed away, and she is now a widow. In a faded dress of common black stuff, she stands in the theatre of that same palace of the Tuileries amidst a throng of *canaille*, to be tried for her life by men whose own lives would be forfeited if either compassion or justice should move them to find her not guilty.

Though so poorly clad, there is no want of majesty in her bearing, and that peculiar carriage of the head which always distinguished her has lost none of its haughtiness. Her fortunes are fallen, but she is none the less the daughter of the Cæsars. She is still young, yet grief has blanched her once bright, fair hair. Her swollen eyes and pallid face bear the traces of tears. There is an expression of mental anguish on her countenance, which she with difficulty subdues, while for upwards of two hours she replies with dignity to the numerous questions put to her. They are for the most part vague, frivolous, vexatious, or insulting. She is confronted with numberless witnesses, who tremble, as they answer, for the safety of their own heads.

There are three, however, from whom the sanguinary tribunal can elicit no charge against the poor prisoner. Their depositions, on the contrary, are in her favour. These three fearless men are the brave Admiral d'Estaing, the ex-Mayor of Paris, Sylvain Bailly, and the syndic Manuel, who had resigned his office, declaring that he could no longer endure the continual shedding of blood. He further horrified the revolutionary tribunal by acknowledging that he had spared life and shown mercy at every opportunity. No long time elapsed before these three heads fell under the guillotine as those of traitors to the republic.

The queen was, of course, declared guilty and condemned to death. On the 16th of October she arrayed herself carefully for the sacrifice, with the assistance of the wife and daughter of the Concierge, who were kind to her and obtained her a white dress, which, like Madame Roland, she preferred for the occasion to black. But she was much startled, poor thing, when, instead of the close carriage which had been used to take the king to the scaffold, she found that, as the last indignity that could be put upon her, she was to take her place in the common cart that bore several other victims to their doom. For a moment she was overcome by a feeling of horror and terror. She retreated a few steps; then, by an effort recovering herself, advanced and entered the cart.

Never perhaps had a denser crowd thronged the streets of Paris, or filled the windows of every house on the line of the route with more eager spectators; 30,000 men were under arms, cannon were placed in the squares, on the bridges, and at the corners of the principal streets, and gendarmes, horse and foot, escorted the wretched vehicle from the Conciergerie to the place of execution. No sooner did it appear than loud shouts of "*Vive la République! À mort la tyrannie!*" were raised. But Marie Antoinette seemed to hear them not. Pale, rigid, motionless, she more resembled a statue than a living being. Only when the cart stopped before the avenue of the Tuileries did she raise her eyes, and during the long, earnest gaze she cast on the château it was evident that she struggled with emotions difficult to overcome. Yet she mounted the scaffold with a firm step. And perhaps some spark of pity took the place of gratified revenge in the eager, jostling crowd that filled the vast square and clung to every available post and doorway affording foothold and a view of the scene of the execution. For the wild shrieks of savage joy that hailed her on issuing from the prison were gradually hushed as the mournful *cortège* advanced. Nor were they renewed, even when Sanson's assistant walked round the scaffold and held up, for their gratification, the unhappy victim's head.

Thus perished poor Marie Antoinette,— her fate affording one of the most terrible examples of the vicissitudes from which even royalty is not exempt. Whatever were the faults of her earlier years, — and they were many, — she alone was not to blame for them; while the sorrows of her latter years, the painful humiliations she underwent, and the cruel death to which she was condemned, must always command the deepest sympathy and pity.

The work of the guillotine was now so heavy that Sanson complained to the Revolutionary Committee of the expense he was put to for assistants. On the 24th of October the Girondins to the number of twenty-one perished on the scaffold; among them was the husband of Madame de Genlis. It was then that the first pang of remorse shot through the heart of Camille Desmoulins. He stuttered forth a cry of self-reproach, and wept. Some few of the Girondins

The Trial.
Photogravure by Goupil and Company from
Painting by Cain.

Peint par Cain.   Photogravure Goupil & Cie.

fled; but, weary of lurking in concealment in caves and forests, they either committed suicide or died the miserable death of starvation. On the 6th of November the Duc d'Orléans (Philippe Égalité) was arrested, condemned, and beheaded. On the 9th Madame Roland, after five months' imprisonment, ascended the scaffold. Two days later her husband stabbed himself, to save by suicide his daughter's inheritance — forfeited had he been publicly executed. By fifties and sixties the guillotine thinned the population of Paris daily, and the same work was going on as briskly in the provincial towns. The once black mud of the capital had changed its hue, and sandals and training Grecian robes bore too visibly traces of it.

Robespierre was marching on bravely towards the absolute power he coveted, — whether as Dictator or "Son of the Supreme Being, Redeemer of the human race, the Messiah of the prophets," as the woman Catherine Théot, the pretended prophetess, proclaimed him, mattered to him not. He was clearing the ground rapidly. So many were denounced that the tribunal could no longer spare time for interrogating the accused persons separately. Several were therefore brought in together, told in insulting language that they had conspired against the "republic one and indivisible," and then were despatched without further delay to await their turn at the guillotine, as the hard-worked Sanson could take them.

It was in this way that the poor Princesse Elisabeth was sent to the scaffold on the 10th of May, 1794. The day had been devoted to clearing the prisons of a "large batch on hand of clergy and aristocrats." Among them the princess met a number of old friends of the late queen's household. "She, at all events, can have nothing to complain of," said Fouquier Tinville; "she may fancy herself at Versailles again." Then came the turn of Danton — even the terrible Danton — who had established the tribunal that now pronounced his doom. "I ask pardon," he said, "of God and men for having done so." He had declared that, in order to terrify and to vanquish, all that was needed was "*l'audace, encore l'audace, et toujours l'audace.*" Yet audacity failed him when urged on by those who were willing to support him, but, like himself, had not the courage to make the first spring. There was a question of bearding the human tiger in his lair. For Robespierre, deceived by the impunity with which he continued his work of extermination, had the vanity to believe that all France was at his feet; while, on the contrary, he was execrated, and his downfall ardently longed for.

Danton met a fate which he had been so active in contributing to bring on many others far more courageously than Camille Desmoulins. The latter, like so many of those red-handed revolutionists, made a very cowardly exit, and would have retracted his recommendation to form a committee of clemency (which was the charge against him) if Robespierre would but have relented and been clement in his case. Robespierre was, however, only too glad to put such turbulent spirits out of his way; and as the vituperative tongue of the widowed Lucile could not be silenced, she soon followed her husband to the scaffold. Two abortive attempts to assassinate Robespierre were made on the 4th Prairial,— 23d of May, 1794, — one by a young girl, Cécile Rénault, ambitious, it seemed, of rivalling Charlotte Corday. And it was at the instance of a woman that vengeance was soon to overtake the execrable monster.

At that wonderful *"fête* to the Supreme Being" arranged by Robespierre for the 20th Prairial (8th of June), and which was in some sort an imitation of the *Fête Dieu*, there were in the procession a few daring Conventionists who, laughing with each other at the absurdities they were taking part in, allowed their jesting and sarcasms to reach the ear of the great Robespierre. Arrayed in a violet silk coat, girded with a tricoloured scarf, and on his head a broad-brimmed hat, with a long floating white plume, he preceded by fifteen paces the other members of the Convention, "as grand and as grave as a cathedral Swiss at the head of a parish procession."

"Ah! look now; does not he play the god to

admiration?" "Does not he look like the high priest of the Supreme Being?" These and other gibes marred his enjoyment of the loud *vivas* for Robespierre from the populace, who liked the show. He is said to have arrogantly compared his colleagues on that occasion to "Pygmies seeking to renew the conspiracy of the Titans against the gods." Perchance, he might have prolonged his despotic and murderous career, and even have proclaimed himself the Supreme Being he was so anxious to set up as the god of the republic. But the passionate love of the furious Tallien for the beautiful Madame de Fontenoy, whom he married, and who used her influence over him to turn his mission of persecution at Bordeaux into one of mercy, prevailed also when she bade him take courage, confront the tyrant at the Convention, and denounce him.

And how easily his downfall was accomplished! In the course of the last nine days he had sent 345 persons to the scaffold, and none had dared raise his voice against it. Yet, at the first interruption of a domineering speech, at the first utterance of "Down with the tyrant," "Down with the Dictator," the cry was taken up and repeated with frantic enthusiasm. They who, trembling for their lives, had been his most abject slaves, were now loudest in accusing him. In vain he shrieked and yelled with rage, because none would listen to him. In vain he called them

" brigands, intriguers, and scoundrels." "Perish the traitor!" "Perish the tyrant!" were the only responses vouchsafed him.

To avoid the scaffold, Robespierre put a pistol to his mouth and fired it. A shattered jaw was the result, but not death. The guillotine was not robbed of its prey, and on the morrow, the 10th Thermidor (28th July), the infamous tyrant, his second self Saint Just, and some others of his allies in crime, ended their blood-stained career on the Place de la Révolution. The propitious event was hailed throughout the land with an enthusiastic shout of joy.

CHAPTER XII.

General Paoli. — The Bonaparte Family. — General Cartaux. — The Siege of Toulon. — Serjeant Junot. — Robespierre's *Protégé*. — General Hoche. — Provisionally Suspended. — Bonaparte a Prisoner. — Junot's Defence of His Friend. — The Irony of Fate. — The Future Emperor. — Railing at Fate. — Junot in Love with Pauline. — A Faithful Friend. — A Hand, a Heart, and £48 a Year. — Fréron's "*Jeunesse Dorée.*" — The "*Bals des Victimes.*" — Marie Antoinette's Laces. — Bonaparte's Star Looms Clearer. — Agitation and Alarm. — Bonaparte Reinstated. — The 13th Vendémiaire. — Bonaparte's Recompense.

THE old Corsican general, Paoli, had raised the standard of revolt in his native isle, after his return in 1792. His fervid harangues to his excitable countrymen stimulated so greatly their patriotic ardour that, wherever lukewarmness seemed to betray itself when freedom and independence were named, thither the more enthusiastic of those islanders carried fire and sword. Several acts of incendiarism having occurred, and no ready means being at hand to stay their ravages, the consequence was that on the 19th of July the greater part of the little town of Ajaccio was in flames.

Amongst the sufferers from this calamity was the widowed Madame Lætitia Ramolino Bonaparte. With her three daughters and four sons, she fled for refuge on board a French vessel, then about leaving the harbour. The whole party crossed over to Marseilles, and a decree of Paoli, whom the Corsicans had named generalissimo, and governor of the island, having banished the Bonaparte family, Madame Lætitia claimed the protection of France. There, later in the year, they were joined by Napoleon, who had been engaged with Salacetti and others in an unsuccessful attack on Ajaccio. Joseph and Lucien shortly after obtained employment in the Commissariat department, and Napoleon's many applications for active service at length brought him an order to join the Fourth Regiment of Infantry, and with the step in advance from second to first lieutenant. The regiment was in garrison at Nice, and before our young lieutenant could join it, some deaths had occurred which gave him, on his arrival, the rank of captain.

But it was the retaking of Toulon, which the inhabitants had given up to the English, that afforded Bonaparte the first opportunity of distinguishing himself. Général Cartaux, all gold lace and embroidery, a very superb personage, apparently, for an officer of a *sans-culotte* government, was the commander-in-chief of the expedition. Général Dutheil, who held the chief command of the artillery, was temporarily absent, and Dammartin, the second in command, being in the first skirmish disabled, was replaced by Capitaine Napoleon Bonaparte, with the brevet rank of *chef de bataillon*. The great skill displayed in his arrangements for the taking of Toulon, which, from the strength of its fortifications and the difficulties of its position, was named " Little Gibraltar," excited the admiration no less of Général Dutheil, on his return, than of the commander-in-chief, Dugommier.

The brilliant Cartaux had been dismissed for incompetency by the military department of the government, after he had informed them of his plan of the campaign ; in which they could see no ingenuity except brevity. In that it was a model of its kind.

"The artillery," he wrote, "will storm Toulon for three days ; I will then attack it with three columns and carry 'it."

It was one of those sieges where much skilful strategy was needed to render courage and numbers of any avail. Bonaparte, on this occasion, was wounded in the thigh, and his horse was shot under him. Seeing one of the artillerymen slain at his battery, he, with much *sang froid*, stepped into his place, and fired a dozen balls himself. The general attack began on the 16th of December, 1793, and was continued on the 17th, when Général Dugommier was wounded in the knee and right arm. He was also much exhausted by fatigue, and Bonaparte begged him to withdraw and repose himself. " You may do so," he said, "in perfect security, General, for Toulon in fact is taken, and after to-morrow you may sleep there."

The 18th was a terrible day to both besieged and besiegers. Furious cannonading; flames of burning buildings; sinking of vessels; drowning of thousands of the inhabitants in their haste to get on board the English fleet, and to fly from the fury of the revolutionary government, and from such atrocities as it then was inflicting on the revolted Lyonnese. Toulon escaped total destruction only by the efforts of the galley-slaves, who broke their chains and freed themselves in order to save the city. Barras proclaimed them the only honest men in Toulon.

On the 19th, as Bonaparte had promised, the commander-in-chief slept there. At his recommendation, the skill and intrepidity of the young artillery officer were rewarded by his promotion to the rank of general of brigade. "You had better promote him," wrote Général Dugommier, "or he will surely promote himself."

It was at Toulon that Bonaparte first met those two devoted, lifelong friends, Duroc and Junot. During the siege Bonaparte needed to write a few lines to his general. "Can any one here serve me as secretary for five minutes?" he inquired of a serjeant standing near him. "I can," was the reply. While engaged in writing at the hurried dictation of his officer, a shell whizzed by, grazing the earth at his feet, and scattering it over him and his paper. "Good," said the serjeant, continuing to write, "I shall not want for sand." This was Junot, the future Duc d'Abrantés. Both these young men became intimate at that time with the younger Robespierre. Shortly before the 9th Thermidor the latter was recalled to Paris by his brother, when he was especially anxious that Bonaparte should return with him to be introduced to Maximilian, as an officer likely to do the republic some service.

But Bonaparte could not be persuaded. His star did not seem to lead that way. Besides, he did not like the Jacobins, and Robespierre's proceedings made more persons anxious to avoid than to seek his acquaintance. "Who knows, had I yielded," said Bonaparte, "by what steps he would have rapidly promoted me?" Doubtless, they would have been the steps of the scaffold. To such promotion Robespierre had already destined the promising young soldier Hoche, who was his own especial *protégé*, but whom he pronounced a "dangerous man," as soon as he gave proofs of ability.

Hoche was then a prisoner in the Conciergerie. Being protected by the Conventionalist Carnot, he was allowed to linger on there until Carnot himself, with some threescore or so other obstacles in that path to supreme power the great Robespierre believed he was treading, should first be removed. Happily, the 9th Thermidor intervened. Carnot immediately released Serjeant Hoche. A violent cough had settled on his lungs, and, owing to the want of medical attendance and to other prison privations, so weakened him that he could not, when liberated, ascend the stairs without assistance. Serjeant Hoche, however, lived to become Général Hoche, the "Pacificator of La Vendée," and to distinguish himself during his short career of three years by his humanity to the suffering people of that country. He died in his twenty-ninth year. His constitution had been undermined by neglected illness in the horrid prison cells of the Conciergerie; and to that, rather than to poison, his early death is to be attributed.

Had he lived, Bonaparte would have had a powerful rival to contend against. For Général Hoche, though he had not had the advantage of studying the art of war at the royal military colleges, but had derived his skill as a tactician from habits of observation and early experience, is said to have shown, as a strategist, no less ability than Bonaparte. He was probably a man of nobler character, too, and of far less selfish aims. At all events, he has been considered the only man of that period capable of effectually checking the ambition of Bonaparte, and of frustrating, had he lived, the results of the 18th Brumaire.

But those ardent young soldiers of the Revolution had many enemies among their less able and older companions in arms, who looked on their rapid promotion with very jealous eyes. Bonaparte was destined soon to feel this. On returning to Nice, the young general of brigade, released from the severe restraints which straitened means had imposed on him, began to devote some brief moments of leisure to playing the *cicisbeo* to the handsome young wife of one of the deputies of the people, then stationed with the army of Italy. These gallant attentions were interrupted by an order from these deputies to repair to Genoa, secretly to survey its fortress and that of Savona, and to obtain other information for military objects. On his return he was put under arrest, — at the instance, it was said, of his enemy, the Corsican officer Salicetti. The deputies declared that his conduct in Genoa had been more than suspicious, and that having entirely lost their confidence, they provisionally suspended him.

He was accused, it appears, to the commander-in-chief of being a "Terrorist," a terrible charge at that moment. For the chief of the Terror had just lost his head on the scaffold; and those who had been his most humble slaves, while hastening to cast from themselves the imputation of being his partisans, were yet by no means unwilling to fasten that stigma on others. For fourteen days he remained a close prisoner. The faithful Junot, whose bravery during the siege had raised him to the rank of subaltern officer, — with the right to add a single epaulet to his uniform, but scarcely enough additional pay to cover the expense of it, — contrived to convey to his friend several plans of escape. But Bonaparte would not attempt them. By ruse or by force, Junot determined to save him; for once arrested, an acquittal was rare, whether there was or was not any real charge to sustain. Junot, therefore, fearing that Bonaparte's life was in danger, took upon himself the *rôle* of advocate, wrote an elaborate defence of his friend, and presented it to the deputies.

Junot was not ill-qualified for his self-imposed task. Unlike many of the rough soldiers who became generals and marshals of France under the empire, Junot had received an excellent education. He was of a good old Burgundian *bourgeois* family of Bussy le Grand. His father, though by no means a wealthy man, was in easy, comfortable circumstances. Before the National Assembly issued a contrary decree, in 1789, no *bourgeois* family could place a son in the army with any expectation of his ever ranking as an officer, however able and deserving he might be. Junot's father, therefore, destined his son for the bar, and he began his studies in law under a private tutor, his futher education being pursued at the college of Châtillon-sur-Seine.

But to the ardent, active-minded Junot, the

camp was more attractive than the forum, and military distinction more valued than forensic honours. Yet, when, for the only time in his life, he essayed the part of advocate, he might at least assume that he had not been wholly unsuccessful. For Bonaparte, some few days after Junot's warm defence of his character and conduct had been submitted to his judges, was informed that a decree of the representatives provisionally liberated him, in consideration of the services he had already rendered, and might again render, the republic.

The changes incidental to the Thermidorian reaction had placed an old artillery captain, named Aubry, at the head of the military committee. Considering Bonaparte too young for the grade of Brigadier-General of Artillery, he conferred on him, in exchange, that of General of Infantry, with a command in La Vendée. Bonaparte hastened to Paris to remonstrate against this change. The civil war in La Vendée did not attract him. Aubry, however, was inflexible. Bonaparte, being no less so, declined the command then offered him. He was, in consequence, erased from the list of generals, Cambacérès amongst others (oh, the irony of fate!) signing the act of his erasure. This again reduced him to the penury from which he had but so recently escaped. But Junot, who had followed him as the companion of his misfortunes, was occasionally supplied by his father with funds, which he insisted on sharing with his impoverished general.

Junot's father did not approve his son's conduct in leaving his regiment to follow the fortunes of an unknown officer. "Who and what is this Général Bonaparte?" he wrote. "Général Bonaparte," replied Junot, "is one of those men of whom Nature forms but few, and casts on our globe perhaps once in a century."

Bonaparte was also very kindly received in Paris by Madame de Permon, his mother's early friend, and herself a Corsican, but of Greek origin. Bonaparte is described at this time as positively ugly from excessive thinness. His height was five feet two inches, his complexion more yellow than sallow. His hair, rarely smoothed by brush or comb, was very slightly powdered. It was cut short along the forehead and over the ears, but hung down his back, in lank, straight pieces, without the slightest wave or turn of a curl in them. His usual dress was a long gray overcoat, a shabby black cravat, carelessly put on, and a round hat, either placed far back on his head, or so forward that it shaded and nearly concealed his eyes. His long, thin, bony hands were gloveless; "his means," he said, "would not allow of his indulging in the purchase of such superfluities as gloves."

The want of them, however, could scarcely then have been a noticeable defect in dress. "Sans-culottism," at the period in question, had become so firmly rooted in the habits of the people that neatness in dress, whether with men or women, was the exception, rather than, as formerly, the rule. Elegance or distinction in appearance or manners was rare indeed. Too many unfortunate persons, among the seven or eight thousand who left the prisons after the fall of Robespierre, had lost their all in the Revolution. Homeless, their property confiscated, and houses pillaged of their contents, they took refuge in the prevailing "sans-culottism" of the day, and concealed their poverty by the outward display of extreme republicanism. Poor Bonaparte, then, with his gloveless hands, his ill-made, unblacked boots, and the general slovenliness of his attire, was but one of many in a similar unfortunate position.

Yet that there was something extraordinary in him was often remarked, and perhaps oftener felt. For with all the disadvantages which then beset him, there was, we are told, in his eagle glance, a power to awe or command, and in his smile an irresistible sweetness that rarely failed to subdue.

He and Junot — between whom a brotherly attachment sprang up — would stroll for hours together in the Jardin des Plantes. Bonaparte, irritated by his forced inaction, would rail at Fate — personified by Salicetti — who had "destroyed his future," he said, "in the morning of life, as a flower snapped from its stem."

The young soldier friends (Junot was two years

younger than Bonaparte) haunted the gardens and retired parts of Paris in preference to more frequented spots. The solitude that seemed so congenial to both owed its charm to different motives. Junot had been introduced at Marseilles to the Bonaparte family, and had fallen deeply in love with the beautiful Pauline, then a very young girl. It was therefore to sigh forth his lamentations on the rankling pain he suffered from Cupid's shafts, and to urge his friend to speak favourably of him to Madame Lætitia, that Junot sought shady groves and lonely streets. The moody Bonaparte, meanwhile, by whose side he sauntered, pouring into his inattentive ear his lovelorn tale, was brooding over the wrong that had been done him by the sudden check to his military career.

Now and then Junot's torrents of eloquence became so fervent that they interrupted Bonaparte in the weaving of his plans and schemes for future advancement. He would then suddenly turn to his companion and exclaim: "All you possess, Junot, all that you can fairly call your own, is a single epaulet. Pauline cannot boast even of so much as that. What, then, is the total? Nothing!"

"My father," Junot would begin —

"Your father," Bonaparte would interrupt, "is hale and hearty, and it is to be hoped will make you wait yet many a year for your share of his property."

"But my pay — 1,200 *francs* a year?"

"Yes, your pay, when it is paid, is 1,200 *francs* a year. But that is no competency; and until you can offer Pauline — I will not say a fortune, but a competency at least, Madame Lætitia certainly will not listen to you."

"My father shall write to the *citoyenne* Bonaparte."

"No, Junot; you must wait, and not dream of marriage until more prosperous days arrive. And rest assured they will arrive, even should I be compelled to seek them in some other part of the world."

Bonaparte's thoughts often turned towards America at this period, and he looked to Junot to follow him whithersoever fortune or his star might lead. And he looked not in vain. Junot's devotion to him was strong as the fidelity of a faithful dog to his master, which is perhaps a far more intense feeling than that which usually animates the human breast.

When, a few years later, the handsome, extravagant Général Junot, the brilliant Duc d'Abrantès, Governor of Paris, was reminded by any circumstance of the above conversation — which is given here on the authority of Madame Junot, to whom he repeated it — he was always highly amused at the idea of his ever having offered his £48 a year, together with his hand and heart, to the wealthy Princesse Borghèse, then reputed the most beautiful, and perhaps heartless, as well as the most extravagant, woman in Europe.

But to return to the cloudy days that preceded the opening of the brilliant career of the lovelorn subaltern and the discontented young general. For six months or more they continued their plaints and their promenades, the difficulty of providing for daily wants daily becoming greater. Famine, that scourge of France, was again stalking through the land. Bread was scarce, and there was a failure in the arrival of other provisions in Paris. The discredit of the assignats, and the disturbances in the south of France, added to the general distress. The siege of Lyons had thrown thousands of workmen out of employment, and utterly ruined their employers. Their wives and children were starving, or dying miserable deaths in their wretched homes. The mulberry-trees having been destroyed, the silkworms had died. The looms were burnt or broken, and the men who should have worked them roamed about in bands, committing frightful depredations.

These troubles were the result of the royalist reaction, which threatened France with a second Terror. The oppressed became the oppressors, and by their odious exploits and sanguinary reprisals lost even the right to complain of their predecessors in crime. A change of parts only had taken place. This new terrorism was not confined to the Southern bands of assassins, who styled themselves brotherhoods, or companies, of the Sun, and of Jehu. The capital was also in a frightful state of anarchy. Several thousands of young men of the *bourgeoisie* and the *noblesse* placed themselves under the guidance of Fréron, the journalist (the son of the severe but distinguished critic), naming themselves Fréron's "*jeunesse dorée.*"

They usually assembled at the Palais Royal, wore a distinctive dress — *costume à la victime* — and their hair fastened up with combs (called *cadenettes*) in imitation of the usual arrangement of the hair of the victims of the guillotine. Armed with short canes, the tops heavily loaded, they paraded the principal thoroughfares in bands, inflicting blows and wounds on the persons they suspected of terrorism. Their own excesses and cruelties were, however, but a continuation, in another form, of that Reign of Terror which suffering, bleeding France had hoped was ended by the events of the 9th Thermidor. These reactionists had their public balls; society, or what remained of it, was so thoroughly dispersed and impoverished that there was no possibility of giving private ones. They gave them the horrible name of "*Les bals des victimes;*" and there, with culpable levity, the young people who had lost fathers or mothers or other near relatives by the guillotine, danced together with much glee the *in memoriam* "*Contre-danse des victimes.*"

THE "BALS DES VICTIMES" 179

These balls might also have been called "calico balls." Silks, velvets, jewels, and lace were not worn there, because nothing of the kind was then made, and no one had money to buy them had they been readily obtainable. Costly wardrobes, jewels, plate, and furniture existed somewhere,— the pillage of the great hôtels, and the property of their guillotined owners. But for the time being, such things had either been sent out of the country, or, in secret cupboards and recesses, were carefully locked up out of sight, together with whatever yet remained of hard cash; for a gold piece of twenty *francs* was then worth between 7,000 and 8,000 *francs* in assignats, and was daily increasing in value. The second-hand dealers in *objets d'art* and other valuable property were the chief gainers by the wholesale confiscation, destruction, and prohibition of all that was rare and beautiful in art. The queen's magnificent laces, worth many thousand pounds, were bought by the actress Mdlle. Devienne for a few hundred *francs*. As soon as it was safe to do so, she appeared on the stage covered with these laces, and glittering from head to foot with diamonds.

Meanwhile cotton reigned supreme at the victim balls. Odds and ends of various colours composed the scanty dress, resembling the marvellous concoctions of the present day, which reveal to all beholders the numberless defects and deformities of the human frame. The male victim attire was as tasteless and unbecoming as the female costume. This would, indeed, have mattered little had it represented a mere caprice of fashion; but it represented a faction, — a faction whose frequent acts of violence prevented the reëstablishment of order and peace, which the country so much needed and the afflicted people were longing for.

The continual collisions between the partisans of the several sections and factions which divided the government, inflamed public opinion and led to insurrection. Once more, drums were beating, the *tocsin* sounding, and the Palais Royal and Tuileries Gardens were the scene of tumultuous assemblages. The struggle between the chiefs of the royalist and democratic factions had begun, and Bonaparte's star now loomed clearer on the horizon. The royalists were preparing to strike a decisive blow to prevent the establishing of a directorial government. Emigrants were arriving in great numbers, most of them wearing the uniform of the Chouans, the insurgent troops of La Vendée.

At this menace of civil war, the Convention called the army to its aid, and formed a camp close to Paris. The royalists had in great part gained over the *bourgeoisie* to their cause, but the troops were wholly republican. Those in the camp of Sablons were marched into Paris, and surrounded the Tuileries for the protection of the

Convention, who had appointed a committee of five of its members, with authority to adopt whatever measures were deemed necessary for ensuring the public safety. Paris was in a state of extreme agitation and alarm. The inhabitants barricaded their houses. Whichever party might triumph in this struggle, they dreaded its results, and trembled at the thought of the possible revival of the Terror.

The Convention having determined on taking the initiative, Général Menou was charged with carrying out the needful arrangements. Failing, however, to satisfy the Convention, he was superseded, and an order despatched to Général Alexandre Dumas, requiring him immediately to take the command of the armed forces in and around Paris. Général Dumas was absent on leave, and matters were too urgent to allow of waiting for his return. Général de Barras, one of the committee of five, was therefore named commander-in-chief of the army of the interior. But Barras, though brave, had little knowledge or experience of the art of war. He required a second in command,— a man of head and resolution, capable of serving the republic in this moment of peril. He bethought him of the young officer of whose *sang froid* and strategical skill the commanders of the Toulon expedition had spoken so highly, and of which he had himself been an eye-witness; for it was Barras who accused Général Brunet of giving up Toulon to the English, and who arrested him in the midst of his army. Aubry, the artillery officer who had deprived Bonaparte of his rank, was of the reactionary party, and it may have afforded some sort of malicious satisfaction to Barras to reinstate this young man and enable him to avenge himself of his adversary while serving the republic.

If we may believe the "*Mémorial de Sainte Hélène*," Bonaparte reflected for half an hour before deciding to accept the important command offered him. "He was not more anxious to fight against the Parisians," he said, "than the Vendéens. But the defeat of the Convention would be a national calamity, and his confidence in himself told him it was a calamity that he could avert." Having come to this conclusion, he hesitated no longer, but at once obeyed the summons of the committee. A short consultation with Barras ensued, which resulted in the whole direction of the enterprise being confided to him.

To his alacrity in taking measures for vigorous resistance, to his skilful disposition of the troops, and the terrific effect with which the cannon he placed on the steps of St. Roch replied to the attacks of the insurgents, the success of that terrible 13th Vendémiaire, An. IV. (15th October, 1795), was owing. There was fighting in the streets until near nightfall, and the hall of the Tuileries was filled with the wounded and dying.

The insurgent army, however, was driven from all its positions, and the revolt completely quelled. The Parisian sections, whom Bonaparte had vanquished, gave him the name of the "*mitrailleur.*" The Convention, whom he had saved, restored his name to the list of generals. But at the end of the month the Convention, considering their mission accomplished by the restoration of order and the establishment of the republic, resigned office, — giving place to a directorial government, afterwards named, in jest, "Royalty in five volumes." Barras, as the most competent to do the honours, was the first in dignity of the "five kings," otherwise directors; and soon after he was installed in his office he recompensed the services of the young officer, to whom both he and the republic were so much indebted, by nominating him (Carnot says at his suggestion) to the chief command of the army of Italy.

CHAPTER XIII.

Supplying the Army. — A Lucky Fellow. — Bonaparte and His Aide-de-camp. — A Gratifying Change. — First Meeting with Joséphine. — Diane-Hébé. — "*Le Bon Bouilly.*" — Offers of Marriage. — Departure for Italy. — Madame Campan. — *Grandes Dames* of the Empire. — The Impetuous Tide of Victory. — A Wife and a Thousand *Louis d'Or.* — "Soldiers of Italy!" — The Price of an Armistice. — An Independent Conqueror. — Spoken *Rêveries.* — Bonaparte's Views and Aims. — The *Dolce far Niente.* — Joséphine's Victories. — A Portrait of Bonaparte. — An Admiring Contemporary. — "Necker's Intriguing Daughter." — Général Augereau. — The Treaty of Campo-Formio. — Jealous Relatives. — A Present to Joséphine. — The Return to Paris.

AT the outset of their career, fortune, in the sense of mere money making, seemed more propitiously inclined towards Joseph and Lucien Bonaparte than to Napoleon. To be connected, though but indirectly, with furnishing supplies to the army, was no less a sure road to wealth at that time than under the old *régime*. The frauds in that department continued to be extensive, and public interests were sacrificed to private and personal ones as recklessly as ever. Lucien had already married, and without consulting his family. He probably foresaw that his choice, as it proved, would scarcely please them. To Napoleon it was especially annoying; for the new sister-in-law, Christine Boyer, was but the daughter of a humble tavern-keeper, and had for her portion neither riches, beauty, nor *esprit*. She was a simple, amiable, kind-hearted country girl; and personally, by no means unpleasing, though not regularly beautiful. Being devoted to Lucien, who was deeply attached to her, the *ménage* of the youthful pair, even while frowned upon, was a happy one.

"Now, Joseph is really a lucky fellow!" exclaimed Napoleon, somewhat despairingly; for the incident his exclamation referred to occurred some days before he was summoned to take the command of the armed forces of Paris. Very opportunely, a remittance from Joseph had reached him, and with it the information that he, too, was about to marry. Joseph, the eldest, and by far the handsomest of the five brothers, had captivated Mdlle. Clary, the daughter and coheiress of the wealthy financier, M. Clary of Marseilles. Besides giving him his daughter and her fortune, M. Clary, as soon as Napoleon's name began to be on every tongue, supplied Joseph with the means of purchasing the splendid estate of Mortfontaine, renowned for the beauty of its park, its English gardens, and magnificent château.

Fortune indeed, in every sense, was unsparing of her favours to these Bonapartes, distributing them lavishly to each in his turn. At the moment when Napoleon pronounced Joseph a really lucky fellow — perhaps with a pang that he, who felt himself equal to the highest achievements, found the path of glory closed to him — three generals were successively displaced by Fate, as it seemed, that no obstacle might obstruct the opening of his brilliant career. His arrears of pay as brigadier-general were handed to him on his restoration to that rank. Probably a further sum, too; for he had done the Convention good service. Also we find him, very shortly after the events of the 13th Vendémiaire, and before his appointment to the command in Italy, visiting his friend Madame de Permon "in a well-appointed carriage," accompanied by his aide-de-camp, Captain Junot.

"And he himself," we are told, "oh! so changed," — his *toilette* no longer neglected; his hair well-arranged and powdered; his uniform handsome and new, but plain, having only a narrow border of gold embroidery, and in his military hat a tricoloured plume. He has also launched out into such superfluous expense as the purchase of gloves. "His ill-fitting boots are replaced by exquisite specimens of the bootmaker's skill, showing to advantage his small, well-shaped foot." This is a change very gratifying to Madame de Permon; for, like the rest of "the Republican *élite*," he had been accustomed to walk into her *salon* with dirty, wet boots, covered with the black mud of the Paris streets, and deliberately to dry them at the fire.

It was a custom, which, with many others of the *sans-culotte* period, that lady could never with any complacency tolerate, though she risked being denounced as an aristocrat.

Bonaparte has also changed his poor lodging in the *mansarde* on the fifth story of the corner house of the Rue de Condé, for a suite of apartments, *au premier*, in the Rue des Capucines; for his visitors now are numerous. He has shown qualities that make him necessary to the government, and the solitary, degraded young soldier has become a person of importance. Thus, noiselessly, and as by the stroke of a magician's wand, he is raised to a first stepping-stone to honours and dignities unlooked for, probably, by himself at that time; certainly little dreamed of by others, and least of all by the Directory.

His first meeting with the Vicomtesse de Beauharnais occurred at this period. The anecdote which assigns it to a visit from Joséphine, to thank the young general for restoring her husband's sword to her son Eugène, is an extremely questionable one. Général de Beauharnais had been guillotined during the Terror, nearly two years before. It is not likely that his sword would have been more cared for than hundreds of others, and preserved through those scenes of anarchy, bloodshed, and disorder. Weapons of all kinds were constantly in request, and were sought for wherever there was a chance of finding them.

Bonaparte, too, was no participator in those scenes. He was far away from Paris during their occurrence, and it was by no means probable that the restoration of the decapitated general's sword — if perchance Eugène really applied for it — was a request in his power to comply with.

Joséphine herself had had a narrow escape from the scaffold. But it was not as the widow of Général de Beauharnais that she was denounced as a *suspecte*. It was because of her intimacy with Madame Tallien, and her frequent efforts to rescue, through her friend's influence, an innocent victim from the guillotine. Doubtless Bonaparte and Joséphine first met at the Luxembourg, at the receptions of the Directors Gohier and Barras. The dramatic writer, J. N. Bouilly,* — in his "*Mes Récapitulations*," — says:

"I often met the widow Beauharnais in the *salon* of my old friend Gohier. She was an elegant, graceful woman, with an expressive countenance, to which her great goodness of heart lent an added charm. She attracted considerable attention, and was treated with the greatest respect; many traits of heroism being related of her in connection with victims condemned by the revolutionary tribunals, and the means she had employed to shield or save them. She had the dignity of Calypso, with the enchanting grace

---

* The author also of many charming and popular works for the young.

of Eucharis. Gohier was accustomed to call her Diane-Hébé. Both he and Barras, at her intercession, erased the names of many emigrants from the fatal list of doomed exiles; and in Gohier's private room we frequently met, when a similar errand led me also to seek an interview with him."

M. Bouilly had aided in the escape and saved the lives of a great many persons during the sanguinary Reign of Terror. He had, with that object in view, accepted an office under the revolutionary committee, in his native town of Tours. He was a man of the most humane disposition, and — as Madame Ancelot informs us — was generally spoken of in society as "*Le bon Bouilly.*" Joséphine presented him to Barras, and thus, as he says, gave him "an opportunity of sometimes serving old friends in their trouble." For if capital punishment was abolished in France, the horrors of transportation to Cayenne, which replaced it, were even more dreaded than the guillotine. They were, compared with the latter, as the agonies of lingering death to the momentary pang of its speedy release. Those cruel deportations were far too numerous in the early period of the Directory.

It was at one of Barras's receptions that M. Bouilly first saw Bonaparte. Joséphine, he says, directed his attention to him, as he stood at some distance from them, conversing with two or three general officers. "Do not you perceive in his countenance the signs of a great future?" she inquired. Bouilly does not give his answer; but says that he observed the rapid and penetrating glance of his eagle eye, and doubted not that it was quick to perceive the estimable qualities of the woman who was so powerfully to influence his destiny. A few years later he reminded her of those words, when she seemed pleased that they were remembered, as the event had so fully answered what she regarded as her prediction.

Not long after it was announced at the Directory that the Vicomtesse de Beauharnais was about to become the wife of the young Général Bonaparte, the *petit mitrailleur*. Générals Hoche and Coulaincourt had also been desirous of marrying the fascinating widow. But there was a certain air of ascendency in the manners of Bonaparte that seemed to bid his rivals withdraw, and that did not permit refusal on the part of the lady when he pressed his suit. Her friends, says Madame de Créquy, were surprised and annoyed at this obscure marriage. It took place on the 9th of March, 1796. The bride was thirty-three, the bridegroom twenty-seven. Their union excited some surprise also among the few members of the old aristocracy (M. de Montesquiou, the Duc du Nivernois, and one or two others), who had contrived to live through the last few years, and now frequented the Directorial *salons*. It was thought that the charming Veuve de Beauharnais had descended a step or two of the social ladder by marrying this little upstart general. While he, ignorant of the gradations of rank among the old *noblesse*, believed that he had married a *grande dame* of far higher status than Madame de Beauharnais actually was; though no doubt he was truly attached to her. On the 21st of the same month Bonaparte left Paris to join the army of Italy, Joséphine accompanying him, "to share his dangers, and by her grace and her goodness to shed greater lustre on his laurels," says the gallant M. Bouilly.

Eugène and Hortense de Beauharnais — the former then fifteen, the latter two years younger — were left at St. Germain for the continuance of their education. Both of them very freely expressed disapprobation of their mother's marriage. It was long before Hortense could be reconciled to the change from Madame de Beauharnais to Madame Bonaparte, or could overcome her aversion to her father-in-law. Two or three months before the marriage, Joséphine had placed her daughter and her niece Stéphanie with the celebrated Madame Campan, who had recently opened an educational establishment in the Rue des Urselines at St. Germain-en-Laye. Eugène was also at St. Germain, at the same *pensionnat* as Madame Campan's son, and shared with the latter his mother's care and surveillance during Madame Bonaparte's absence.

Soon after the Directory had arranged with the Emperor of Austria for the liberation of Madame Royale, the daughter of the unfortunate Marie Antoinette, and the sole survivor of the five prisoners of the Temple, more peaceful days seemed about to dawn on France. It was then that Madame Campan, who had lived through the Terror at the village of Coubertin, in the valley of Chévreuse, concealed and in poverty, with her son and her mother, was recommended to apply to the Directors for the permission to establish her school. All such institutions had been suspended from the beginning of the Revolution. No course of study was open to youth; and the evil results of this neglect of education were already too apparent. Barras, to whom she explained her wishes and intentions, approved them entirely; and several pupils being promised, her famous establishment was soon after founded.

Though Barras was a man of dissolute life, he had the instincts of his race, and sometimes remembered that he was a gentleman. He was of an ancient noble Provençal family, "old as the hills," as was familiarly said. To this advantage over his colleagues, he certainly owed the part assigned him of doing the honours of the semi-royal court of the Directory. The grand manners, the correct forms of expression, and the social amenities of the despised old *régime*, were coming again into favour. Where, and of whom, could the rising generation of young ladies learn these things better than in the establishment of one who had lived in courts from her youth, who was, as it were, to the grand manner born, and who in solitude and secrecy had preserved it intact, remote from the contaminating influences of the revolutionary orgies? Madame Campan, therefore, became a personage of considerable importance; and under her fostering care were trained most of the future duchesses, princesses, queens, and other *grandes dames* of the empire.

But while Hortense was learning queenly manners at Saint Germain-en-Laye, Joséphine, in Italy, as the victorious general's wife, was receiving the honours initiative of the homage which at no distant period awaited the empress. The series of brilliant victories with which the Italian campaign was opened was the more striking and startling from having been wholly unexpected. Both in Austria and central Italy the bulletins describing the success of the French arms were at first declared to be false reports. But the rapidity of the young general's movements soon convinced the most incredulous. Bewilderment speedily took the place of doubt. For the tide of victory was rushing impetuously onward, towards the frontiers of states that had deemed themselves so safe from its invasion that no steps had been taken to resist, or to turn it aside.

The French government were scarcely less

surprised than the enemy against whom their arms had been turned. For, in conferring on Bonaparte the command of the army of Italy, the Directory — as some writers have asserted — hoped to disembarrass themselves of an aspiring young soldier. He had served their purpose well; but it was thought expedient to put some check on his very evident ambition. The Italian command was not in request; so that no jealousy was raised, no umbrage taken, by the gift of this appointment to Général Bonaparte. Under more favourable circumstances older officers might have coveted it, and the young general have been considered amply rewarded by reinstatement in his former rank. "If he had died in Italy," wrote Carnot, "the Directory would have given him as splendid a funeral as they gave Général Hoche." However, they took the chance of that, and despatched him to Italy with a wife and a thousand *louis d'or*.

The army of Italy numbered but 30,000 men, and was the least numerous of the French armies then in the field. It was also the least in condition to face an enemy. Insubordination had shown itself, and no strict discipline could be maintained. Général Scherer, its late commander, had been recently beaten by the Austrians; and when Bonaparte arrived at Nice the troops were lying in complete inaction, shut up between the coast and the mountains, much dejected, and in want of provisions and clothing. According to most accounts, Bonaparte spoke French at that time with little fluency or correctness. The staccato style of his bulletins and addresses to the soldiers, though so effective, may have originated in some difficulty of that sort. The first time he spoke as a general to his army was on reviewing the ragged, dispirited battalions of Italy. His address at once inspired them with hope and courage, and with confidence in their leader.

"Soldiers!" he said, "you are naked, and wanting food. Much is owing to you; but there is nothing to give you. Your patience and courage amidst these rocks are admirable. But they procure you no glory. I come to lead you to the most fertile plains in the world. Large towns, wealthy provinces, will soon be in your power. There you may obtain riches, honour, and glory. Soldiers of Italy! Will you be wanting in courage?"

The young general's appeal was responded to with enthusiasm; and with this army and an additional 20,000 men, Bonaparte overran Italy, and gained the battles of Montenotte, Millesimo, Mondovi, Castiglione, Rivoli, and others, and was victorious in the engagements at Dego-Saint-Jean, and in the passage of the Bridge of Lodi. Joseph soon after was employed at Rome to negotiate with the Pope — to whom Bonaparte granted an armistice — and to arrange for the transport to Paris of the pictures, statues, and MSS., which, with a good round sum in money, were the price of it. The fury of the people, however, led to insurrection, and General Duphot, to whom Mdlle. Clary — the sister of Madame Joseph Bonaparte, and afterwards the wife of Bernadotte, and Queen of Sweden — was to have been married on the following day, was shot down at Joseph's side.

The whole of the Bonaparte family, except Lucien, seem to have been in Italy, following, in two parties, the fortunes of Joseph and Napoleon. The headquarters of the latter were at the magnificent palace of Montebello, near Milan. There he and Joséphine resided; their surroundings resembling rather a brilliant court than the headquarters of an army. The strictest etiquette was observed between Bonaparte and his officers. His aides-de-camp — Junot (now colonel of hussars, and who had been severely wounded at Lonato), Duroc, Lavalette, Murat, and Lannes — were no longer received at his table, and he was extremely particular in his selection of the guests he admitted to it. An invitation was an honour eagerly sought, but with difficulty obtained.

He dined, in royal fashion, as it were, in public, — the people of the country being permitted to enter the dining-hall while he was taking his repast; when they would walk round with their eyes earnestly fixed on him. Nor was he in any degree embarrassed or confused by the excessive homage then paid him, but received it with the *nonchalance* of one who from all time had been accustomed to it. The *salons* of the palace, as well as a large tent he had had erected outside, in the gardens, were constantly filled with a crowd of generals, the members of the government, and great contractors who supplied the armies. Also, the Italian nobility of the highest rank, and the most distinguished men in Italy, came to solicit the favour of merely seeing him, or exchanging a few words of compliment with him. In a word, all bowed before the young general, — subdued by the greatness of his victories and the singular haughtiness of his manners.*

Already he was no longer the general of a triumphant republic, but an independent conqueror, imposing his laws on the vanquished, and treating as mere *rêveries* all republican forms and ideas. Conferences were opened at Montebello for a definitive treaty of peace between France and Austria, and for considering the affairs of Genoa, etc. The Directory, jealous of the absolute independence assumed by Bonaparte, sent Général Clarke to Italy, under the pretext of assisting him in the conduct of the diplomatic functions that had devolved on him. But Bonaparte regarded Clarke as a spy, and allowed him to take no part in the negotiations.

It was a singular trait in the character of Bonaparte that he was frequently impelled, irre-

* Bonaparte à Montebello, "*Mémoires du Comte Miot de Melito.*"

sistibly as it seemed, to unbosom himself almost to the first person he encountered, and to explain with the utmost unreserve the ambitious views and aims that constantly occupied his thoughts, — as though he were really thinking aloud, caring for no reply, unmindful of the impression he was creating, and merely desiring to relieve his mind by giving utterance to the crowd of ideas that oppressed it. He indulged to a great extent in this sort of spoken *rêverie* while in Italy, when strolling in the groves and gardens of Montebello with M. de Melzi and Comte de Melito. He would talk almost incessantly for two or three hours together, they very rarely interrupting him by a brief remark, and he not appearing to expect it; for he very rarely conversed, he simply talked.

On the occasion of one of these promenades, he said: "What I have accomplished so far is nothing. I am but at the outset of the career that lies before me. Do you suppose that it is for the glory of those lawyers of the Directory, the Carnots and Barras, that I triumph in Italy? Do you think it is for the sake of founding a republic? What an idea! A republic of thirty millions of men! — and with such manners and vices as ours! How is it possible? It is a chimera, this republic, which has fascinated the French. But it will pass away as so many others have done. What the French need is glory, the satisfactions of vanity. But as for liberty, they know not what it means. Look at the army. Our recent victories and triumphs have already restored the French soldier to his true character. I am everything to him. Let the Directory but attempt to deprive me of the command of the army, and they will quickly learn what power *they* have over it. The nation wants a chief, — a chief illustrious by glory. It wants no theories of government, no phrases, no ideological discourses. The French know nothing about them, and do not understand them. They want toys, baubles, with which they can be amused, while allowing themselves to be led; provided, however, that the goal towards which one is marching them be adroitly concealed from their view."

The peace negotiations dragged on for some months; and as Bonaparte desired no definitive treaty, he availed himself of the inactivity of the plenipotentiaries to make an excursion to the Lago Maggiore, accompanied by Joséphine and Joseph's intimate friend, M. de Melito, to whom Bonaparte had also taken a fancy, and treated very confidentially. The natural beauties of the Isola Bella; its rich vegetation, lovely walks, baths, and soothing atmosphere, had their accustomed effect even on the restless-minded Bonaparte. Readily he seemed to yield to the *dolce far niente* frame of mind they inspired. His attentions to Joséphine were then constant, and marked by extreme devotion. No doubt, at that period, his affection for her was great, and her influence over him no less so; and both, it is more than probable, might have been retained to the end, as beneficially for him as for her, had poor Joséphine been but as wise as she was charming.

While Bonaparte gained victories in Italy, Joséphine gained hearts. Respected and loved by the people for her amiability of disposition and readiness to do good, — of which many opportunities were afforded her in the course of that desolating war, — the wife of the conqueror was no less admired by the *haute société* of the Italian courts for the charm of her manners, her personal grace, and last, though not least, the elegance of her *toilettes*. The proud Italian signoras, when, greatly against their will, they paid their visit of ceremony to Madame Bonaparte, were agreeably surprised by her distinguished appearance and air of high breeding. They were not prepared by the reports that had reached them to meet such a woman; and generally they left her with a far more favourable opinion of the ladies of the republic than the greater number of the stars of the Luxembourg *salons* merited.

On the other hand, the first shock was great to many men, and ladies too, when the little general presented himself. Fancy had accorded him a stature and bearing in proportion with the height of his fame and the loftiness of his deeds. "I was strangely surprised," said one who had taken a journey to obtain a glimpse of the conqueror, "and could hardly believe that it was he, when a young man entered, of stature below the middle height, thin as a strip of parchment, and his hair cut in a singular fashion, — square over the ears and hanging down his back in long tresses. Half a dozen aides-de-camp, a number of general officers, and several foreign plenipotentiaries, attended him. In the midst of so much gold lace and embroidery, glittering stars and crosses, he was distinguished by the plainness of his dress. It was a long, straight coat, buttoned closely up to the throat, a general's sash and sword, and a tricoloured plume in his hat. The chiselled beauty of his features, I had heard so much of, did not strike me. I saw they were prominent, and the more so perhaps from his remarkable thinness. But when he took off his hat I perceived in the stern, thoughtful brow, and searching eye of the youthful warrior, the signs of a man capable both of forming and executing vast projects."

But while victory everywhere followed the French arms in Italy, discord triumphed at home in the Directory. Two of its five members, Carnot and Barthélemy, were wholly opposed in their opinions and views to the other three, Barras, Rewbell, and Larévellière. At the same time the royalists were plotting to overthrow the Directorial government and reinstate the Bourbons, though unsupported by the sentiments of the people. To which party the victorious general, with an army ready to obey his nod, would lend his powerful aid seemed at the moment doubtful. "All ideas of personal ambition yet slumbered in his mind," says the contemporaneous historian Anquetil. "He had but the glory of France in view; the deliverance of oppressed peoples; the splendour of the republican arms. Never was the passion of liberty allied to so much greatness of soul, so much moderation and genius."

Bonaparte, however, in determining to lend his support to the revolutionary party in the Directory, was influenced wholly by views of personal ambition, to be more fully developed later on. He had no sort of sympathy with it, as he said himself, in one of those moments when, in the fulness of his heart, he poured forth his thoughts to his friend Melito. He was aware of the crisis at hand, — a struggle similar to that of the 13th Vendémiaire. The Bourbons had entertained hopes of attaching him to their party, because he had shown some favour to the court of Turin, and for his own military objects had endeavoured to preserve quietude in Piedmont. "I shall not leave Italy," he said, "to pay court to the lawyers of the Luxembourg; nor will I contribute towards the triumph of the Bourbons. Some day I shall weaken the republican party; but for my own advantage, not that of a worn-out dynasty. The favourable moment is not yet come. The pear is not yet ripe. *En attendant* — one must act with the republican party."

M. de Talleyrand, too — whose name "Necker's intriguing daughter" had contrived to get effaced from the list of emigrants — was in active correspondence with him. The same lady — who was all-powerful during this most corrupt of all governments — had induced Barras to give the ex-Bishop of Autun the *portefeuille* of foreign affairs. He also had been in doubt towards which side he should lean, for M. de Talleyrand despised the Directory. But with his usual perspicacity, though he had not seen Bonaparte, yet from his victories, his bulletins, his addresses to his army, he divined the man who was to overthrow the Luxembourg government. The cordial support of M. de Talleyrand, and the benefit of his counsels, were, therefore, secured to the victorious young general, so long as it should be his fate or his fortune to prevail.

Général Bernadotte had been recently despatched to France with thirty standards taken on the field of battle. Général Augereau now arrived at the Luxembourg to lay sixty more of these trophies of war at the feet of the five kings. The commander-in-chief did not choose to leave his army himself, until defeat or triumph had sealed the fate of the Directory. The fighting of their battle in Paris he left to Augereau. "I shall remain to sign peace if necessary," he said. "Should I leave that to another, the glory of my victories would pale before the people's enthusiasm for him who, by signing the treaty, should seem to have given them the blessing those victories have obtained; and of which, therefore, that other would reap the benefit."

Général Augereau made his appearance at the Directory covered with gold and diamonds. He wore on every finger rings of antique design, the spoils apparently of the vanquished. "And they might possibly," says Carnot, "have been those of which Hannibal despoiled the Roman knights." Of every three words Augereau uttered, two were oaths; thus he surpassed in this respect other revolutionary generals, whose every other word only was an oath. He was loud in disparaging his general-in-chief, of whose victories he took to himself the credit. "Bonaparte was inexperienced," he said, "but possibly might some day make a good general. His numerous mistakes he had helped him out of, — in fact, it was he who had done all."

Augereau, however, prevailed for the Directory on the 18th Fructidor, An. V. (4th September, 1797), and received as a recompense the command of the army of the Rhine. The Treaty of Campo-Formio was signed by Bonaparte on the 17th of October. One of its conditions was the release of the four French prisoners confined in the fortress of Olmutz. Général de La Fayette was one of them. He had been captured by the Austrians in 1792, when, after the fatal 10th of August and the imprisonment of Louis XVI. and his family, he left France and was crossing a part of the Austrian territory on his way to the coast to embark for America. Général Berthier and M. Monge, the famous mathematician, were despatched to Paris with the treaty. The Directory immediately ratified it, and recalled the conqueror from the scene of his victories.

During their stay in Italy, Bonaparte's family, jealous of the greater honours paid to Joséphine than to themselves, and annoyed that he also exacted from them much deference in their manner towards her, began already to play that insidious part whose object was to weaken her husband's affection for her, and to sow dissension between them. Elisa Bonaparte had married M. Felix Bacciochi, adjutant-general of the army of Italy; and Pauline's beauty had captivated Général Le Clerc. Madame Lætitia and her youngest daughter, Caroline, — then about twelve years of age, — with Louis and Jérôme, both mere youths, were received into Joseph's family when Bonaparte was recalled to Paris.

Joséphine, attended by numerous servants, preceded the general by several days, carrying with her many treasures, — presents and spoils amassed during the campaign. One small chest contained objects esteemed so rare and precious that she would not allow it to be removed out of her sight, even when she was entertained on her homeward journey at Turin. When, following shortly after, Bonaparte also stopped at Turin, the court desired to give a *fête* in his honour. But he would not allow it. He received the ministers, but would not take any formal leave of the king. On the morning, however, of his departure, a splendid, high-bred Sardinian horse was sent to him. The queen (Madame Clotilde, sister of Louis XVI.) had hung round the animal's neck a necklace of precious stones, — a present to Joséphine. It was said to be the only valuable article of jewelry she possessed. She indeed no longer wore jewels, having sacrificed everything of that kind to the needs of the country.

Bonaparte is said to have been much moved at receiving this present, — a very mournful one, under the painful circumstances in which Piedmont was then placed. As he could not refuse the offering, he presented jewelled boxes and diamond rings to the officers who had brought the presents, and liberal gifts of money to their servants.

On parting from M. de Melito he said: "I confess to you, *mon cher* Miot, that I no longer am able to obey. I have been invested with power to command, and cannot renounce it. My decision is taken; if I cannot be the master, I shall quit France. What I have done here shall not be given to the lawyers of the Luxembourg." The same evening he left Turin, crossed Mont Cenis on the morrow, and continuing his journey *viâ* Bâle, thence to Rastadt, reached Paris on the 6th of December, 1797.

CHAPTER XIV.

Signs of a Change. — The Regency of the Revolution. — The Prince of the Republic. — Enter Aspasia and Pericles. — Fruits of the 18th Fructidor. — An Attempt to Veil Vice. — Barras's Grand Dinners. — A Long Stride Forward. — The Return of Old Friends. — Building a Fortune. — The Contractors' Wives. — Monsieur and Madame Privas. — *Adieu! Ma Bonne Dame.* — Results of the Revolution. — M. de Talleyrand. — The Luxembourg *Fête.* — The Peacemaker. — "*La Grande Nation.*" — The Fraternal Embrace. — Examining the Crown Diamonds. — Rival Beauties. — Imperial Rehearsals. — The *Tricolor* Insulted. — A Hasty Departure. — The Château of La Malmaison.

IT was long before the brutalising mark left by the excesses of the Revolution on all who had participated in them was to any great extent effaced. Yet when, after nearly two years' absence, Joséphine returned to Paris, she observed that a great change had taken place in what was termed the society of the capital. This change may have been more vividly impressed on her by the warm welcome she received, by the unusual attentions paid her, as the wife of the victorious general, whom an enthusiastic reception awaited, and by the fact that the small hôtel she had taken in the Rue

Chantereine was besieged throughout the day by visitors. A change, however, in manners there certainly was.

The frightful depravity of the period obtained for the reign of the "Viscount King Barras" the epithet of the "Regency of the Revolution." It was the actor Dazincourt, no very severe moralist, who thus named it. Barras was one of the members of the Legislative Assembly who voted for the death of Louis XVI., and against the proposed appeal to the people. It was, indeed, such stern regicides who alone were eligible for the office of Director. They were supposed to be the purest republicans, holding it criminal to indulge in the superfluities and luxuries of life, — virtuous citizens, who had beheld with horror the extravagance and frivolity of the court of Versailles, and whose hearts had ached for the suffering people. Having brought the vicious Louis to the scaffold for his crimes in not checking those evils, and through much shedding of blood purified the land, they were expected to establish the reign of wisdom, justice, peace, and plenty — liberty, equality, and fraternity, and all other republican virtues comprised in the suggestive term, "sans-culottism."

But no sooner was the Convention abolished, and the Directory, that was to usher in the much longed for millennium in France, established, than the noble De Barras, as its ornamental head, gave the rein to tastes and habits which for a time had been held in subjection by the force of circumstances alone. At once he assumed the airs of a prince of the republic; and although the public treasury was said to be empty, he found wherewithal in its coffers to buy the fine estate of Grosbois, and another at Surènes. He had his packs of hounds, his hunters, his mistresses, and a whole retinue of lackeys. This drew around him a circle of courtiers,— the Aristides, the Brutuses, and other stern patriots of the Convention, — no less obsequious and intriguing than those who had bent the knee before royalty at Versailles. Nor did the Lucretias of the republic disdain the *cercle intime* of the *maîtresse-en-titre*, the beautiful Madame Tallien, — not yet divorced from her second husband, but every day threatening it, and every day with that threat bringing to his knees the jealous, complaining Tallien to sue for pardon to his frail, but lovely, Spanish wife.

In the Luxembourg *salon* the brilliant Teresa reigns supreme. She and Barras enter together, — he in the absurd theatrical costume the Directors have invented for themselves, and in which alone Barras, who is as vain and handsome as he is dissolute, appears to any advantage. The rest seem rather ill at ease in their stage finery; rather ashamed of their ruffles and jabots, their pearl-coloured satin vests, their gold-embroidered mantles, their buskins, and their Henri Quatre hats,

Barras.

Photo-etching from Drawing by Raffet.

with long floating plumes, surely unsuitable for stern republicans.

Madame Tallien rests one elbow on Barras's shoulder, and he with his arm encircles her waist. She is not only queen of the *salon* and queen of beauty, but also queen of *la mode*. She is the first to appear with rings on her toes; her silk stockings being made with divisions like the fingers of gloves. Her feet are incased in sandals fastened with jewels. She disdains, very wisely, the flaxen wig then in favour, and wears her own black hair, unpowdered. It is cut rather short and arranged in close curls round her head, after the manner of an ancient bust in the Vatican. Her dress is of finest Indian muslin, bordered with gold, and made on the model of the tunic of a Greek statue. The long open sleeves are fastened on the shoulders with fine cameos, lately brought from Italy. The waist-belt has a similar fastening. She wears no gloves, for her arm is a model for a sculptor. But around her statuesque form an Indian cashmere scarf, one of the finest specimens of Eastern looms, and difficult to obtain at that time, is draped *à l'antique*.

The modern Aspasia is said to have had a truly regal appearance in this dress. Women gazed on her with envy, and, as they are wont to do, detected weak points even in a faultless piece of perfection. But men were accustomed to regard her as formed in a mould which nature had destroyed without vouchsafing to an admiring world a second copy. The events of the 18th Fructidor, by saving the republic, saved, as was said, Capua and its enjoyments, which Barras valued still more. Perhaps the parallel hardly holds good in this case, for Barras was no Hannibal reposing after great victories. If he had shown any bravery, it was merely for personal defence. The changes and chances of the Revolution had put power into his hands, but he valued it only because of the ease and pleasure and dissolute enjoyments with which it enabled him to surround himself.

Firmly seated, then, on the luxuriously cushioned Directorial throne, Barras and Queen Teresa decreed that, the effusion of blood being stayed, and the Carmagnole costume and Phrygian bonnet now rarely seen, other souvenirs of the sanguinary past should also be effaced. In the *salons* of the Luxembourg should be begun the attempted return to the civilisation of former days,— the days of the demoralised old *régime*. If vice could not be made to withdraw her hideous visage from the Directorial receptions — and wholly to exclude her was, alas, an effort beyond the power of these reformers — she could, at all events, be compelled to veil it.

The gross forms of expression, the more than rough manners of the Terror and Convention, which were rooting themselves too deeply in the language and habits of the once amiable and most *spirituelle* of nations, should henceforth be sternly frowned down. All who could find favour at the Directorial court must be prepared to imitate the head of that court; whose republican virtues shone with a twofold lustre, adorned by the *grande politesse* of his manners, his strict observance of *les bienséances*, and social *convénances*, which the republican bond of brotherhood now demanded from each of its members. The model that Barras kept steadily in view, in his revival of the part of *grand seigneur* of the old *régime*, was the libertine and arrogant Comte d'Artois. At the same *bijou* pavilion, La Bagatelle, the orgies of its former royal owner were reproduced, and Citizen Barras assumed the same haughty, insolent airs and overbearing manners towards his numerous attendants as had so unenviably distinguished the *vrai chevalier français*.

Very grand, indeed, were Barras's grand dinners, prepared by famous *chefs* of the late royal or aristocratic kitchens, and supplied from equally celebrated cellars with choicest wines that, like many other good things, had been safely stowed away somewhere during the Terror. These were no Spartan banquets. The people might be doomed to appease their hunger with a piece of black bread, — for the distress was great, and there were many, far above the ranks of the people, hiding their misery and poverty from the light of day in wretched garrets, glad to receive a piece of black bread, — but of bread the whitest and finest, and of all the other good things of life, there was no stint at the Luxembourg.

Two or three pairs of sharp eyes had detected the royal arms on the table linen. All was, in fact, so perfect that the invited guests, either shamed by the consciousness of presenting a very unflattering contrast with these dainty surroundings, or, warned by a gentle private hint, actually began to put on clean shirts, to wash their hands and faces, to get their boots blacked, and a brush-down given to their shabby coats — and their *culottes* also, unless in their principles too decidedly *sans-culottes* — before appearing at the well-spread hospitable board of King Barras.

This was decidedly a long stride forward towards the desired goal. It was remarked, too, that those who ventured, whether servants or visitors, still to *tutoyer* the superb Barras and the stately Teresa, did so in a faltering, ill-assured manner. For "thee" and "thou" were going out of fashion and favour, and "citizen" and "citizeness" were even much frowned upon. Among the people these revolutionary forms still prevailed; and "Citizen Minister," "Citizen General," etc., were the official modes of address, until the proclamation of the empire. They were, however, by general, if tacit, consent, banished from society, and "Monsieur" and "Madame" were welcomed back as old friends, — especially where the *élite* were timidly venturing again to appear.

It is not surprising, then, although so very much remained yet to be done before society could be considered reformed, or recomposed, that Madame Bonaparte, comparing the social changes she saw on her return with the state of things she had left, should have been as much surprised as she was pleased by it. The still cherished motto of the republic was, of course, "Liberty, equality, and fraternity," — " or death " no longer formed part of it. But for the rest the Citizen Directors and Citizen Ministers proudly bore the inscription on the buttons of their several fantastic official uniforms. Yet in spite of this, it was evident that, as a principle, it was now accepted, and acted upon, in a very modified sense, when compared with that in which it was announced in the full tide of the Revolution.

No separation, however, of the different classes of which society was composed could yet be established. In Barras's *salon*, and even in a more marked degree in the *salons* of the other Directors, there assembled indifferently — together with a few *ci-devant* dukes and marquises — generals, army contractors, men of letters, and men who lived by their wits; women of the ancient nobility, with actresses, reputable and otherwise, and women of openly infamous life; returned emigrants, and a few tamed patriots of the Reign of Terror. Among the latter was Fouché, very anxiously seeking some post under the Directory. But public feeling was then so strong against him that the Directors could not venture to employ him. The atrocities he had been guilty of in the South, *con amore*, as it seemed, surpassed in cruelty even the orders he had received from the sanguinary chiefs of the Terror. Through Barras's influence, however, he obtained an interest in the furnishing of the government supplies; thus, as he said himself, beginning the building of his fortune after the manner of Voltaire.

The eager desire to make money was, indeed, the one sentiment, the one aim, that alone was common to this assemblage of persons, differing so greatly in every other feeling, in their language, their education, manners, and station. Even ladies would pay assiduous court to Barras, or to Madame Tallien, to obtain for themselves, or for a *protégé* with whom profits were divided, an interest in that most profitable of all speculations, the furnishing of the government supplies.

Money was scarce, yet there was a feverish desire for amusement, — for balls, theatres, luxurious living, expensive dress; and only army contractors appear to have been able fully to gratify those desires. Their wives were, for the most part, women who may be said to have sprung from the ranks, — often the very lowest ranks. They made themselves fine as peacocks with satins and diamonds and feathers, and affected to be leaders of fashion when promoted from the cellar, or called down from the garret, to figure in the *salons* that had belonged to their betters. But, at all events, they generally were anxious to adopt, as far as they could learn them, the airs and graces of that old *régime* to whose ruin they owed their rise in the world.

The return to Paris of several *grandes dames*, who had found the means of buying permission to reënter France, seemed to promise a gradual reorganisation of *la bonne compagnie*. And probably more than one of the contractors' wives, ambitious of being received in the Faubourg St. Germain, may have followed the example of a certain Madame Privas, who was desirous of qualifying for that honour, and also of opening her own *salon* to the *beau monde*. Arrayed in velvet and plumes, she sought an interview with Madame de Genlis, — paying her visit in an elegant carriage, and attended by a negro servant in Moorish costume.

She stated that M. Privas had supplied the army with flour, and fortunately — with an expressive smile — when wheat was scarce. He had lately bought a fine hôtel in the Rue St. Dominique, and an estate at St. Aubyn, in Burgundy. In a word, she and her husband were rich — very rich. They wished, she said, to do honour to the splendid fortune they had acquired. They were fond of society; but only that of people quite *comme-il-faut*. She wanted, therefore, a lady to receive for her, to put her in the way of the old etiquette, of which — as she was a mere child when the Revolution broke out — she declared she had really lost all recollection.

Having read Madame de Genlis's work, "*Adèle et Théodore*," Madame Privas went on to say, she had at once exclaimed to Privas: "This is the lady for us." Privas having cordially agreed with her, she set about inquiring where Madame de Genlis was to be found; and learning that she had returned to France, and, poor lady, in very pinched circumstances, she came to offer her the position she had spoken of. She would give her a salary of 12,000 *francs*. She would also promise not to tyrannise over her; and even an intimate friend or cousin should be welcome, if she desired it, to a room in the house.

"Madame, I thank you for your obliging offer, which I have the honour to inform you it is not in my power to accept," replied Madame de Genlis, with an air of *grande dame* that surprised Madame Privas.

"You refuse it! Why, I offer you much more than you can get for your books. And you would besides have friends in us, — friends with a fortune of five millions. *C'est beau, ça! Eh?*"

"Madame, I have answered you. Such an arrangement is impossible."

"Well, adieu, then, my *bonne dame*. Privas will be much disappointed. We both made sure you would jump at this offer. And as you may be likely to think better of it, there is my address; write to me." Making a deep curtsey, and tossing her plumed head, Madame Privas flounced out of the room.

"And France, then, is come to this!" exclaimed Madame de Genlis, when her strange visitor had taken her departure, — "that the fortunes and estates of so many unhappy persons now suffering in exile and poverty, of so many heirs of massacred victims, should fall into the hands of such persons as these Privas! The woman spoke of her fortune of five millions; she has, then, an income of 250,000 *francs* [ten thousand pounds] a year, — perhaps, too, my father's château of St. Aubyn, which she spoke of; while I, his daughter, have to work for my bread. This, then, is the result of the Revolution!" Madame de Genlis, however, had hailed the first outburst of the Revolution with much enthusiasm. Had she forgotten that she once possessed (perhaps her subsequent troubles may have compelled her to part with it) a very remarkable *bijou de circonstance*, commemorative of the fall of the Bastille?

But hark! The conquering hero comes! All Paris for some days has been anxiously looking forward to his arrival; and wreaths and garlands, and triumphal arches, decorated with the colours taken during the Italian campaign, have been busily preparing. M. de Talleyrand has shown more than his usual hospitality and civility in entertaining Général Berthier and M. Monge, the bearers of the treaty of peace. He has artfully extracted from them all the information they could furnish respecting Général Bonaparte's habits, disposition, and supposed ambitious aspirations. He sees wealth and his own elevation in the young general's probable rise to political, no less than military, eminence. And it is now that he attaches himself to his fortunes, to rise with him, so long as he has self-sustaining power; but when his vaulting ambition o'erleaps itself, to heap ignominy on him in his fall.

M. de Talleyrand accordingly received the hero with an effusiveness rarely evinced by him. "The fraternal embrace" was given with, apparently, all the cordiality, and warmth of feeling, of an elder brother welcoming back from the wars the youngster whose distinguished valour in the field had won for him the victor's crown. Setting aside the claims of the Minister of War, whose duty it was to present Général Bonaparte to the Directors, he took upon himself that office. Perhaps it gratified and amused him to observe their mortification. Compelled to dissemble their fears and their jealousy, and, in deference to the sincere enthusiasm of the people, to seem to participate in the general joy, they gave the brilliant *fête* at the Luxembourg in honour of the "Conqueror of Italy and Pacificator of Europe."

"For this *fête*—given on the 20th Frimaire, and on a Decadi, the republican Sunday—a grand altar, "*l'autel de la patrie*," was erected in the great court of the Luxembourg. It was surmounted by allegorical figures of Liberty, Equality, and Peace, and decorated with the trophies of war. At noon, cannon proclaimed that the *fête* was begun. But from an early hour crowds had surrounded the palace, braving the drizzling rain of a chill December morning to obtain, though they should have to struggle for it, but a glimpse of the hero of the *fête*. Surrounding the altar, but on a sort of platform that raises them above it, the five Directors recline in luxuriously cushioned velvet armchairs. Barras is in the centre. The ministers, the *corps diplomatique*, and legislative authorities, less gorgeously attired, yet a dazzling show, are arranged on either side of the Directors. Of the thousands of seats for spectators, not one is unoccupied, nor is there an inch of standing-room vacant.

The "Marseillaise" and the "*Chant du Départ*" are sung by the pupils of the Conservatoire. Then the "*Chant du Retour*" is begun. But the voices of the singers and the sound of the accompanying instruments are suddenly overpowered by the applauding shouts of the assembled thousands. "*Vive à jamais Bonaparte! Vive le Pacificateur de l'Europe!*" It is as a peacemaker, then, that the man who is to kindle the flames of war throughout Europe receives his first public ovation. It appears to have taken a considerable time to calm down the enthusiasm of the ladies, whose handkerchiefs, fans, gloves, and scarfs waved a welcome to the hero from all parts of the vast hall. But, when the fervour of their welcome was a little subdued, the Hymn of Liberty was sung by the choir of the Conservatoire, — all present rising from their seats and joining in it. Even the magnificent Directors stood, holding their plumed hats in their hands, to do homage to republican liberty.

The Treaty of Campo-Formio, ratified by the Emperor Francis, was then laid by Bonaparte on the altar of *la patrie*. M. de Talleyrand, departing from his taciturn habits, pronounced a long eulogistic discourse, in which he hailed the young general as "*l'homme des siècles*," spoke admiringly of "his simple habits; his disdain of luxury and splendour, as the ambition of vulgar souls; of his delight in poetry; his especial love of the poems of Ossian, so well calculated, he said, to wean the mind from the gross things of earth and all worldly considerations."

This rhapsody ended, it was Bonaparte's turn to address the Directors. The deepest silence prevailed. Every ear was strained to catch the tones of his voice, which, full, clear, and impressive, carried the pithy, telling, incisive sentences of his short address, distinctly to the most distant part

of the hall. France was then first named by him
"*la grande nation.*"

Barras's response (supposed to have been prepared for him by M. de Talleyrand) was long — too long, impatient listeners declared; but it was complimentary. Repeating almost the exact words that the devoted Junot wrote to his father, he pronounced him one of those prodigies of whom Nature was sparing, — one of those great men she produced for the admiration of the rest of mankind only at very long intervals.

Barras concluded by bidding the victorious young soldier take command of the army of England (an army that existed only in name), and crown his illustrious career by the conquest of that island. Seemingly overcome by profound emotion, he then fell with the whole weight of his portly person into the arms of the little general. This was the fraternal embrace (*l'accolade fraternelle*) given in the name of a grateful country, and the customary finale of all proceedings on important public occasions like that now in question. Bonaparte, unprepared for this brotherly demonstration of the national feeling, had well-nigh fallen prostrate under it. He, however, sustained the shock with admirable calmness, and a seriousness that checked a general inclination to laughter in the profane lookers-on. But his own stoicism almost gave way when a similar attack was made on him by the four other Directors in succession. They appeared to be malignantly bent on stifling him in their fraternal embraces, and burying him under the weight of their gorgeous mantles, their tall plumes of feathers, and broad-brimmed hats.

Bonaparte, however, survived to attend the grand banquet that followed the ceremony of the morning; also to be present at the ball given to him in the evening at the Théâtre de l'Odéon, when Paris was illuminated. It was the first ball on a grand scale and with any attempt at splendour of decoration that had taken place since the breaking out of the Revolution. The ladies failed not, even those of slenderest purses, to stretch a point to do honour to the occasion. Many diamonds that had been hidden away for some years shone forth again in full splendour that evening. Madame Tallien made a magnificent display. Diamonds of large size and great lustre adorned her neck, her arms, her waist, glittered in her hair and on her sandals, and bordered her Roman tunic.

A story was afloat that a royalist, present at that ball, had found an opportunity of attaching a paper to the lady's tunic, having first written upon it "*Respect aux propriétés nationales.*" This drew upon the jewels the scrutinising attention of many persons. Madame Tallien, noticing this, asked of one of them:

"Why, monsieur, do you look at me so seriously and earnestly?"

Napoleon.

Mezzotint by G. W. H. Ritchie, after Painting by David.

"Madame," he replied, "I am not looking at you, but am examining the crown diamonds."

The little Directorial papers — of which a whole host, light, lively, and satirical, but of varying political principles, appeared after the Terror — vehemently denied that there was any truth in that story. But at all events it was generally remarked, "*Se non é vero é ben trovato.*"

That Joséphine had exquisite taste in dress is well known. She had not the superb beauty of Madame Tallien, nor the Madonna-like charms of Madame Tallien's rival, Madame Récamier, then in the bloom of youth, — just twenty-one, and two years younger than the lady who reigned as queen at the Luxembourg. But without any fear of eliciting odious comparisons, Joséphine could take her place beside those ladies. Her age was then thirty-four or thirty-five, — a period of life when the traces of time on the female face are usually very slightly perceptible. Joséphine, so skilful, too, in the art of beautifying, could throw off a dozen years with ease, and, aided by her unstudied natural grace and elegance, and a *toilette* perfectly adapted to her height, her form, her figure, with just enough and no more of ornamentation, win a full tribute of admiration in the presence of her younger rivals.

Such a triumph she achieved on the evening of the ball; and Bonaparte was as proud of it as of any of his Italian victories. He saw that

Madame Bonaparte attracted around her all who had any pretensions to be classed as the *élite* of the assembly; while the *bonnes dames* of the *bourgeoisie*, and the contractors' wives, in their diaphanous Greek and Roman costumes, stood afar off and studied her air and manner, hoping to catch, and to retain for their own use, some inkling of the aristocratic ease and grace which distinguished the victor's wife. Joséphine began her novitiate for the throne at her receptions in Italy. The ladies of the Bonaparte family now returning to France with Joseph, who had fled from his Roman embassy, were also about to learn and rehearse in Paris their *rôle* of imperial princesses, during Bonaparte's absence in Egypt.

Of balls, *fêtes*, and theatres he had soon had enough. Scarce a month had elapsed since his return, and already he was weary of inaction. He had no intention of reposing on his laurels. Having visited the northern coast, it was his opinion that the scheme of an invasion of England was impracticable, at least at that time. Also, information received from M. Gallois, who had been sent to London during Lord Malmesbury's and M. de Talleyrand's ineffectual attempt to negotiate a peace at Lille, confirmed him in it. The project of the expedition to Egypt was therefore brought on the *tapis*. It was first suggested by M. Monge, with whom, while the Campo-Formio negotiation was pending, Bonaparte was in frequent communication. He adopted the idea with ardour. M. de Talleyrand favoured it, and the Directors were glad to consent to any scheme that should remove the restless and ambitious young general out of their way.

The disturbance that occurred at Vienna when Général Bernadotte, who had been sent thither as ambassador, displayed the tricoloured flag in front of his residence, seemed likely to put an end to the Egyptian expedition. For Bernadotte left Vienna, and Bonaparte was ordered to repair to Rastadt, with the fullest powers to offer, or, should he deem it expedient, demand reparation. This pleased him well. But he expressed so openly his satisfaction at once more being the sole arbiter of peace or war that the jealous Directors took alarm, rescinded the order for his departure, and sent François de Neufchâteau in his stead.

Barras undertook to inform him of the change, and went to Bonaparte's residence for that purpose. "They were closeted together in his private room," says M. de Melito, who was present, "less than a quarter of an hour, when Barras left hastily, scarcely noticing the presence of Madame Bonaparte as he passed through the *salon*. The general soon followed, slamming the door violently after him." He made no reference to what had passed between him and Barras; but, bidding a hasty adieu to his friend, returned to his room to make, as he said, some preparations. That same night he was on his way to Toulon. He feared that the expedition to Egypt should be countermanded.

It had been arranged that M. de Talleyrand should proceed to Constantinople as ambassador, to persuade the Sultan, if possible, to look favourably on the occupation of Egypt by the French.

It was, however, mere cajolery on his part. He had become doubtful of the success of the expedition, and ever guided, as he said, by commonsense, did not choose to commit himself by too rashly participating in it.

Fouché declared that "Bonaparte flattered himself with the idea of governing Egypt, either as sultan or prophet." It is, however, more likely that he had then an idea that he was likely at no distant period to govern France. His brothers, Joseph and Lucien, watched the action of the Directory in his interest during his absence. And he did not leave without securing to Joséphine an income of 50,000 *francs*, in addition to her own of 25,000, and placing a sum of money at her disposal for the purchase of a country house. Her choice fell on the pretty Château of La Malmaison, destined to become so famous.

CHAPTER XV.

The Scientific Party. — Departure for Egypt. — False Hopes. — The Returned Exiles. — Memories of the Past. — The *Salon* Talleyrand. — Madame Grandt. — A Political Debating Club. — Madame de Staël. — A "*Chevalier des Dames.*" — Joséphine's Thursday *Réunions*. — Joséphine's Extravagance. — Artists and *Littérateurs*. — "L'Abbé de l'Épée." — "*Les Deux Journées.*" — "*La Belle Laitière.*" — Le Château de Morltfontaine. — M. de la Trénise. — The Battle of Aboukir. — The Return from Egypt. — Reproaching the Government. — The Martyr's Prayer. — A Presentiment Fulfilled.

BONAPARTE was accompanied on his expedition to Egypt by his stepson, Eugène de Beauharnais, who, as one of the general's numerous aides-de-camp, then began his military career. Tallien, too, leaving his beautiful wife to do the honours of Barras's establishments, and to receive the homage, persistently paid at this time, of M. de Fontenoy, her first husband, availed himself of an opportunity of joining the party of scientific men, savants, and artists, who were to follow the army. This addition to the army of Egypt was suggested by M. Monge in the interests of science, literature, and art; and the Directory readily consented to all arrangements that Bonaparte approved, for the sake of disembarrassing themselves of an ally whose projects and restless ambition were so fraught with danger to the Directorial government.

Joséphine joined her husband and son in their hurried journey to Toulon, where they embarked on the 19th of May. Bonaparte is said to have evinced deep emotion at parting with his wife, and to have promised her that Eugène should receive from him a parent's watchful care.

On her return to Paris the little hôtel in the Rue Chantereine (now Rue de la Victoire, in compliment to Bonaparte) became the centre of attraction to the *beau monde*. M. de Talleyrand, whose own sentence of banishment had been so lately reversed, was able to obtain the erasure of many distinguished names from the list of proscribed exiles,—always, of course, for an ample consideration. He may have shared the profits of this traffic with Barras, who, besides being charged with doing the honours of the Luxembourg, was also at the head of the department of police. Such matters, therefore, came under his immediate cognisance; and it was notorious that gross corruption, disorder, and peculation prevailed in every department of the government. This, together with the extravagance of Barras and his affectation of reviving the trappings of state, brought the chiefs of the Directory into contempt with the returned exiles.

The greater number were royalists, and believed that, when the favourable moment for putting his designs into action should arrive, Général Bonaparte would prove a General Monk. Meanwhile, as he was absent, they paid assiduous court to his wife. Under other circumstances they would probably have held themselves aloof; for there were doubts of her having been presented at the court of Louis XVI. — a distinction which the *débris* of the old *régime* regarded as an impassable gulf between them and less fortunate individuals who had not been thus sealed of the number of the *élite*. Joséphine claimed to have been presented to Marie Antoinette in 1789. The serious troubles of the court began at that time; and soon after it was announced that no presentations would take place until further notice. Nor were they again formally resumed.

But whether presented or not, Joséphine, for her own sake, as well as for the possible advantages to be derived from her husband's future career, was welcomed everywhere, visiting and visited by all Paris, — rarely, however, appearing at the Luxembourg; such being the will of Bonaparte, who disapproved her intimacy with Madame Tallien, and hated the dissolute Sybarite Barras. But as emigrant friends were recalled, by the favour of M. de Talleyrand or otherwise, a more select and congenial social circle was formed. In this remnant of the old French society there was doubtless less gaiety than formerly, less sprightly *badinage*, less sparkling and *spirituelle* conversation.

The elastic spirits with which the French are for the most part endowed rarely allow them to brood long over bygone sorrows. But those returned exiles, though there were among them several women of rank who had been remarkable for their wit and vivacity, generally had fled from France to escape the fate that had befallen husbands, sons, or other near relatives, during the Reign of Terror. On reëntering a society in which some few faces perhaps were known to them, while so many were new and strange, sad thoughts would naturally overwhelm them. Like Talma, when unable from emotion at once to proceed with his part, on reappearing on the stage after the Terror, they might have replied, as sufficiently excusing this irrepressible agitation of mind: "Citizens, I have lost all my friends on the scaffold!"

Gaiety and the flow of soul doubtless were often checked by the sudden intrusion of saddening memories of the past; and gloom would overspread those *réunions* of the *renaissance* of society, composed as they were of elements so discordant. Even when much weeding out had taken place, and the master mind of Napoleon invented his famous "system of fusion," the old and the new *régime* did not readily amalgamate. It was gratifying, then, to returning emigrants, at this early stage of the reorganisation of society, when M. de Talleyrand opened his *salons* twice in the week at the elegant hôtel he had taken — formerly hôtel Créquy — in the Rue d'Anjou. The official residence of the Minister of Foreign Affairs was the hôtel Galifet, and there, as the *corps diplomatique* became more numerous, he found it expedient to give his official dinners.

By some means M. de Talleyrand had contrived to amass wealth during his expatriation. This, with his official salary and other sources of income, enabled him to live in a princely style, of which the Parisians had begun to lose the recollection. His private circle was for some time very limited; he did not open his doors to the mixed assemblages that thronged the Luxembourg. In consequence, his establishment obtained the name of a *maison insociable;* yet it was regarded as a sort of charmed circle into which all were anxious for admission; for the renegade bishop was in all respects the same *grand seigneur* and model of courtesy as of old. He was, perhaps, a shade more cynical, and there may have been more of mockery in his smile than once there was of levity; more bitterness in his irony, too, since he had lost faith — if perchance he ever had any — in that grand wonder-working principle, *la liberté régénératrice*, which was to inaugurate the reign of wisdom, virtue, and justice in France, and eventually to regenerate the world.

M. de Talleyrand had escaped the stigma of having voted for the death of Louis XVI. Returned emigrants of the old French society thankfully remembered this when they accepted the refuge and welcome he offered them in his elegant and perfumed *salon*, while they conveniently forgot that, nevertheless, he was then the minister of three regicides. One drawback to the enjoyments of his luxurious *salon* the ladies especially found in the presence of the beautiful Madame Grandt. Madame de Staël, who was anxious to number Talleyrand amongst her lovers, was deeply aggrieved by his admiration of this lovely woman. "What was the mere beauty of that stupid person compared with her intellect, her superlative eloquence?" But Talleyrand was not needy, like Benjamin Constant, Louis de Narbonne, and some others, of that train of followers whom interest attached to her. If he conspired, he chose rather to do so in complicity with fortune, as Bonaparte said, than with Madame de Staël and her lovers.

The old French fashion of suppers was revived at the hôtel d'Anjou, — suppers at which Brillat-Savarin did not disdain to assist. The host, however, never partook of the good cheer he provided for his guests, though he shared in the sprightly *causerie* it seems to have inspired. It was then, too, that Madame Grandt, who did full honour to the supper, indulged also in her most brilliant sallies, — the remarks of this reputed beautiful simpleton being often so telling, so stinging, that it was sometimes suspected they were prompted by the "protector," as he called himself, of this lovely *ingénue*. However, repose and enjoyment appear to have reigned in the abode of M. de Talleyrand more than elsewhere at that period.

The *salon* of the Swedish ambassadress was a political debating club, of which the ambassadress took the lead, as a planet around which numerous satellites revolved, receiving light or inspiration from her. In her *salon* the conferences of the great republican forum, the Club de Salm, were rehearsed; and there was planned the successful scheme that, on the 18th Fructidor, overthrew the royalist plot for bringing back the Bourbons. Madame de Staël preferred the republic. The Directorial government met with her full approbation, — a proof that her political opinions were as valueless as are those of women generally.

She had some influence over Barras, who, hating political discussion, and wanting the impassivity that distinguished her ungrateful friend Talleyrand, readily yielded to her wishes to place or pension her friends, as she suggested, in order to escape from the infliction of an eloquent harangue. The lady who reigned at the Luxembourg was therefore less in disfavour with her than the divinity who presided at the hôtel d'Anjou. She pronounced her "*belle, bonne, et spirituelle,*" and saluted her graciously when they met in the Directorial *salons*. But she avoided placing herself beside her, as she was accustomed to do with Madame Récamier; whose inanimate beauty, as she believed, though not always rightly, served but as a foil to increase the effect of her own great mental gifts.

Madame de Staël had not passed through the events of the Revolution without acquiring and retaining in her manners, habits, and feelings, many of the characteristics of that stormy period. She was then about thirty-two, and is described by a writer of the time, and a professed admirer of her intellect, as greatly resembling her father; but having an eager, almost ravenous, expression in the eyes, and something masculine and assured in her countenance. Her complexion was scorbutic, her lips were dry and arid, and her movements and gestures imperious. Her voice was sonorous, and her utterance rapid and energetic. The frequent distractions, arising from a secret and continual preoccupation of mind, that were peculiar to the sublime Necker, were observable also in his daughter; who, after a few moments of this inward communing, would suddenly give expression to some vehement opinion, some fiery thought, or cutting epigram, fresh apparently from the mintage of her brain.

In a word, says the same writer, she was neither imposing nor pleasing, and one's first impressions were not in her favour. "She gave me the idea of creative genius, taking the form of a woman destitute of beauty, in order that men who were so rash as to enter into disputation with her might, when subjugated, feel their humiliation less keenly." This is sufficiently fanciful. But it is from the pen of M. Bouilly, a recognised "*chevalier des dames*" Speaking of the lady who always received him so graciously, and who some years before had advised him to decline her father's offer of the post of secretary, because she discerned in the talent displayed in his early writings that a better career was open to him, something that should look like a compliment was to be expected.

This M. Bouilly was for many years a highly esteemed and welcome guest in most of the best Parisian *salons*, literary, artistic, and dramatic, and wherever talent and high character received their due meed of honour. He was no less in request, at this time, in the *salon* of Madame Bonaparte than in that of Madame de Staël; though in the tastes of those ladies, and in the bestowal of their friendship, they would seem to have been swayed by influences that placed them far as the poles asunder. They bowed to each other graciously when they met. But the hero of Italy, by his laconic replies, had so checked the flow of enthusiasm with which the eloquent Madame de Staël had been prepared to overwhelm him, that there could be no approach to intimacy between her and the hero's wife.

While La Malmaison was preparing for occupancy, and the victor's share of Italian spoils — pictures, bronzes, marble statues, mirrors, etc. — were being transferred thither for its adornment, Joséphine held her receptions at her hôtel in the Rue Chantereine; and she continued to do so until Bonaparte's return from Egypt, — passing only occasionally a short time at La Malmaison with Hortense and her niece Stéphanie. "Madame Bonaparte," says M. Bouilly, "honoured me with a general invitation to her Thursday *réunions*, when all that yet remained of those perfect models of grace and good-breeding that once made the charm of French society assembled around that amiable woman." There might sometimes be met the once celebrated Madame d'Houdetot, whose wit and beauty inspired Jean Jacques with a passion so intense; also Madame Fanny de Beauharnais, Joséphine's aunt and a literary celebrity, who occasionally looked in also at Madame de Staël's, where ladies were not accustomed to make long visits.

Some members of the Bonaparte family — Pauline oftener than others — attended these receptions, — with the double object of acquiring some notions of the *convénances* of society, with which they were wholly unacquainted, and of observing with malevolent eyes all that passed, especially all that by straining might be interpreted unfavourably and thus reported to the absent brother. At this period Bonaparte availed himself of every spare moment to write passionate love-letters to Joséphine, and sent her large sums of money. Yet she had rarely a crown in her pocket, and disorder and distress prevailed in her household, owing to her extravagance in dress, and thoughtless profusion generally.

It suited the views of Bonaparte that Joséphine should live expensively, and keep up her establishment to the fullest extent of the means he provided her with, and that she should receive all who had any claims to talent, rank, or distinguished merit. But he looked to her also for order and method in her expenditure. In this latter respect she failed — ignominiously failed; but in the former she carried out his wishes successfully. Men of elevated rank, the most distinguished orators of the tribune and the bar, men of literary fame, and artists of celebrity met in her *salon*.

David (who, in laying aside the toga, appears to have resumed his right mind), and his pupils, Gérard and Girodet; Grétry, and the younger composer Méhul, with Lesueur, and the famous Cherubini — whom Joséphine called her master — formed a distinguished artistic group.

Of *littérateurs* who had contrived to save their heads, there was first Joseph Chénier, accused of not doing all he might have done to save his gifted brother André from the scaffold; then Ducis, the translator, or adapter, of Shakespeare; Lebrun-Pindare, the poet and epigrammatist; Arnaud, Legouvé, Desaugiers, Longchamps, Després, and, not the least distinguished among them, Hoffman, the critic, — forming together a brilliant galaxy of talent and genius. Nor must we forget Joséphine's friend, Bouilly, whom she one evening invited to read in her *salon* his drama of "L'Abbé de l'Épée," then accepted for production at the Théâtre Français, and which achieved so brilliant a success. Well indeed it might when the cast included such names as Monvel, Grandménil, Dazincourt, Baptiste *aîné*, and Mesdames Talma, Mézerai, and La Chassaigne.

A far greater gratification, however, than the mere success of the play awaited its worthy author on the first night of its representation. It was the release from unmerited imprisonment of the Abbé Sicard, the successor of the Abbé de Épée, the humane founder of the famous institution for the instruction of the deaf and dumb. The drama was founded on an incident connected with it, which so moved the audience that the poet, Collin d'Harleville — who was in a box opposite that occupied by Général Bonaparte, then very recently named First Consul — being urged by those around him, rose, and, addressing the general, said: "We demand the release of the worthy Abbé Sicard, now lying in prison, the victim of injustice and persecution." The audience applauded, and, taking up the poet's words, repeated the demand that the able and humane teacher of the deaf and dumb should be released and restored to his office.

Bonaparte probably was unacquainted with the matter. Joséphine was with him, and he appeared to appeal to her. Presently an aide-de-camp announced to the managers that the cause of the *abbé's* detention should be inquired into, and Monvel, who played the Abbé de l'Épée, informed the audience of it from the stage. Immense applause was the result. So promptly were the general's orders carried out, that on the evening of the following day the Abbé Sicard, in person, made his appearance at M. Bouilly's residence to thank him for his liberation from prison, where, as he said, but for the touching scenes of his play, he might have been long detained, unheeded, or forgotten.

Bouilly's operetta, "*Les deux Journées*," had the singular result of making him so popular with the Savoyard water-carriers of Paris that he had difficulty in excusing himself from receiving gratis from each of them, all the year round, an ample supply of water. Bouilly's libretto was charmingly set to music by Cherubini. Its subject was the escape of a distinguished member of the *noblesse*, condemned by Robespierre to the scaffold, but who, aided by a faithful Savoyard, was conveyed beyond the barriers of Paris, to a place of safety, in a water-carrier's barrel. The whole fraternity of water-carriers felt themselves complimented by M. Bouilly's play; and, although they were unable to prevail on him to accept the overflow of their grateful feelings in water, which, in those days of scanty supply, was no mean offer, he did not refuse a presentation bouquet of enormous proportions, to which each man had contributed a choice flower.

The incident that formed the subject of the play was said to have actually occurred. Many lives were probably saved during the Terror in a similar manner. The charming Mdlle. Contat, disguised as a milkwoman, with donkey and pails, and accompanied by a man, in appearance her farm-servant, led safely through Paris one who had formerly been her enemy, but who, in an hour of extreme danger, implored her forgiveness and aid, which, as regards the latter, she effectually, and at the risk of her own life, gave him.

At this period of social revival, although the Directorial government was daily and deservedly growing in disfavour, a feeling yet prevailed that a time of greater security was drawing near, — a cessation of intestine divisions, and of that spirit of anarchy which had brought so much evil on France. The social circle became greatly extended; *salon* after *salon* was gradually reopened. But where could be found a more brilliant circle than at the Château d'Ivry? Where a more genial, *spirituelle*, and accomplished hostess than that same Louise Contat, now Comtesse de Parny, with her gift of improvisation and witty repartee? The gallantry of the old French school, with gaiety and good breeding, were said to have taken refuge in her *salons*, whither, twice a week, the *élite* of Paris, and the most distinguished members of the world of literature and art, eagerly flocked,— forming, as a contemporary writer remarked, " veritable federations of the celebrities of the epoch."

Another recently formed grand establishment, kept up at great expense, was the princely Château of Mortfontaine, where Joseph Bonaparte lived in luxurious style, receiving the most distinguished generals, the principal employés of the government, and the most intriguing of the women of the *beau monde*. Madame de Staël was a frequent guest; Madame Bonaparte a rare one.

Conjointly, Joseph and Lucien — the latter the more ambitious of the two — watched the action of the Directory in the interest of the absent Napoleon. Lucien had not a rich wife and a wealthy father-in-law, like the fortunate Joseph; yet he, too, lived in a handsome hôtel, in the Rue Verte, Faubourg St. Honoré, and received more numerously than Joseph.

But a different section of society visited Lucien and Christine. The latter, it appears, had readily acquired the manners of a woman of the world, and without detriment to the natural grace and goodness of heart that made her also so charming a woman. *La grande gaieté* reigned at Lucien's establishment, and even much frivolity. There, youth and beauty delighted to congregate, the host and hostess themselves were so young. There, dancing was always kept up with unflagging spirit through the greater part of the night. None was more constant in his attendance than that *beau danseur* of the period, M. de la Trénise, whose name and fame are immortalised in the third figure, La Trénise, of the first set of quadrilles; in which he was accustomed to display his terpsichorean airs and graces with so much effect as *cavalier seul*.

But, notwithstanding Lucien's apparent levity, trifling, and love of pleasure, he was more earnest and active than Joseph in furthering Napoleon's views, and in keeping him well informed of the state of affairs and the decline of the Directorial government. It is probable, as stated by Fouché, that Lucien proposed to share power with him; to establish a duumvirate, Lucien being the head of the civil government, Napoleon taking the supreme command of the army and the department connected with war. But this division of the supreme power was in no way contemplated by Napoleon.

His Egyptian expedition, though brilliant, had not been satisfactory in its results. He had taken

Malta on his way to the East, and he had gained there, but with immense loss, a victory over Mourad. But the ill-success of the siege of St. Jean d'Acre, the destruction of the French fleet at the battle of the Nile, the disposition of the conquered yet desperate people to revolt, determined him, after he had repaired by a new victory some of those disasters that had befallen both the land and naval forces of France, to return to Paris and there watch the course of events.

The battle of Aboukir furnished him with the opportunity. The bulletin — setting forth in exaggerated terms the importance of this victory — was circulated throughout the capital, and commented upon with enthusiasm by the Bonaparte family. Thus was prepared the triumphal entry of the conquering hero into the capital — henceforth *his* capital. Suddenly, unexpectedly, but most opportunely for the realisation of his plans, it is about to take place. Joséphine was in the secret; but less discreet than her brothers-in-law, and not dreaming of the possibility of failure, she could not refrain from exclaiming exultingly: "Ah, if he were only to arrive now — what a joyful surprise! How soon he would restore tranquillity and set everything in order" (alluding to the dissensions in the government).

" After hearing that speech," said Fouché (who had succeeded in obtaining the direction of the police but had not yet fathomed the Bonaparte plot), " and noting the tone in which it was uttered, I was prepared to see him any day fall from the clouds amongst us." In less than a fortnight the young general appeared, and both Fouché and Talleyrand, at that time, seem to have really admired his audacity, and to have entered with ardour into the intrigue that was to place him at the head of affairs.

His journey through France had been a triumphal progress from town to town; and this deserter from the army of Egypt, this violator of the quarantine laws at Fréjus, whom a strong government would have deprived of his commission and punished severely, was greeted, from the moment of his landing to his entry into Paris, with frantic enthusiasm. The sensation his arrival produced was extraordinary. The nation seemed to hail him as its liberator, and to proclaim its want of a chief, and the general feeling that under the auspices of fortune that chief had arrived.

And this expression of national delight at his return was received by Bonaparte as the welcoming of a sovereign back to his kingdom. As a sovereign, from the tone he assumed in his proclamations, he seemed from this time to regard himself. The feeble Directory strove to dissemble its resentment, but comprehended that its days were numbered. With singular arrogance, the great man reproached the government on the unhappy state of the country.

"What have you done," he said, "with that France which I left you so brilliant? I left you peace; I now find war. I left you victories; I find reverses. I left you the millions of Italy; yet throughout the country I find naught but misery and spoliation. What have you done with those hundred thousand Frenchmen who were my companions in glory? They are dead. This is a state of things that cannot, must not endure. In less than three years it would lead us to despotism."

If despotism had not already arrived, one might infer from this address that it was near at hand. Barras had been in treaty with the Bourbons. He had in his pocket the promise of a pardon and a pension from Louis XVIII., and was prepared, with others who were in the secret, to deliver over the government of France into his hands. But the long cherished hopes of the Comte de Provence were not yet to be realised for many a year. The prayer of the martyred Suleau, uttered in 1792, had been granted. The tutelary deity he had invoked for his country — the despot and man of genius — had appeared. "Until France," he said, " has bowed in silence beneath the iron rod of an inflexible master, haughty as Richelieu, she cannot again be reunited as a nation. I would call to her aid an enlightened and magnanimous usurper, capable, by his superb and striking Cromwellism, of making himself both admired and feared by the people he forces to respect and bless their servitude." Surely this describes Bonaparte, the imperious master that kneeling France was awaiting.

Within a month of his return, the 18th and 19th Brumaire had abolished the Directorial government. Barras had sold Grosbois to Général Moreau and chosen Brussels for his residence, where, on the plunder of his five years' reign, he lived for many years *en prince;* while in the first days of the closing year of the eighteenth century the Consular government was established, with Général Bonaparte as its chief.

"I have a presentiment," said Jean Jacques, "that the little island of Corsica will one day astonish Europe;" and astonish it she truly did in the brilliant career of one of her sons. Without being invited to preside, Bonaparte, on entering the council-chamber, took his seat, *sans cérémonie*, in the president's chair, and with it the lead in the government.

CHAPTER XVI.

Love and Jealousy. — Madame Récamier. — The Word "Divorce" First Uttered. — Joséphine in Disgrace. — Reconciliation. — Ineligible Visitors. — A Change of Scene. — "Get Up, Little Creole, Get Up." — Taking Possession. — A Forgotten Inscription. — "*Vive le Général Bonaparte!*" — Violets and Snowdrops. — Joséphine's *Coup d'Essai*. — Death of the Trees of Liberty.

HE powerful feelings of love and jealousy, no less than ambition, agitated the minds of both Lucien and Napoleon Bonaparte while engaged in accomplishing the *coup-d'état* that was to change the destinies of France. Notwithstanding his professed devotion to his "*bonne et douce* Christine," Lucien was then madly in love with the beautiful Madame Récamier. He thought himself the more supremely wretched that his devotion having, as he fancied, touched the lady's heart and moved her at least to pity, she yet subjected him to the most rigorous and heart-breaking treatment.

Madame Récamier had a devoted husband, to whom she was a devoted wife. Nevertheless, such was the state of morals at that period that Lucien could not understand the coldness and reserve she displayed towards him. Under this tumultuous state of feeling his political energy seemed to acquire fresh vigour. Yet the active and prominent part he took in the proceedings of the 18th and 19th Brumaire, did not so entirely engross his attention but that he found some moments to give to the vehement urging of his suit. It was in M. Récamier's château of Clichy-la-Garenne that his plans for the 18th were partly matured; his political objects being as freely explained to his hostess as the pangs of his violent love. She, however, was sufficiently discreet to conceal the former and to abstain from encouraging the latter. Madame Récamier was accustomed to be thus adored. So many bruised and wounded hearts were constantly laid at her feet that she had learned to hear their sighs and contemplate their pangs with stoical indifference. This gained her the reputation of being a mere cold and inanimate, though beautiful, statue.

Napoleon had received the wound to his feelings from his wife; or rather the malevolence of the Bonaparte family towards Joséphine seemed likely, on Napoleon's return from Egypt, to cause not merely estrangement between them, but separation. For the word "divorce" was uttered, and its realisation would have greatly pleased them. When his landing at Fréjus became known, she and Joseph Bonaparte set out for Lyons with the expectation of meeting him. But he had taken a different route from that they expected, and arrived in Paris before them. The tale of poor Joséphine's indiscretions — a mingled tale of truth, exaggeration, and falsehood — was then poured into Bonaparte's ears. And Joséphine, alas! was not there to welcome her warriors home, to greet her husband and son with smiles, and to refute with her winning voice — which the former had said was to him as the sweetest music — the malicious accusations of Lucien.

Doubtless Joséphine was then greatly loved by Bonaparte. He was aware of her propensity to forget there was a limit to her or to his means, when a new and tasteful *toilette*, elegant and expensive jewelry, and pretty things in general were temptingly brought under her notice. This was a vexatious, an embarrassing habit in the wife of a soldier of fortune, even though his prospects were brilliant. But it was as nothing, compared with the acceptance of favours that self-respect should have told her to refuse, or, as broadly insinuated, if not positively asserted, with more serious offences against him still. Bonaparte was deeply wounded — cut to the quick.

Returning with Eugène to his deserted home, disappointed and grieved, he shut himself up in his room to indulge alone in gloomy thought. A few hours later Joséphine arrived, and, after being affectionately received by her son, hastened, all happiness and eagerness, to embrace her husband. But the door of the apartment in which her liege lord had taken refuge was closed against her. Tears, entreaties, reproaches, availed not. A harsh reply, or command to withdraw, alone was vouchsafed to her. After some hours of this misery, Bonaparte allowed Eugène and Hortense, who had come from St. Germain-en-Laye to welcome the hero, to enter his apartment. So long and so earnestly they pleaded for their mother, that at length signs of relenting appeared. An anxious silence ensued; when the sighing and wailing of poor Joséphine outside were heard, and at last overcame what yet remained of unwillingness to yield.

The door was thrown open; explanations ensued, and reconciliation followed. Lucien, who had expected a totally different result, came in just in time to witness it. The divorce was therefore adjourned to a more convenient season. It would probably never have taken place but for the persistent urging and enmity of the Bonapartes, and the fretful jealousy of Joséphine; over whose head it hung menacingly as the sword of Damocles for the next nine years. Had it occurred at this time it would have raised up a powerful party against the "usurper" (as Bonaparte was generally and rightly considered on the 19th Brumaire). It would have served as a pretext for calling into action the spirit of resentment that smouldered in so many hearts against the author of the Constitution of the year VIII.—a constitution that supplanted the Abbé Sieyès's fantastical scheme, and, by the changes it introduced into the representative system, overthrew the barriers that opposed a return to despotism.

Joséphine had an important part to play in smoothing down many asperities obstructing Bonaparte's progress from the Consular arm-chair to the imperial throne. The reorganisation, he said, of the "*système sociable*" must take precedence of that of the "*système social.*" And this, which none of his female relatives could have accomplished for him, was to be done solely by the attractive Joséphine.

The Luxembourg, which had been the residence of the Directors, was for many reasons declared by Bonaparte an unsuitable abode for him and his colleagues. There must be no souvenirs of Barras and his dissolute parody of a court intruding themselves at the receptions of the First Consul and Madame Bonaparte. Most of the women who had frequented the Directorial *salons* were ineligible for admission to those of the Consulate. Madame Tallien was to be permanently erased from Joséphine's visiting list, as she already was from several others.

The name of Tallien, associated with so many sanguinary deeds, inspired horror. But when the modern Aspasia consented to bear it, she redeemed it — so many people thought — from much of its infamy, by connecting it with acts of mercy and the downfall of a bloodthirsty tyrant. But lately she shone the star of the Luxembourg revels; now, she is in total eclipse, but is destined to shine forth again with greater refulgence than ever, as Princesse de Chimay; and in years to come, loved and regretted, to die in the odour of sanctity.

But Joséphine has promised her lord that she will see this once favourite friend no more, — this "*notre dame de bon secours*," as those who remembered only her kind, compassionate heart, when kindness and compassion were such very rare virtues, were wont to name her; as they named Joséphine "*notre dame des victoires*," after Bonaparte's sobriquet of "*le petit mitrailleur*" gave place to the appellation of "The Conqueror of Italy."

"We take up a different position. A change of scene is requisite. We form a new epoch," he said. Bonaparte therefore decided that for him the most suitable residence was the Tuileries. The Third Consul, Lebrun, he thought, it would be well to allow an apartment in the palace, while to the Second Consul, Cambacérès, an hôtel on the Carrousel should be assigned. Of the chiefs of the different governments that France had had since the fall of the monarchy, Bonaparte was the first that had dared to take up his residence in this ancient royal domicile. It was his second innovation. The first was the placing of his name at the head of the public acts. Until that time they had been published in the name of the republic. But having resolved on the change, no time was lost in putting his resolve into practice.

His installation was announced for the 19th of January, 1800. The republican party exhibited some alarm. The royalists viewed his project with favour, — fancying that, the Tuileries swept and garnished, Louis XVIII. would be called on to take possession. But the pear was not yet ripened for him. Bonaparte was in high good-humour on the morning of the 19th. "Get up, little creole, get up," he said to Joséphine; "you sleep in the home of your masters to-night. And we will go there with some *éclat;* will speak to the eyes and the hearts of the people. They like a pompous show."

But the "we" did not include Joséphine. She and Hortense, accompanied by Madame de Lavalette and Madame Murat (Caroline Bonaparte, then fifteen, and three days a bride), went early to the Tuileries. There, in the apartment of Consul Lebrun, in the Pavillon de Flore, Joséphine received a number of ladies, all, like herself, elegantly attired for the occasion; all profuse of compliments and congratulations; all full of enthusiasm for Général Bonaparte, and anxious to see the pompous show they had been promised.

But of pomp there was so little that, but for the grand military display, the *cortège* of the chief of the state would have been ludicrous rather than imposing. His own plain carriage, with its six magnificent white horses, — a present from the Emperor of Austria on the signing of the Treaty of Campo-Formio, — was the most striking object in it. Paris resounded with the acclamations of the people when it appeared: the First Consul seated on the right, the Second on the left, the Third on the seat facing them, three aides-de-camp riding on either side. The *vivas* for the "*vainqueur pacificateur*" showed unmistakably that their enthusiasm was wholly for him. And no doubt it was heartfelt. They, all classes in fact, and not the people only, were yearning for what he promised them, — peace and prosperity, and security for life and property.

The First Consul's carriage entered the court of the Tuileries, preceded and followed by a score or two of *fiacres*, their numbers concealed by pieces of paper of the colour of the vehicles. These pompous equipages contained the members of the Consular Council of State, ministers, and others, — M. de Talleyrand, an ambassador or two, being the only persons who had a private carriage, and that of the plainest description, that republican susceptibilities might not be wounded. It was but quite recently that any conveyance better than the ordinary *fiacre* was even tolerated. And had it been otherwise, few could obtain them, — direst poverty having fallen on so many of those to whom the elegancies and luxuries of life had been most familiar.

The grand court of honour of the Tuileries was in a miserably dilapidated state. The gaps in the walls were patched up with boards, and on one of the rough board guard-houses, run up during the Revolution, there still remained the inscription :

"10th of August, 1792.— Royalty is abolished in France, and will never be reëstablished."

It is said not to have escaped the eagle eye of the First Consul, who alighted from his carriage close by to mount his horse, in order to pass the troops in review. He wore on this occasion a magnificent sabre, also a present from the Emperor Francis Joseph. Though not quite so thin as formerly, he was still slight, active, and of youthful appearance, — very strikingly contrasting with that of the two sub-consuls : Cambacérès, heavy, slow in his movements, and of grave aspect ; Lebrun, of wonderful rotundity, middle-aged, but less severe of countenance.

Of the military pageant they were merely spectators, entering the palace with the rest of the members of the new government to contemplate their triumphant chief receiving the homage of his soldiers, and to behold him uncover and bow low as the tattered and powder-stained colours of some of the regiments were borne by the ensigns past him. It was an inspiring sight to the crowd that thronged the Place du Carrousel. With what fervour they shouted their *vivas* for their new master, "*le Premier Consul; le Général Bonaparte.*" "The French love glory," he said. "To give them glory is to give them happiness;" and truly each man that day seemed to be intoxicated with glory, or with enthusiasm for it.

The ladies, too, drank deeply of it, and found it even more exhilarating than champagne. They were all aglow with it, and felt not the searching, chilling air of January, as they stood at the open windows of the houses which then closely hemmed in the Place du Carrousel; while numberless banners, handkerchiefs, and scarfs, were waved from those windows by groups of *belles* in Grecian costume. It was not the season of flowers, yet they welcomed him with the first flowers of the year, and contrived to sprinkle a shower of violets mingled with snowdrops, if not upon him, as nearly as was possible around him. And when he bowed his thanks, and favoured them with one of those famous "irresistible smiles that partially revealed his superb white teeth," enthusiasm become delirium, and instead of throwing flowers on his head they would gladly have thrown themselves at his feet.

"*Ah! quelle journée pour Bonaparte!*" wrote a lady who was present. "He was great, truly great, that day!" He had certainly achieved a great success; and his installation banquet, given in the grand hall of the Tuileries, to his officers, the ambassadors, ministers, and chief employés of the government, was no less a success than the pageant that preceded it.

The banquet ended, the gentlemen hastened to Madame Bonaparte's initiatory reception. Most of them were formally introduced, — perhaps one should say presented, though there was no appearance of presuming on her new dignity by an assumption of any unusual airs and graces. She was unaffectedly cordial, as she was accustomed to be; exquisitely dressed, as was her habit also; yet close observers — jealous ones, probably — fancied they detected in her tone and manners a tinge of what they termed graciousness. They were also disposed to take objection to her seating herself in the centre of a sofa (a more elegant one than any royal abode in France was supposed to contain at that time), and ranging her small circle of ladies on either side of her.

However, the greater number present were pleased with the modest *coup d'essai*, or prelude to the grand scenes that were to follow, while Bonaparte, no less keenly observant of his guests than they probably were of him, expressed his full conviction that the more salient traits of the French character were not destroyed by the Revolution, though some violence might have been done to them. "They will naturally spring forth again," he said, "for vanity and the taste for pomp and show are as strong in the nation as ever."

That same night two "trees of liberty," planted in '92 in the Tuileries gardens, disappeared. They were dead, certainly, as were most of those trees scattered about Paris. The air of the capital seemed not to agree with them, and one after another, but always in the dead of the night, they were removed. No less speedily — for with Bonaparte, to resolve was to act — the grand court of his palace was cleared of the planks and rubbish that for eight years past had been collecting within it. With them, of course, disappeared the old guard-houses that had long given nightly shelter to thieves and assassins, and announced to passers-by that royalty was abolished; and with their disappearance the work of repairing, restoring, and refurnishing the Tuileries began. Henceforth it was his ordinary residence. The Senate assembled at the Luxembourg, and the Palais Royal became the Palais du Tribunat.

CHAPTER XVII.

Clearing the Ground. — "*Le Gouvernement, c'est Moi.*" — Fouché and Talleyrand. — The Sociable Fusion. — Proposals for Peace. — Setting Out for the Wars. — Across the Alps to Marengo. — Impelled by Fate. — Celebrating Marengo. — The *Fête* of Flowers. — Hope Deferred. — Bribing M. de Talleyrand. — A National Recompense. — The Offer of St. Cloud Declined. — Bonaparte's Toast. — Général Junot. — In Search of a Wife. — An Ancient Pedigree. — Madame de Permon. — A Midnight Ceremony. — Duroc and Hortense. — The Peace of Lunéville. — The Peace of Amiens. — Carnot's Remonstrances.

THE years 1800 and 1801 were years of preparation, or of clearing the ground for laying the foundations of the empire. Before that desirable result could be attained, much that the Revolution had accomplished must be abolished, much restored which, like royalty, was supposed to be banished forever, and much constructed on an entirely new plan. Bonaparte was in effect, if not in name, already the sovereign of France; but this he then cared more to conceal from, than to reveal to, the people. He especially favoured the expression "the government;" "the intentions of the government;" "the acts of the government," etc. But had he been required to say who and what constituted that government, he might have replied "myself," so entirely did it centre in him.

The Abbé Sieyès, when Bonaparte laughed at his Constitution, and compared his Grand Elector — an office designed for him — to a fattened pig in a sty, had quietly put his Constitution into his pocket, resigned his consulship, and accepted, as compensation, a share of the money left in the treasury by the Directors, and from Bonaparte the estate of Crône. Afterwards, as one of the Senate, he objected to the nomination of Fouché as Minister of Police. Bonaparte replied that "the evil done in the past must be forgotten; the good only remembered." What good Fouché had done it would be difficult to discover. He had displayed greater ferocity of character than Tallien during the Terror, and it is not recorded that, like the latter, his ferocity was vanquished by the voice of love.

But Bonaparte, though he, too, disliked him, saw his fitness for the office he gave him, and thought to turn him to account. And doubtless he served his interests well, though without forgetting his own, as also did M. de Talleyrand, again Minister for Foreign Affairs. Fouché and Lucien were sworn enemies, and at daggers drawn. The former had greatly ingratiated himself with Joséphine during Bonaparte's absence. Knowing that she was in great straits for cash, he put her name on the list of recipients of the fund obtained by a tax on gambling, and sent her from it, as her share, a thousand *louis d'or.*

Joséphine's acceptance of it was made known to Bonaparte by Lucien. It was one of those offences that was so galling to him on his return from Egypt. Nevertheless, he employed Fouché, whose influence soon rivalled that of M. de Talleyrand, while the sway he obtained over Joséphine was more pernicious to her in every respect than Bourrienne's, which had excited Bonaparte's jealousy.

As soon as the First Consul had securely possessed himself of the reins of power, he began to put into practice his social system of political fusion. The ex-Director, Carnot, who had contrived to evade undergoing his sentence of transportation to Cayenne, was made Minister of War, and every department of the government was thickly sprinkled with Jacobins. His object was to reconcile opposing parties; to induce them to follow his banner, and to attach them all to his interests. Conjointly with this scheme, the "sociable fusion" was to blend the society of the Faubourg St. Germain with the *parvenue* society, civil and military, of his own creation.

By means of this fusion, or blending of many discordant parts into one smooth and compact whole, he proposed to heal the wounds of France, and to raise her both politically and socially to the enviable position of "*la grande nation,*" par excel-

lence, which he had in name already proclaimed her. Those whose business in life was the pursuit of ease and pleasure were to dress, dance, and amuse themselves unstintingly,— that there might be abundant employment for those whose lot was labour, and no lack of occupation in those various branches of industry on whose flourishing condition the general prosperity of the nation largely depended. As for glory, was it not the mission of the victorious general, the accepted, if not chosen, ruler of France, to cover his country with glory, and to hold up the *"grande nation"* to the admiration and envy of the peoples and monarchs of the whole world?

And how Fortune favoured her hero! Notwithstanding the plots and intrigues that vexed and thwarted him at the outset, though many doubtless were fabricated to serve the objects he had in view, yet France was delivered from the horrors of anarchy. The gaiety and gallantry of the national character began to reappear, and science and the arts again to be cultivated.

The lower classes certainly needed yet a good deal of breaking in. Many among them would still have liked to have gone on dancing the Carmagnole and sporting the *bonnet rouge*. They were not of the class that had suffered much by the Revolution, but were its abettors. The guillotine had not thinned their ranks; there was reserved for that the lately introduced conscription,

— an idea borrowed from Austria. But the sword of the conqueror is for a brief, a very brief, space sheathed, and efforts for peace are the order of the day.

George of England, however, refuses them a favourable response. But proposals direct from the First Consul were made more for the satisfaction of the French people, who were anxious for peace, than with any expectation that they would lead to an English alliance. Bonaparte, indeed, did not desire it. Negotiations with Austria were also then pending, and were allowed slowly to drag on until all was ready for a new campaign. Then, suddenly withdrawing his plenipotentiaries, he declared war. He thought a new victory necessary to restore that *éclat* to his military reputation which the Egyptian campaign had in some degree dimmed, as well as to cement his authority, and to conceal with new laurels the death and burial of liberty.

To be gay in his absence, and to entertain, were Bonaparte's last orders to Joséphine when he bade her adieu on setting out to join the reserve *corps d'armée* at Dijon, on the 6th of May, 1800. On the 18th he and the whole of his army had crossed the Great St. Bernard. On the 9th of June, having passed the Po, he encountered and beat the Austrian forces at Montebello. On the 14th he again met them in the plains of Marengo, and gained over them one of the most signal victories the republican arms had yet achieved. A preliminary treaty was arranged, and signed on the following day, by Générals Berthier and Mélas.

The latter — the Austrian commander-in-chief — was eighty-four years of age, and full of vigour and activity, though he had lost his battle. Bonaparte and his army had fallen upon him, whence least expected, from the Alps, like an avalanche, and before he was aware that his antagonist was even in Italy. Sudden, unexpected attacks were chief characteristics of his mode of warfare, and rarely or never failed in their object, while he retained his youthful activity, or was present to head his troops and inspire them. On the 2d of July, eighteen days after the battle of Marengo, he was again in Paris, where those who were left in charge of the government had, in anticipation of his probable death, spent the two months of his absence in discussing — and none more eagerly had put forward their claims than Joseph and Lucien — who should succeed him. The wildly perilous attempt, as it was thought, to cross the Alps with an army, had given rise to hopes and expectations destined to be quickly dispelled.

Bonaparte was fond of attributing his success to Fate, and probably to a great extent had brought himself to believe in the predestined career he was anxious to impress on others was irrevocably traced out for him. His whole family, more or less, were influenced by the same idea.

It appears to have had its origin in the exclamations of Bonaparte's father when dying at Montpellier of an illness which, acting on the brain, subjected him to frequent attacks of delirium. He called, it is said, with much earnestness, for his absent son Napoleon. "Where is he?" he asked. "Where is he? He whose sword shall make kings tremble — shall change the face of Europe — where is he? He will defend me from my enemies; he will save my life."

These words inspired his family with awe. They were regarded as a prophecy and reverently treasured up. Cardinal Fesch, who was present, firmly believed that Bonaparte in all his acts was irresistibly impelled to the course he took by supernatural agency. Yet it would seem that he did not so firmly believe in it himself; for, when referring to Cæsar, he said: "He did wisely to speak of his fate or fortune, and to appear to believe in it. It is a means by which the imagination of all may be acted upon without wounding the self-love of any."

But whether Fate or his own audacity was supposed to have led him over the Alps and to a victory on the plains of Marengo, certain it is that throughout France his great achievement excited the utmost astonishment and admiration. Never had the national vanity been more truly flattered; never had the hope that happy days were yet in store for wounded France penetrated more deeply the hearts of the people; and never had the nation been more sincerely disposed to evince its gratitude towards the man to whom it owed so much glory, and to whom it looked for that most earnestly longed-for blessing, a solid peace, as the fruit of his brilliant victory.

There needed no orders for public rejoicings or general illuminations. Joy, real joy, thrilled in every heart, and all were anxious to express it by some outward and visible sign. For two nights the old city seemed transformed into a fairy domain, of which the Tuileries, with its gardens, was the enchanted palace. In varied and glowing colour light streamed from every window, from every portal, and made brilliant the fronts of the gloomiest dwellings. The trees were then in full leaf; but, artistically placed amongst the masses of foliage, were innumerable small coloured lamps, from which there gleamed and flashed ruby, emerald, and diamond rays.

The public buildings were, of course, resplendent. Patriotic sentences, the temple of Janus, the victor's name, the goddess of Peace, the horn of plenty, with other devices, were conspicuously displayed on illuminated transparencies. As at the levelling of the Champ de Mars, when all the inhabitants of Paris vied with each other in labouring towards its completion, so now all eagerly proffered their services in preparing this Marengo *fête*. The short night, or rather the long twilight, of that season was scarcely favourable to it, and but scantily rewarded the immense labour and expense incurred. But enthusiasm banished all sense of weariness, and enabled the Parisians, the inhabitants of Lyons, and other populous places, to trudge in triumph the streets of their respective cities for two consecutive nights.

So far as Paris was concerned, when the lamps were extinguished the rising sun shone on a floral *fête*. For miles around flowers in great abundance were sent in, either to decorate the houses, or in splendid bouquets, as offerings to the victor of Marengo and to Madame Bonaparte. All France rejoiced in this victory; but, as the conqueror well knew, it was less because the Marengo triumph was in fact the reconquest of Italy, than because it placed the nation in a better position, if her demands were reasonable, to make terms with Europe. With the new order of things, smiling peace and plenty would then begin to reign in fair France.

It was this they looked and longed for; this hope they fêted. With peace in view, "political hate and dissension appeared to have become extinct, and were at least suspended. All fear, all suspicion, disappeared, and none regretted that so much power had been confided to a man who, they believed, would so nobly use it. So great, so unexpected a victory justified everything." But peace before all things was looked for, and peace the victor promised — a speedy peace; yet many hearts began to sicken of hope deferred before the promise of an Austrian peace was fulfilled.

Meanwhile, however, hostilities between France and the American states were brought to an end by a treaty signed in September at Mortfontaine. It was celebrated there with so much magnificence that the First Consul was displeased with Joseph's princely hospitality. He reproached him with playing the *grand seigneur* with other people's money, — alluding to M. Clary, Joseph's wealthy father-in-law, who had furnished funds for the 18th Brumaire. Without such aid the result would probably have been a very different one. Yet Bonaparte felt himself humiliated by the assistance M. Clary had rendered towards the success of his schemes.

He had the strongest aversion to those bankers and *traitants* who farmed the revenues. He was aware of the frauds and exactions which the dissolute Lucien permitted, and so largely shared in, as Minister of the Interior. He was no stranger to Bourrienne's peculations, and intended that all such abuses should promptly be swept away. He knew, too, that M. de Talleyrand was largely bribed by foreign powers to induce him to enter into their views, — a general peace appearing probable, — which sent him portraits and snuffboxes, enriched with diamonds, rubies, and emeralds. M. de Talleyrand, and Fouché also, realised immense sums from the emigrants who eagerly petitioned them to obtain leave to return to France, though their intercession was very rarely needed.

It was a part of Bonaparte's system to favour the return of the emigrants; for he desired that the Quartier St. Germain should again be flourishing, that he might seek among the daughters of the remnant of the old *régime* for wives for his plebeian aides-de-camp, generals, and marshals. Several marriages were then on the *tapis*, and many things relative to the reconstruction of society were under consideration and rehearsal at La Malmaison. Alterations, additions, and embellishments had been made in that charming and favourite abode of Bonaparte and Joséphine. La Malmaison was then his only country residence; but a few days after his return from Italy, the Commune of St. Cloud petitioned the Tribunat to place at his disposal the palace of that name, with its gardens and extensive domain.

Their request was very favourably received, and although it was generally believed to have been suggested with the full knowledge and approval of the First Consul, they were none the less eager to concede the palace to him. They wished, however, to invest this concession with the character of a national recompense. It was, therefore, proposed to offer him the palace of St. Cloud under the name of the Château de Marengo, — following the example of England in naming Marlborough's palace after the victory of Blenheim.

But Bonaparte very astutely declared that, while feeling himself honoured by the offer of such a gift from the nation, he was yet compelled to decline it, as well as to reject all concessions the Tribunat might desire to make to him personally. He could accept nothing while exercising the functions of magistracy with which he was then invested. He reminded them that the concession of St. Cloud must be the result of a law proposed for the purpose, and that the Constitution gave exclusively to him the right of proposing laws. It was evident, therefore, that he could not propose the gift of St. Cloud to himself. The Tribunat must, consequently, limit themselves to notifying in a general manner that the palace of St. Cloud was placed at the disposition of the government. After a short interval this was the course taken.

Both royalists and republicans found matter for serious reflection in this explanation of the First Consul's view of the relative position in which he and the nation stood towards each other. Both seemed to see the goal towards which he would lead them, and both urged him on, — hoping to urge him towards his fall. For it is characteristic of the French to be eager to destroy that which they have been most eager to set up. But Bonaparte was wary, and took no step in advance that did not give him a firmer grasp of power. Many who believed that they had fully fathomed his views were surprised and thrown off their guard, when, on the 14th of July, at a grand banquet at the Tuileries, in celebration of the "birth of liberty," he gave as a toast: "To the anniversary of the 14th July, and to the French people, our sovereign!"

A general promotion soon after took place; also the presentation of a hundred "*armes d'honneur*" to officers and soldiers who had most distinguished themselves at Montebello and Marengo. These weapons — swords and pistols — were of the finest workmanship; some of them were inlaid with silver and gold, or enriched with precious stones. They were highly valued at the time, and afterward those preserved as heirlooms became far more prized, both because of their fewness and the occasion of their presentation, than the decorations of the Legion of Honour.

In this public recognition of the services of the army, the Second and Third Consuls took no part, except as witnesses of the homage paid to their distinguished colleague. From him alone promotion came; he alone was the source whence wealth and honours were looked for. Nor were those who had died on the battlefield forgotten by him. A handsome monument was ordered to be erected to the memory of the brilliant young Général

Desaix, who perished at Marengo, and was buried with military honours at St. Bernard, — a stone cross marking the spot where he was laid, and an inscription recording the circumstances of his death.

For Général Junot, Bonaparte's first aide-de-camp, the post of Commandant of Paris was created. A fine hôtel, and an income adequate to the fulfilling of his duties with *éclat*, of course were needed, and equally of course provided. And who so capable as the brave, devoted Junot of imparting to those whom he entertained a high idea of the nobility of mind, and the great qualities of head and heart, which he himself believed his chief possessed. Junot, the most interesting of all Bonaparte's generals, has been named "chivalry personified." His attachment to him was wholly free from any feeling of interest or self-seeking. Scarcely could he speak of their close friendship of a few years back, or hear his valour and his victories referred to, without some signs of a struggle with an irrepressible emotion.

But the Commandant of Paris must have a wife. It is the command of his chief, who will not allow that woman should have political power, but is of opinion that she should have the conduct of a part of the things of this world, and that to rule a household is one of them. Junot must therefore go forth, like Cœlebs, and search the *salons* for a wife. He has a very susceptible heart, and since the days when he sought the hand of the beautiful Pauline, he has breathed vows of eternal love to many a fair damsel. He has been the captive slave of Madame Récamier, and that lady has smiled with benignant pity upon him, as she was heartlessly accustomed to do on the many victims to her beauty.

Latterly he had been a constant frequenter of Madame de Permon's *salon* — the favourite resort of returned denizens of the Faubourg St. Germain. For Madame de Permon's family claimed lineal descent from Andronicus Comnenus, the last of the Greek emperors of the Comnenus dynasty, who reigned in Constantinople in the twelfth century. She was therefore highly considered in the Faubourg St. Germain. Chérin, the *juge d'armes*, is reported to have gone off into a genealogical ecstasy, when he examined the family pedigree and its proofs, laid before him by Prince Demetrius Comnène, the lady's brother.

Madame de Permon was a widow, and by no means rich; but with just enough rescued from the devouring jaws of the Revolution to receive her friends twice a week in a neatly furnished *salon,* — neatness being the only mark of distinction which her straitened means permitted. She was the first of her class who opened her *salon* after the 18th Brumaire. Music and conversation formed the staple of the entertainment; and the music was sufficiently good to attract the Abbé

Morellet, who again, after long seclusion, reappeared in society; also the composers, Grétry, Méhul, and Cherubini. Of course in such society there was no lack of *esprit* in the conversation.

Thé à l'anglaise is offered the guests, and later in the evening lemonade and biscuits. Those who seek suppers must look for them at Lucien and Joseph Bonaparte's receptions, at M. de Talleyrand's, and those of the wealthy *parvenus*, to whom the Revolution has sent riches; for former princely houses have become dwellings of the poor.

Madame de Permon had been a beauty, of the pure Grecian type, and still retained considerable attractions. Junot was assiduous in his attentions to her. But it was for love of her young daughter, Laure, that he was so eager to secure her good graces. Laure was a charming and talented girl of sixteen; accomplished and *spirituelle* beyond what young girls of that age usually are, — as those acquainted with the writings of the Duchesse d'Abrantès will readily believe. The marriage of Laure de Permon and Général Junot was one of mutual inclination; and it speaks well for the character and habits of the latter that Madame de Permon — who was a very exacting and haughty dame — consented to give her daughter to him.

The marriage at one moment seemed likely to be broken off, because of Junot's hesitation with reference to the religious part of the ceremony. It, indeed, seems not to have occurred to him until the preparations for it by the Permon family brought it under his notice. Madame de Permon would not even listen to any suggestion that it should be omitted. He offered no objection to it himself; but he thought Bonaparte would imperatively forbid the Commandant of Paris to risk the consequences of braving republican prejudices, by the public revival of an obsolete, or as then considered superstitious, rite.

The private performance of the ceremony in the home of the bride's mother is proposed by Bonaparte. She declines to accede to it. Poor Junot is in despair. Bonaparte is rather amused. But as the benediction of the Church on her daughter's marriage vows will alone satisfy Madame de Permon, — to whom, and to her husband, Bonaparte in his student days was under considerable obligations, — he yields to her wishes. The ceremony, however, is to take place at midnight, in the church of their district; the family and immediate friends of the bride and bridegroom alone attending. Thus were the future Duc and Duchesse d'Abrantès married.

Bonaparte was anxious that France should be reconciled to Rome. With this view he employed his influence in Italy to place the Bishop of Imola on the now vacant papal throne. Accordingly, the bishop was shortly after installed, as Pius VII.

A strong mutual attachment existed at this time between Général Duroc and Hortense. Bonaparte would have consented to their marriage, but Joséphine opposed it. She said: "The daughter of the Vicomte de Beauharnais should marry a gentleman." Duroc, if of humble birth, was a man of some education, and of good manners. As a favourite aide-de-camp of Bonaparte, his prospects were of course brilliant. Hortense had resolutely opposed a marriage her mother had arranged for her with Rewbell's son, while Bonaparte was in Egypt. She now took greatly to heart her refusal to consent to a union that promised her happiness. It was a severe blow also to Duroc, who, if not afterwards Joséphine's enemy, certainly was not her friend.

When, some years later, at the time of the divorce, her grief was the subject of conversation, and it was thought that Duroc's great influence with Bonaparte might prevail with him in her favour, he replied: "I shall say not a word against her, but, decidedly, not a word in her favour. She once scrupled not, and from mere caprice, to sacrifice the happiness of two lives." Which would seem to imply that he thought what was to befall her a just retribution. He might have said three lives — for Louis Bonaparte was not less unhappy than Hortense. But at all events, before the worst came, a period of gaiety and grandeur, which for awhile did duty for happiness, was yet to intervene.

THE PEACE OF LUNÉVILLE

Peace with Austria, a continental peace, was at last signed at Lunéville, in February, 1801. Moreau's brilliant victory of Hohenlinden — which Bonaparte, though jealous of the victor's fame, celebrated with great *éclat* — contributed to hasten this desired result of the long-pending negotiation, — while the indignation expressed by the people towards the authors of the Jacobin and royalist plots, and the joy evinced at their failure, convinced foreign Powers that France regarded the preservation of the First Consul's life as necessary to the well-being of the nation.

The system of justice and moderation already introduced had resulted in many wise and humane acts, and the reform of many abuses. Bonaparte seemed, indeed, so firmly seated in his consular armchair as "Napoleon, First Consul for life," that England, hitherto holding aloof, determined, towards the autumn of the same year, to entertain proposals of peace. In May, 1802, a treaty was signed at Amiens by Lord Cornwallis and Joseph Bonaparte. With it the Concordat was also proclaimed in Paris. There was joy — heartfelt joy — throughout the land. France was at peace with all mankind. She was reconciled to the Church; and once more the Catholic religion was the religion of the French people.

The ban of the Church was withdrawn from the recalcitrant Bishop of Autun, and he was said to have been released from his ecclesiastical vows. This, however, was doubted, as he did not then marry Madame Grandt, who now sat at the head of his table when he entertained the *corps diplomatique* at his suburban château at Auteuil. Joséphine at this time also urged on Bonaparte that the religious ceremony should complete their nuptial tie. It would have been a favourable moment for setting so good an example. The family clamoured against it; but it is more likely that his refusal to comply with Joséphine's wishes was prompted by secret motives of his own.

The most brilliant period of the Consulate begins with the signing of the Treaty of Amiens. Foreigners of distinction flocked to Paris. The Tuileries, St. Cloud, and even La Malmaison, began to assume a semi-royal aspect, — so much so, that the stern republican, Carnot, presumed to remonstrate with the First Consul on the royal pomp he affected in his court, and on the inclination evinced by Madame Bonaparte to play the part of queen, by assembling around her a circle of ladies whose names and former rank flattered her vanity.

Carnot, who was Minister of War, received an intimation from Fouché that he would do well to send in his resignation. Carnot was disgusted. Despotism was then to be the result of a ten years' struggle for Liberty!

CHAPTER XVIII.

Fête of the Concordat. — An Old Fashion Revived. — A Fortunate Coincidence. — The Consular Court. — Private Letters from Paris. — *La Politesse* Still Survives. — A Bridal Dress. — Reviving the Old *Régime*. — La Marquise de Montesson. — The Honour of Cousinship. — The Restraints of Etiquette. — The Consular Household. — Improvements in Paris. — Reading the Great Man to Sleep. — Teaching Grand Manners. — Mademoiselle Georges. — Lucien's Second Marriage. — The New Coinage. — A Court Mourning. — A Disconsolate Widow. — Pauline Becomes "a Real Princess." — Pauline's Ears. — Splendour and Simplicity. — M. le Prince and Madame la Princesse. — The Presentation. — Bitter Tears.

THOUGH the signing of the Concordat was proclaimed simultaneously with the signing of the Treaty of Amiens, yet a special *fête* was reserved for it. Bonaparte doubtless desired to associate the reconciliation of France and the Church with some striking event immediately and personally connected with himself, as well as with that national blessing — a general peace. Addresses innumerable — congratulatory, and expressive of deepest thankfulness to "the restorer of religion in France" — were received from all parts of the kingdom. It was by that title that Chateaubriand, then the *protégé* of Madame de Staël, dedicated to him his much admired work, "*Le Génie du Christianisme.*"

The consular court set the good example of attending the daily mass in the chapel of the Tuileries. Nor was it omitted in the little oratory of La Malmaison, during the frequent visits of the First Consul and Madame Bonaparte to this favourite suburban retreat, where the construction of a fine range of greenhouses, with other embellishments and additions to the château, much interested and occupied the latter. Piety, or the semblance of it, had become the rage, like the revival of an old and once favourite fashion; and, after so many years of unblushing and unabsolved vice and crime, many were truly glad to avail themselves of the opportunity afforded them of confession and absolution. The churches were generally well filled; and this return to old habits, if jeered at by some profane scoffers as a return to old superstitions, was doubtless accepted by most persons, and especially among the poor, as a consolation and a blessing.

The restoration of their curés to the inhabitants of the rural districts of France, and the amnesty to the enthusiastic and priest-ridden people of La Vendée, served to swell by tens of thousands the favourable votes of the *plébiscite*, when the question was put to the country: "Shall Bonaparte be First Consul for life?" The response, so overwhelmingly affirmative, and to which the Senate added the right of choosing his successor, was fêted, conjointly with the Concordat, on the 15th of August, — a day that had long been celebrated by the Church with extraordinary pomp, being the festival of St. Louis, and which happened, by a fortunate coincidence, to be the birthday of Napoleon.

It would seem that, in spite of his confidence in himself and his star, he then needed some guarantee of that kind as an assurance of the stability of his position. During the three months preceding the *fête* of the Concordat he had passed more of his time at La Malmaison than at the Tuileries, and, as it appeared to some persons, in a singularly unusual state of inactivity. But Napoleon was meditating vast changes, forming great projects for the reëstablishment of justice and order, which could only be proposed and carried out by an independent ruler, whose power ceased only with his life.

The amnesty, which permitted the return of all emigrants, except those who had taken service in the armies of unfriendly foreign Powers, or held office in the households of the French princes, was a bold and generous stroke of policy, resolved and acted upon at this period. He was meditating also his famous Code-civil, and the organisation of public instruction, by establishing *lycées* or colleges in the several large towns of the kingdom, as well as schools for the special study of law, mathematics, the natural sciences, etc.

He may also have been mentally arranging his consular court. For no sooner had the voice of the sovereign people proclaimed him Consul for life than he set about appointing his household. Earlier than this there was really no marked attempt at any display of pomp and parade, beyond that which a large attendance of troops, numerous aides-de-camp, and the generally improved appearance of the military afforded. Memoir writers of the period who speak of the new order of things at the Tuileries as bordering on luxury, with the display of the etiquette surrounding a monarch, must have intended to compare it with the "sans-culottism" that preceded it, and with which all who had passed through the revolutionary period were most familiar.

A very different tale was told in certain private letters that reached England from a member of the diplomatic mission which followed that of Lord Cornwallis to Paris, to look after English interests there, while he was negotiating the peace at Amiens. The young Englishman referred to (whose letters the present writer has read) expressed extreme astonishment at the general appearance and habits of the company who assembled in the *salons* of the Tuileries. At those wonderful *quintidi* dinners of from two to three hundred persons — dinners which lasted about twenty minutes, so far as Bonaparte concerned himself with them — each guest took his seat where he pleased, or where he chanced to find a vacant one, if he arrived a little late.

The scapegrace, Jérôme, whom no lectures could reform, would come in just as he jumped off his horse, his dress splashed, his boots dirty, and his riding-whip in his hand. The guests generally were much in the same plight,— their gross habits at table, and the barrack manners and oaths of the military men, being as amazing as disgusting to those who had expected to find in "*la grande nation*" some traces of *la grande politesse*, for which it had once been so highly renowned. Barras's banquets were far more like royal repasts. But then Barras had once been a real *grand seigneur*, and could assume the airs and graces of the olden time. As he liked playing at royalty, he would probably soon have revived the etiquette of the *salon*, had not the need of other and more important revivals displaced him.

Happily, however, *la politesse* was not a lost art in France. For the ladies, in manners at least, whatever might have been the case in morals — though it would have been difficult to have gone in that respect much farther astray than was customary in the court and society of the Louis Seize period — the ladies, be it noted, had not deteriorated to the same extent as the men. The *corps diplomatique*, who then, for the first time, were formally presented to Joséphine, were as pleasingly surprised by her distinguished air as the Italian courts had been, and by the ease and grace with which she received them, as well as by the few genial yet appropriate words she addressed to them severally on presentation.

Hortense was also pronounced charming, — not exactly pretty; but having an abundance of light auburn hair, large, deep blue eyes, a sweet voice, an elegant figure, and much of the winning grace so attractive in her mother. Poor Hortense; she was then about to be married to Louis Bonaparte, who, though but in his twenty-fourth year, from his infirm state of health had the appearance of a man of middle age. Both Louis and Hortense had the strongest repugnance to their union. But Napoleon insisted, and his will was law to his family. Her bridal dress of English *point d'aiguille*, together with lappets of the same lace for Madame Bonaparte, and a roll of flannel for M. de Talleyrand, had been sent from London with the British envoy's baggage, that they might share the privilege of passing with it unexamined through the custom-house.

To be graceful and gracious, greatly admired as *une femme distinguée*, and even much loved for kindness of heart, were not sufficient to Napoleon's mind for filling with *éclat* the position he designed for Joséphine. The title he proposed to assume when the right moment arrived was, no doubt, already determined. That of king, or "Consular Majesty," which the English government is said to have proposed to acknowledge for the renunciation of Malta, he had rejected. As soon, therefore, as he had appointed his military household, — four generals, to command the consular guard, with eight aides-de-camp, and Duroc as governor of the palace — he suggested to Joséphine that it was desirable she should take lessons in the art of playing the sovereign with due effect. Joséphine kept a secret with almost as much difficulty as she kept a crown in her purse. This taking of lessons, which was Napoleon's expression, amused her, and she revealed his whim to Madame Junot.

He desired to form his court on the model of Louis the Fifteenth's; eventually surpassing it in splendour, but retaining the same forms of etiquette. There were but two ladies of Joséphine's intimate circle who knew or remembered aught of the court of the "Well-beloved" in its brilliancy. One was the little old humpbacked Marquise de La Rochefoucauld, who was distantly related to Joséphine. She was still lively and *spirituelle*, very caustic in her remarks, but by no means in love with the Louis Quinze period. To its depravity and extravagance she was in the habit of attributing the troubles of the succeeding reign, and the many bereavements as well as loss of property she had personally sustained by the Revolution.

But there was the Marquise de Montesson, — by a left-handed marriage Duchesse d'Orléans, and thus stepmother of Philippe Égalité. This lady looked back to the days of the monarchy with real or affected regret. All that had been unpleasant in her position, as regarded her relations with the court, was effaced apparently by the lapse of time. She and the duke had lived in much retirement after their marriage. He had sought the consent of Louis XV. to their union, as the lady refused to be his mistress, and entreated Madame du Barry to intercede for him. As the duke appeared very urgent for the match, and the favourite believed that the king would forbid it, she replied: "Marry her at once, *gros papa*" (the duke, like most of his family, was exceedingly stout), "and afterwards we will get his consent."

The duke acted on this suggestion. Louis XV. treated the matter with much indifference; but Louis XVI. was highly indignant at so terrible a *mésalliance*, and, contrary to the advice of MM. Turgot and Malesherbes, the marquise was forbidden to appear at court. But when troubles began to surround Louis and his queen, and they were compelled by the people to leave Versailles and take up their residence at the Tuileries, the Marquise de Montesson, forgetting the affront she had received, begged permission to pay her court to them. Permission was given. She was very graciously welcomed, as "*ma cousine*," and with some emotion, by both king and queen, as under the circumstances was natural; for there was revealed to them that the duke had married a high-minded woman, though she was not of royal birth. After being admitted to the honour of cousinship, she sometimes whiled away an hour or two with the unfortunate royal couple in playing a game of backgammon.

Madame de Montesson was, of course, no longer young, but was still considered charming; and, as we all know, so long as a woman is charming, nobody thinks of her age or dreams of her being old. She was fully acquainted with the usages of the court, and with the ancient traditions of the old *régime*. Napoleon would have revived, especially for her, the office of *surintendante* of the household; but Madame de Montesson declined it. She, however, willingly proffered her services, to indicate to Joséphine — whose kindly nature prompted her to give a genial welcome to all — those shadows and shades of difference of manner to be observed in receiving and dismissing persons of different social standing, or, to whom, for other reasons, more or less consideration was due.

This was something to be acquired for future use rather than to be put into practice then. Republican pride would have rebelled against it. Even Joséphine herself, for whom Fate had destined a crown, was sufficiently a daughter of the

Revolution to smile at all this etiquette; and to say: "It was perhaps appropriate for princesses, born to the throne and accustomed to the restraints it imposes; but she who had had the happiness to live so many years simply as a private person, ought, she considered, to be less exacting, less severely punctilious, in her intercourse with those who knew and remembered the circumstances of her former life, as well as she knew them herself." And although she learned to wear her crown and mantle of state, and to sit on her throne right royally, she was ever unfailingly indulgent in the matter of etiquette, and always pleased, as she said, to throw aside its restraints.

Four prefects of the palace — MM. de Luçay, Rémusat, Didelot, and Cramayel — were charged with the superintendence of the *fêtes* and amusements of the consular household, the regulation of the formalities to be observed, and the surveillance of the theatres. Four ladies were also appointed — Mmes. de Luçay, Rémusat, Talhouet, and Lauriston — *dames du palais*, though not yet so named. Their office was to attend Joséphine by turns, in weekly succession, and to introduce the wives of the ambassadors, who came to pay their court to her. The prefects attended, like the ladies, each in his turn; also the four generals of the consular guard, and two of the eight aides-de-camp.

These were the elements of the consular household which, in the autumn, when Napoleon took possession of St. Cloud, and the *grand salon* of that palace was thrown open for Joséphine's first reception, had expanded into a sovereign court. St. Cloud was to be the autumn residence, yet La Malmaison was still the favourite one. It was there that the First Consul often retired to ponder over the many vast undertakings which, eventually, were carried out so beneficially to the nation. There was first planned the Napoleonic capital, — the modern Paris, which, with its wide streets, squares, gardens, and promenades, fine quays, spacious markets, triumphal arches, columns, pyramids, bridges, and many other embellishments, was to replace the fever-stricken alleys, narrow turnings and windings of the muddy, gloomy, pestilential old Paris of the Bourbons.

The gardens and shady avenues of the park of La Malmaison were favourable to meditation, and, as Napoleon often went thither for that purpose, the cross-road between the château and the Palace of St. Cloud was thoroughly repaired, or rather it was made, — for roads that could be traversed without risk to life and limb, or a frequent breakdown of carriage and horses, were few, or scarcely existed at all, before the time of Napoleon. Only from palace to palace, for royal journeys, were they kept tolerably clear.

The occasional short visits which were made

at this time to the favourite château were to Joséphine, and probably no less so to the First Consul, like breathing a pure fresh air on emerging from a stifling atmosphere.

There it was permitted to unbend. There Joséphine gave her social breakfasts to her most intimate friends, — generally to ladies only, who discussed with her the important subjects of dress and fashion. But occasionally two or three gentlemen were honoured by admission to this very select breakfast circle. Then, of course, the usual theme of conversation was varied, and music and the theatres received a share of their attention; while to those of artistic tastes it was real enjoyment to examine the pictures and treasures of art in which La Malmaison was rich, — a perfect museum, in fact.

In Joséphine's *boudoir* stood a splendid harp; it was a favourite instrument then. Sometimes she would sit down and strum a few chords, but it was more for the display of her finely modelled hands and arms than as a prelude to a further performance; for she was not musical, but she had mastered one tune, with which she sometimes favoured her ladies while they were occupied with their tapestry, — an art in which she herself really excelled. Amongst her few accomplishments she numbered that of being an excellent reader. The dulcet tones of her voice had always a charm for Napoleon. One of her duties, therefore, was to read the great man to sleep. When he retired for the night, and it was announced that he was in bed, Joséphine, with some romance or poem he had chosen, would sit at the foot of his couch and read. At first he listened attentively, but gradually the soothing influence of her voice prevailed, and heavy breathing revealed to her that she might close her book, her lord having sunk comfortably into the arms of Somnus.

This was the home life of La Malmaison, when Napoleon still condescended to be in an amiable mood. There the newly married young wives of his generals, for the most part pupils of Madame Campan, essayed the grand manners of which that lady herself afforded them so faultless an example. She had, however, forborne to instruct them in the court etiquette that prevailed at Versailles in her youthful days, when *les grandes dames* were presented, or paid their court to, the queen.

This omission M. Despréaux, the husband of the once celebrated Mdlle. Guimard, was summoned to La Malmaison to supply. His wife, so high in the favour of Marie Antoinette, on the fall of the monarchy renounced her profession, and retired to her country house at Pantin. But M. Despréaux, when suitably recompensed, did not disdain to impart the grand manner of the old *régime*, and its stately airs in the dance, to the wives and daughters of the grandees of the new order of things; to assist, in fact, royalty in *déshabillé* to wear its court dress with *éclat*.

He was of service, too, at the rehearsal of the private theatricals to be afterwards performed at St. Cloud. These amateur exhibitions were as much the rage then as they had been under the monarchy, and were no less royally bad; or, as Napoleon was accustomed to say of the plays performed by these amateurs, "admirably parodied." Equally in Joséphine's court as in Marie Antoinette's, it was deemed indispensable that ladies of high station should attempt to qualify themselves to rival the professionals of the Théâtre Français.

It was at this time that the celebrated Mdlle. Georges made her *début* as the pupil of Mdlle. Raucourt, though she had been on the stage from mere infancy; her father, M. Weymer, being a provincial manager. She was then but sixteen, highly talented, and perfectly beautiful. She was received by the playgoing critics with enthusiasm, as already a great actress. Of course all Paris was madly in love with her. The dissolute Lucien Bonaparte was one of her most ardent worshippers. He had just returned from his mission to Spain. His *douce et bonne* Christine had died during his absence, and was buried by his order on the lawn in front of his Château of Plessis-Chamant. Over her grave he erected a white marble monument, and until married again, which was not long after, he carried her miniature about with him in his breast pocket, as consolation.

Madame Jouberthou, however, soon came to his aid; and his marriage with her was even a more rankling thorn in the flesh to Napoleon than the former *mésalliance*, as he considered it, with poor Christine Boyer. Lucien and Napoleon are said to have been rivals for the good graces of Mdlle. Georges, and Joséphine's jealousy was in consequence greatly excited. But the great man's *aventures galantes*, as they are termed, and which for the most part are, no doubt, mere invention, have been given by others in full detail, and need not be dwelt upon here.

The most eminent actors and actresses of the Théâtre Français, as well as men, and women too, distinguished in the world of letters, with artists, musicians, and talented people generally, were received with princely hospitality by the genial and generous host and hostess of Mortfontaine. They were welcomed, too, on a footing of friendly equality, to which, except in rare instances — as in the case of Talma — Napoleon no longer admitted them. With the objects he had in view, the part of *grand seigneur*, which Joseph played so well, would perhaps have been scarcely consistent; nor was Napoleon either in his tastes or his temperament so well qualified for it.

Many of the changes and innovations introduced in the course of this most eventful year of the consulate — which required but to change its name to connect it with the empire — gave rise to much surprise, even some murmurs, resulting, however, in nothing more serious than a few piquant epigrams. One, though not the first in order, was his bust on the new coinage, supplanting the allegorical figure of the republic, with the inscription, "Napoléon Bonaparte, Premier Consul;" on the reverse was a laurel wreath, within it the value of the coin. On the old coins of the monarchy there were impressed on the rim the words, "*Domine, salvum fac regem.*" Napoleon would have changed *regem* to "*rempublicam.*" M. Lebrun, the Third Consul, ventured to object to *Domine*, lest possibly it should be supposed by some persons to apply to the First Consul. "It is not at all likely!" he exclaimed, harshly. However, after some discussion, it was agreed to substitute for the ancient Latin inscription the French one, "*Dieu sauve la France,*" and thus avoid the possibility of any error in its application.

The court mourning ordered for Général Le Clerc, who died at St. Domingo, whither he had been despatched in the preceding year by Napoleon, as commander-in-chief of the expedition to that island, excited more attention than the change in the coinage. It showed more plainly whither the First Consul was leading the nation. The mourning was notified officially to the *corps diplomatique* and to the ministers of the republic resident at foreign courts. The Senate and the heads of the several departments of the government paid a visit of ceremony to Napoleon, while their wives, in deep mourning, offered their *condoléances* to Joséphine.

Général Le Clerc was no distinguished officer; but he was the husband of the First Consul's sister. She had, very much against her will, and by no means at his request, accompanied him to St. Domingo. Their marriage was "a garrison" one, which some two or three years later her brother would not have permitted. However, he now insisted that she should leave France with him, though husband and wife mutually detested each other. Pauline kept her bed and feigned illness; but Napoleon, not heeding her complaints or entreaties, had her conveyed in a litter on board the admiral's vessel, in which the general was about to sail.

She led a very dissipated life while at the island, and hastened back to France as soon as the general died. Many persons found the beautiful Pauline greatly changed. It was attributed to the climate of St. Domingo, and to grief, poor thing, for the death of her husband. She brought with her a coffin supposed to contain the mortal remains of the deceased Général Le Clerc. But it was reported — widely re-reported, and generally believed, though it may nevertheless have been a false report — that the coffin she sat beside, and watched with so much pious care, contained diamonds and other valuables to the amount of seven millions.

Paris and its gaieties soon restored the fair widow's beauty, and revived her spirits, enabling her to bear without much tear-shedding the death of her little son, Dermide. He was so named by Napoleon, at the same time that he named Bernadotte's son Oscar, in the enthusiasm of his admiration of the heroes of Ossian's poems. Pauline's widowhood was not of long duration. The Prince Camille Borghèse became violently enamoured of her. Notwithstanding his immense fortune, and the large settlements he proposed to make, Napoleon, for some unexplained reason, would not, at first, accept the prince as his brother-in-law. But scandal began to whisper strange tales, and to connect with them two nameless persons, distinguished as a "certain prince," and a "certain fair widow." This came to Joséphine's ears.

Pauline, like the rest of the Bonaparte family, detested her sister-in-law. Frequent estrangements between her and Napoleon, and many hours of unhappiness, were the result of their jealousy and unjust prejudices. Joséphine, consequently, was not sorry when occasion offered of calling his attention to the backslidings of his slander-loving sisters. In the impending imperial court doubtful *liaisons* could not be sanctioned.

Forthwith, therefore, lest consent should be given too late, Napoleon signified his approval of the match, and Pauline became a princess; and "a real princess" before either of her sisters, or her brother's wives, as she was fond of proclaiming.

She had no love for the prince; but she liked his wealth, and his title, and the position they gave her. For the rest, her strongest feeling was adoration of her own beauty, which has been generally allowed to have been perfect. Yet one defect she had, that, if not skilfully concealed, must have greatly marred the effect of her finely formed head and classic features. It was the singular ugliness of her ears. They are described as resembling two straight pieces of semi-transparent gristle, without the curves and folded edges which form the beauty of the ear. Madame de Contades — a rival of Madame Tallien in the Luxembourg *salon* — once took occasion to mortify the vanity and self-love of Madame Le Clerc, by directing attention to her ears, when, as was her habit, she was reclining on a sofa waiting for admiration. "If I had such ears I would cut them off. Recommend her to do so," she said, addressing one of Pauline's adorers.

Of course this occurred before the 18th Brumaire, at a time when open rudeness of speech and manners, with practical jokes, highly amused republican society.

But the scene is now changed, and Madame

Le Clerc, become Princesse Borghèse, is preparing to mortify Madame Bonaparte. The bridal visit is to be paid at St. Cloud. The princess calls it "her presentation." Her dress is to overwhelm Joséphine with despair, by its unapproachable splendour, elegance, and exquisite taste; profound secrecy has been enjoined; not a hint of its colour, material, or the nature of its ornamentation, is permitted to transpire.

The appointed day arrives. Joséphine has learned that she is to be crushed into insignificance by the splendour of the princess. She, a mistress of the art of dress, at once decides for simplicity in her own *toilette;* but simplicity, artistically combined with so much elegance that the splendour of her rival shall serve but to heighten its effect. Her dress, of the finest Indian muslin, is bordered with gold embroidery, and gracefully draped to suit the elegance of the wearer's figure. Her hair, banded with pearls, is dressed *à la grecque*, and pearls and antique gems form her sole ornaments.

Her ladies, when she enters, express their admiration by ejaculating *ravissante*, and other exaggerated epithets which revolutionary fervour had introduced into ordinary conversation, and so shocked the ears of Madame de Genlis and other purists, on returning to France. Napoleon is also enraptured. His rapture is expressed by the exclamation, "*Joséphine, je suis jaloux! Tu es divine!*" He kisses her on the forehead, and pinches her ear violently. "You must have some conquest in view," he says. "No?" Half an hour elapses; Napoleon's patience is exhausted. He will wait no longer for "the official visit," as he calls it, of the prince and princess.

Soon after his departure, the clatter of horses' hoofs is heard. A carriage so grand, with its gilding and emblazonry, that it might have belonged to the *Grand Monarque*, enters the *cour d'honneur* of St. Cloud. It is drawn by six richly caparisoned horses, and a numerous retinue of outriders surround it, all bearing torches, — for the days are short, and the roads not lighted. All belonging to the domestic staff of the household are stationed at intervals on the grand staircase. Presently the large doors of the *salon* fly open, and in a loud voice the *huissier* announces Monseigneur le Prince and Madame la Princesse Borghèse.

All rise. Pauline sees with satisfaction that she creates a sensation. Even Joséphine cannot wholly conceal it. The princess wears pale green velvet, embroidered in gold, mixed with diamonds. The front of her dress is a *tablier* of diamonds, with diamond stomacher, and sleeves partly covered with the same brilliant gems. A diadem of large emeralds and brilliants encircles her beautiful brow, and emeralds and diamonds adorn her arms, wrists, and throat. She has upon her the whole of the family diamonds of the wealthy house of Borghèse, besides her own, of the value of many millions. She makes a dazzling show; but her beauty seems to be extinguished under the weight of so much magnificence.

She has, however, the mortification of crossing the room to Joséphine, who had risen, but advanced not to meet her, as Madame la Princesse had expected her to do. But for this disappointment she finds consolation in the opportunity afforded her of displaying the gold and diamonds with which her long green velvet train is embroidered. Congratulations, embraces, kisses (women's Judas kisses), are exchanged with all apparent amity; and Joséphine and Pauline are seated side by side.

The latter is compelled to acknowledge that Joséphine's toilet is charming. But — oh! horror! She suddenly perceives that the furniture and draperies of the newly furnished *salon* of St. Cloud are of a colour that, while it gives full effect to Joséphine's dress, absolutely renders hers hideous. To be seated on blue velvet and arrayed in green is almost more than her nerves can bear. That she should have prepared for a triumph and encountered a defeat! It is a disaster of so crushing a nature that she hastens to leave the scene of her deep humiliation, to seek consolation in a flood of bitter tears. Poor Pauline!

CHAPTER XIX.

Lord Whitworth. — English Travellers in France. — Renewal of Hostilities. — The Visit to Belgium. — The Return to Paris. — A Change in Costume. — Madame de Genlis. — The First Consul in Full Dress. — Theatricals at St. Cloud. — The Hereditary Succession. — Napoleon's Vast Ambition. — Joseph's Advice to Napoleon. — "*Aut Cæsar, aut Nihil.*" — The Camp at Arras. — A Proposal to Sleep on. — Surrendering a Pigtail. — Arrest of the Duc d'Enghien. — The Execution. — The Empire Announced. — The Legion of Honour. — Regretting the Republic. — The Tribune Curée. — A Man of Strong Prejudices. — An Old Edition of Virgil. — Singular Coincidence. — Wounded Vanity.

THE peace — the general peace — which the French nation had so ardently longed for and so joyously welcomed, was destined to be but of short duration. The vexed question of the cession of Malta, and the extreme irritation felt by Napoleon at the coarse gibes and defamatory libels the English papers were permitted to indulge in, soon brought about a rupture with England. Also, the choice of an ambassador was an unfortunate one. Lord Whitworth was full of pomposity. He had the highest opinion of himself, but nothing conciliatory in his manners. His wife, the disdainful old Duchess of Dorset, also plumed herself on her rank, and was equally unattractive and as little calculated as her husband to win the consideration and esteem of the society she fancied beneath her, but, perforce, now and then grimly entertained. Nor was Général Andréossi a more suitable ambassador for the Court of St. James.

English travellers in France, and they were numerous, — having so long been deprived of their grand tour, their visit to the court of Versailles, or their fortnight's sojourn in Calais, — suffered for the sins of their rulers and their rulers' representatives. For an act of the government ordered "the immediate arrest and detention, as prisoners of war, of all the English then in France, between the ages of eighteen and sixty." A few, warned barely in time, succeeded, after many adventures and hairbreadth escapes, in crossing the frontier. To attempt flight was difficult and hazardous; owing to the scarcity of conveyances, the fearful condition of the roads, and the almost certainty of being betrayed when aid was sought or proffered. A ten years' exile was therefore the consequence to those who failed to elude the vigilance of the government employés; or, where found practicable, to throw gold dust into their eyes.

The renewal of war was a source of anxiety to the nation. The manufacturers of Lyons, and wine-growers of Bordeaux, suffered greatly from it. But Napoleon, elevated by war, was almost compelled to sustain his position by war, in order to prevent discontent and intrigue among his unemployed generals. Again, then, he called them into active service. The French troops invaded Hanover, and reëntered Naples; and the ports of Italy and those of the north of France were closed to the English. Satisfied for the moment with these arrangements for the commencement of hostilities, Napoleon prepared for a visit to Normandy and Belgium.

This visit was a sort of royal progress, resembling that of the *Grand Monarque*, when in 1670, with his three queens (his little Spanish wife, and two *maîtresses-en-titre*, Madame de Montespan and Madame de la Vallière), his godship set out to look at the cities and towns, supposed to be his conquests. His generals had certainly marched their troops into these open towns, while the warrior king looked on at a very safe distance. But his faith in the divinity that hedgeth a king convinced him, when he heard the shout of victory, that the walls of these towns had fallen flat before him, like the walls of Jericho at the approach and the shout of Joshua. The roads, when Napoleon took his journey, were in much the same state as they were upwards of a century before, when a corps of sappers and miners preceded the royal travelling carriage to clear a path for it and its sixteen horses.

But it is a warrior-ruler of a different calibre

who now travels that road, and such obstacles to ready communication with the Belgian cities will soon be removed. Napoleon, however, consents to be everywhere welcomed with no less servility than the people evinced in the homage they so readily paid to Louis XIV. Joséphine accompanies him, attended by two of her ladies, and receives her full share of the obsequiousness, and adulation in manner and language which the authorities, civil and military, and, above all, the clergy, vie with each other in paying them. Flattery so gross was perhaps never before or since heaped on mortal man. To bend the knee scarcely satisfies these slavish Belgians; they would willingly fall prostrate and offer divine honours to their new god.

Reports daily fill the columns of the *Moniteur*, giving full details of the triumphal entry into Brussels, the royal state observed at the First Consul's, and Madame Bonaparte's receptions at the hôtel of the prefecture of Aix la Chapelle, and the fulsome language of the congratulatory addresses so complacently received there. They have an unfavourable effect on the public mind in Paris. Much disgust is openly expressed, and many insulting epithets are applied to Napoleon, which the agents of police, on the *qui vive* in all places of public resort, very summarily silence.

Nevertheless, when, shortly after, he returned to St. Cloud, and thence came to Paris with a pompous retinue to receive the civil and military authorities and the *corps diplomatique*, he was greeted with discourses and harangues as offensively gross in flattery as any that were addressed to him on his Belgian tour. It was the month of August. The Tuileries gardens were illuminated, and an open-air concert was given. This attracted a vast number of promenaders, who vehemently applauded the hero of the *fête* when he graciously stepped out into the balcony. The Tribunat, as though resolved not to be outdone in subserviency by the Belgians, had even proposed to ride out some leagues from Paris to meet him on his return; that they might be the first to inform him that the consular dignity was voted hereditary in his family. This did not fall in with his views; and the intention of the Tribunat being transmitted to him, he positively forbade it.

When Joséphine's next reception took place at St. Cloud, it was remarked that military boots and pantaloons, clanking swords, and cockades, were in a considerable minority; and that silk stockings, shoes with buckles, dress swords, and *chapeaux sous le bras* were the rule. Some of the company had, however, endeavoured to spare their feelings too complete a shock, by an attempt to unite the past and the present. While returning to powder and embroidery, lace ruffles and cravat, they contrived to retain in their costume some reminiscence of the fast vanishing and much regretted "sans-culottism" of the republic. This resulted in incongruities startlingly shocking to good taste. Others, quite undesignedly, had offended in a similar manner; and all under their new finery were more or less ill at ease, — the ladies, of course, excepted. They, naturally, are quicker at comprehending, and more ready to adopt, the changes of costume.

Napoleon, in his own person, ought certainly to have presented a faultless example to his courtiers; for he was then under the guidance of Madame de Genlis, in matters concerning the costume and etiquette of the Louis Quinze period. Her souvenirs were of more recent date than those of her aunt, Madame de Montesson. This lady is supposed to have suggested to Napoleon that Madame de Genlis — lately returned to France — might afford him valuable information on the subjects he was so much interested in, and with which she had been so familiar. He gave her an apartment in the Arsenal, and afterwards a pension of 12,000 *francs*. At first she declined it. But M. de Lavalette was sent to urge her acceptance of it, and to beg that she would write to Napoleon every fortnight, or once a month, as her literary avocations permitted. The formation of his court was often the theme of her epistles; though a lecture on morals, or the critique of a new play, was occasionally introduced.

During the last twelve months Napoleon had

grown considerably stouter. "See how war and the activity it demands agree with me," he said to Joseph Bonaparte. "If I have to bring many of these European sovereigns to their senses, I shall certainly become very corpulent." As yet he was far from that. But *embonpoint* was gaining upon him, and if war agreed with him, his uniform of the chasseurs became him best. He scarcely appeared to advantage in the superb gold embroidered violet velvet coat he wore on the above mentioned occasion, with white silk stockings, shoes with gold buckles, and a very handsome dress sword at his side.

But, especially, the effect of all his finery was marred by a black military stock. Even the uninitiated were struck by its flagrant want of harmony with the rest of his splendid court dress. Ladies, perhaps, ventured slily to glance at each other with elevated eyebrows; but, for the rest, none dared smile, or utter a word in allusion to it. Yet they were inclined to laugh at themselves; and comments were freely passed on the sins of omission and commission, too glaringly apparent in their own attempts to disguise the republican under the habiliments of a courtier of the *ancien régime*.

A theatre on a large scale had lately been added to the palace of St. Cloud. This afforded courtiers in their novitiate the same opportunity of forming their manners and mode of speech after an approved model, as had sometimes occurred in the days of the monarchy. When the actors of the Théâtre Français were summoned to perform at this new theatre, the same ceremonial was observed as when "the king's comedians" played before the court. The national libraries and archives had been thoroughly searched for correct information on such matters.

The First Consul occupied a large box on the right of the theatre; none entered it but himself and his aides-de-camp; who, ranged behind him, remained standing during the whole performance. On the opposite side was Madame Bonaparte's box; where she appeared attended by the ladies of the palace. The two other consuls, the ministers, the ambassadors, and their wives — to whom formal invitations were always sent — filled most of the other boxes. When the First Consul and his wife entered, the whole of the company rose, and were in return graciously saluted. No expression of approval or disapproval was permitted. The play proceeded in silence, and attentive ladies and gentlemen received many a lesson in manners and the old court etiquette from Dazincourt and Molé, Mdlles. Dévienne and Contat, when such pieces as "*Le Cercle*," and similar ones of the *rèpertoire* of the last named distinguished actress were revived.

Napoleon's rigid exaction, at this period, of the same homage for Joséphine as for himself, was the result of his journey to the north of France and

Belgium. He stated as much to Joseph, in the course of one of those violent altercations then so frequent among the Bonaparte brothers, when the question arose whether the hereditary succession should be limited to his descendants, adopted or otherwise, or devolve on his brothers' heirs, failing his own. "Until he took that journey," he said, "he had entertained the idea of a divorce; but the base servility he everywhere met with, both from Frenchmen and Belgians, had convinced him that he could accomplish his aims without having recourse to any such expedient." He further added that he was fully determined on having his wife crowned with him.

Eight months before the coronation took place, some such ceremony had been proposed. But the Tribunat and the Council of State had not then quite settled what title should be borne by the supreme ruler they were about to place over the nation. Napoleon had probably decided it in his own mind; and if he turned their ideas in the same direction, he yet resolved not to assume the title until it should be offered him. He expressed a preference, whether sincere or not, for that of Stadtholder; the office to be held for life, but elective. But the Bonapartes were eager to clutch the supreme power, and to assure themselves of it before the chances of war had removed Napoleon, — an event that might happen any day.

For his brothers well knew that he looked to

"reigning over Europe, and perhaps the world." It was his own expression. But should he ever attain to universal empire, he was aware that it would be preceded by much fighting. He, however, was not favourable to the succession being hereditary in his family. Joseph had but two daughters. The children of Lucien's first marriage were also two girls; and no son that Madame Jouberthou, now Madame Lucien, might bear must hope to sit in the seat of Napoleon. Louis vehemently opposed the adoption of his son as his brother's heir; and Jérôme, not yet twenty-one, had entirely thrown away his chance of imperial rule by marrying Miss Patterson.

There remained the adoption of Eugène de Beauharnais as his successor. This intention he would probably have adhered to, but for his misfortune in having so numerous a family — all eager for wealth and honours; all jealous of any favour shown to Joséphine and her children; and all urging a divorce.

"Divorce her at once," Joseph exclaimed. "You are not married to her. The woman may die, and it will then be said you have poisoned her, — that you found it to your interest to do so."

Napoleon was staggered at these suggestions. His countenance is said to have become of a deathlike paleness. After a minute or two of silence he murmured: "You have forced on me an idea which would never have occurred to me, and with it the possibility of a divorce. In what direction then, under such a supposition, should my views be turned?"

"Towards a German princess," replied Joseph; "or a sister of the Emperor of Russia. Dare only to take that step, and you change your own position, you change ours, before even the birth of a child takes place. All is done by that step alone; the family system is established, and we are yours entirely."

Years elapsed, as all know, before Napoleon was induced to act on this advice, and to gratify his brother's ambitious hopes as well as his own. "It was then too late," say some writers; but, sooner or later, the result would probably have been the same. Joseph afterwards, in his deep dissatisfaction that his counsels were not followed, declared that he was weary of Napoleon's tyranny. "I will have all or nothing," he said. "Let him leave me to pass my life as it suits me, as a private person, or let him offer me a post that will assure me the supreme power after him. In that event I will yield and engage myself entirely to him; but should he refuse, let him expect nothing from me."

These dissensions, this discord, in the bosom of his family, did not escape the cognisance of jealous and vigilant observers. The pretensions of the Bonapartes were commented upon with great severity, — "a family," it was said, "ten years before wholly unknown, and scarcely to be considered French." Lucien, who by some means had amassed an immense fortune, very wisely determined to leave the country. Napoleon had threatened to have his marriage annulled, while he was disposed to set his threat at defiance. This scandal, however, was prevented by the advice of judicious friends, and Lucien and his wife, who is said to have been a remarkably beautiful and accomplished woman, left France for Italy. Except once, briefly and secretly, at Mantua, not until 1815 did the brothers meet again.

Preparations for the descent on England were being carried on with activity; a camp of 30,000 men was formed at Arras. Général Junot, who commanded in chief, had long been anxious to cut off his grenadiers' pigtails; to do away with their use of powder; to exchange their three-cornered hats for shakoes; and to give them a new and less uncomfortable kind of collar. These changes he was allowed to introduce with the exception of cutting off the pigtails, to which the men were so much attached that, if done arbitrarily without their consent, it was thought likely the whole corps would rebel, and cause a mutiny.

Junot undertook to accomplish the much desired change by persuasion. His troops were greatly attached to him. He was a kind, considerate officer, with a dashing manner, and a great reputation for bravery. The scars of deep sabre wounds on the side of his face often inspired those soldiers who had been his companions in arms to tell, when gathered around the camp-fires, of the daring deeds in which those wounds were received. An address from such a commander was likely, therefore, to be favourably listened to. So Junot assembled his grenadiers and harangued them on the advantages of having no pigtail; of the time saved in arranging and binding it; the comfort of being freed from so unnatural and unsoldierlike an appendage; the advantage it offered in cleanliness; and the improved condition that would soon follow in the backs of their coats. They were to think it over, to sleep on it, and on the morrow to report themselves as ready, or otherwise, to be operated upon by the regimental barber.

In the morning a large number of the men presented themselves to their general, already shorn of their pigtails, which they carried in their hands; for many proposed to send them as souvenirs to wives or sweethearts, mothers or sisters. To each of those men who had so readily followed his advice and complied with his wishes he presented a piece of money. This induced others to follow their example, and in a few days, different motives prevailing, the whole of Junot's grenadiers, with the exception of one old sergeant, had submitted to the loss of their tails.

At last, even this veteran, moved by the jokes that were made at the expense of his solitary tail, and pricked in conscience also in holding out so long against the wishes of his general, consented to a surrender. One condition, however, was attached to it — Général Junôt alone should cut it off. The general consented, and celebrated his victory by a review of his troops, unpowdered and shorn, and with the reforms he had planned in their equipment.

The officers' wives and the principal families around Arras were invited to witness Junot's ideal of a crack corps. Of course all were gratified and expressed high approval. But it remained for Napoleon to crown Junot's triumph. He was frequently passing between Paris and Boulogne, and at the first opportunity a review was ordered. Perhaps the great soldier was a trifle jealous when, after long and critically contemplating the troops drawn up before him, the exclamation escaped his lips, "They surpass my guard" (that devoted *corps d'élite*, known later on as "the old guard"). The happiness of poor infatuated Junot was complete.

But while these troops were being drilled and trained for a service they were destined never to perform, plots and intrigues called royalist were being actively organised in England, to be carried out by agents on the Continent. Their object, probably, after having overthrown Napoleon, was to set up Général Moreau, rather than to restore the Bourbons; for Moreau was dissatisfied with the 18th Brumaire, because he had been but the aide-de-camp of the hero of that day, when he had hoped to have been himself the hero. But whichever it may have been, the discovery of the plot of which Georges Cadoudal, and Généraux Pichegru and Moreau, were at the head, resulted in that sad drama, the hasty arrest and immediate execution of the Duc d'Enghien.

A description of Général Pichegru, in the seized correspondence of one of the agents employed on the Continent, was mistaken for that of the duke; and as he chose to live perilously near the French frontier, suspicion was at once directed towards him. M. de Talleyrand would seem to have counselled his arrest and the deed that followed it, — according to a letter, seen and read by M. de Chateaubriand, that had escaped the fire to which, at the time of the Restoration, M. de Talleyrand consigned all correspondence of his relating to the above-mentioned plots that he could lay his hands on in the archives of the Louvre.

It was a deplorable event, which the delay of a few hours might have averted. Napoleon probably did deplore it. He remained for four days at La Malmaison silent and gloomy, seeing no one, and allowing Joséphine to receive no visitors. They dined alone, and dispensed with the attendance of their usual numerous retinue. La Malmaison, always so cheerful, had become as a house of mourning. That the duke had ceased to exist was announced at the same time as his arrest. Joséphine's tears flowed, no doubt, for the fate of the unfortunate young duke, as well as for this first sanguinary stain on Napoleon's career. But entreaties to spare life she could not have added. Life was extinct ere she knew that it had been contemplated to take life. The Duc d'Enghien was shot at the fortress of Vincennes on the 21st of March; and on the 24th M. de Talleyrand gave a grand ball at the hôtel of the Ministry of Foreign Affairs!

The general gloom momentarily inspired by the above sad event vanished as speedily as a passing cloud. On the morning of the 31st Floréal (20th May), the *Moniteur* announced that the Tribunat and the Senate had decided on confiding the government of the republic to an emperor, and on declaring that dignity hereditary in the family of the First Consul. A deputation repaired to St. Cloud with this interesting information. Graciously the new dignity was accepted, as it was "considered useful to the nation." "In no case," he said, "will my spirit be with my posterity on the day it shall cease to merit the love and esteem of *la grande nation.*" The 14th of July was named for the coronation; that the empire might be supposed to be founded on the principles associated with the day sacred to the birth of liberty in France.

But Napoleon intended to bring the Pope from Italy, and the interval was too short to take the necessary steps for obtaining his consent, and for making so long and, at that time, so difficult and fatiguing a journey. The 15th of August was then named. Soon after another adjournment took place. For Napoleon had a far more pompous ceremony in his mind than the members of the government who had proposed it ever dreamed of.

The 14th was therefore utilised for the inauguration of the Order of the Legion of Honour. An order of chivalry, when first proposed at the *fête* of the Concordat, was generally thought incompatible with republican principles. Opposition to it was overpowered by an obsequious majority in the Senate. Yet its inauguration had continued in abeyance, waiting for some event that should confer on it *éclat* and *prestige*. Such an event was found in the proclamation of the empire.

The first distribution of crosses took place at Les Invalides, and much surprise and dissatisfaction was expressed when it was found that the order was not uniform, but consisted of three classes; contrary to the principle of *égalité*. Consequently, all on whom grand crosses were not conferred were annoyed at the open disparagement of their services which a second or third class decoration seemed to them to convey. It was explained that the Legion of Honour was essentially a republican institution; its decorations obtainable by all, without reference to social standing, occupation, or profession. It was simply a mark of honourable service, civil or military.

The republican generals, true sons of the Revolution, received their crosses and grand crosses with the utmost indifference. The prevailing sentiment among them was bitter regret for the effacement of an order of things the nation had passed through so terrible an ordeal to obtain, and which now, just within their grasp, as they believed, was snatched from them by a despot's hand. They did not then look forward to the possession of such honours, wealth, and dignities as the empire had in store for them; nor foresee how soon, as princes and dukes, grand dignitaries and marshals, of that empire, republican prejudices would vanish, and their martial breasts swell with pride; not only under the grand crosses of the Legion of Honour, but under a double or triple row of such baubles, presented by other despots.

On the troops assembled at Boulogne the new decoration was next conferred. This was an imposing spectacle, though wind and rain greatly interfered with the arrangements, and falsified the prediction of the morning, that there was to be a day of "emperor's weather." It had already begun to be a popular notion that the elements would be propitious and smile on all *fêtes*, or public celebrations, at which the new emperor would be present. But like the trust in these days sometimes put in "queen's weather," the expectation was too often unfulfilled. The camp at Arras was not forgotten; many of the men were decorated, and their commander received the grand cross and a pension of 30,000 *francs*. But Napoleon never gave the brave and devoted Junot the well-deserved marshal's baton.

An amusing and singular anecdote — well known perhaps to many, but which will bear repeating — is told in connection with the proposal of the tribune Curée to confer the dignity of emperor on Napoleon. In the course of this tribune's speech on that occasion he said: "Time is hastening on. The Bonapartean era has completed its fourth year, and the nation now desires a chief as illustrious as its destinies." When this appeared in the *Moniteur* it greatly roused the anger of the learned M. Langlès, a member of the Institute, and keeper of the manuscripts in the National Library. "I knew it," he exclaimed; "I saw from the first that he aimed at sovereignty. Soon the crown of France will not suffice him. He will have the pretension to reign over Europe. Ah! poor nation; for this man's insatiable ambition you will indeed have to pay dearly." He had been strongly prejudiced against Napoleon, even when all Paris was fêting him as the conqueror of Italy, and had refused to accompany his expedition to Egypt when requested. "Then I order you," said Napoleon. "I receive orders only from the government," was the reply.

The events of the 18th Brumaire having raised Napoleon to the Consulate, the members of the Institute of France waited on him to offer their congratulations. He remarked that M. Langlès was not with his colleagues. Determined not to join them, he expected his dismissal to follow. However, no change was made. Another visit from the Institute followed the proclamation of the empire; but again no M. Langlès appeared, and still, to his surprise, he was not removed from his office. He was, however, so devoted to its duties that an equally competent successor was then difficult to find.

A few days after the coronation had taken place M. Langlès appeared one morning at the house of an intimate friend, with a very sardonic smile on his face and a very old quarto volume under his arm.

"Ah! ah!" he said; "so your usurper chose to play the part of Cæsar."

"What do you mean?" inquired his friend.

"You know," replied Langlès, "that he employed the tribune Curée, to propose his elevation to the imperial dignity. Now, read the historical note in this ancient edition of Virgil. It is in the sixth book of the "Æneid," where the sibyl Deïphobe, after conducting Æneas to the infernal regions, and when the great criminals pass in review before him, fixes her eyes on one of them, and pointing him out to the Trojan hero, says: 'This man, for gold, sold his country to Cæsar, and imposed on it a powerful master!' Now, who is 'this man?' Look at the note at the bottom of the page. It is '*Cureus tribunus.*' Thus," continued M. Langlès, "this Bonaparte, wishing to adorn himself with the aureola of a Cæsar, discovers this obscure individual Curée among the tribunes, and employs him to deck his head with an imperial crown."

"It is a strange coincidence," said his friend, "but I should doubt that Napoleon knew of it."

"Well," replies M. Langlès, "perhaps there are not in France three copies of this edition; but I am none the less convinced that the usurper was acquainted with it. If not, who the devil would have thought of selecting such a man as this Curée to propose the empire?"

Under a promise of secrecy from whom obtained, the old volume was shown to Joséphine, and the passage above quoted explained. Thus it was brought under Napoleon's notice. He was exceedingly struck by the singular allusion, which seemed to interest him greatly. But, on returning the book, he said to M. Bouilly (it is he who gives the anecdote, and who was M. Langlès's friend):

"You may be fully assured that the tribune Curée did not sell his country for gold."

"I am convinced of it, Sire," replied M. Bouilly;

"but your majesty must allow that in proposing, with the free will of France, to decern the imperial crown to you, '*dominum potentem imposuit.*'"

Napoleon, regarding this reply as a piece of adroit flattery conveying an appeal for place or patronage of some sort, inquired what he could do for M. Bouilly. What did he desire?

"Sire, I desire nothing," he replied. "Placed on the *juste milieu* of the social ladder, though I hope not to descend, I yet have no ambition to mount higher."

"It is, in effect, the happiest of positions, to one satisfied with it," he rejoined, in a tone of slight asperity. Perhaps the vanity of Napoleon was wounded at meeting with a man who was able to reply that he could do nothing for him.

CHAPTER XX.

The Coronation. — Arrival of Pius VII. — The Nuptial Benediction. — The Eventful 2d of December. — The Pontifical *Cortège*. — The Crown of Charlemagne. — The Crowning of Joséphine. — The Emperor and Empress. — The Presentation of the Eagles. — Madame Decadi's Marriage. — Louis XVIII. and Gustavus IV. — The Iron Crown. — Doing Credit to the Empire. — The Governor of Paris. — The Arch-Chancellor. — *Un Artiste Culinaire.* — Full Dress Dinners. — A More Genial Host. — The France of Other Days. — *Une Altesse Sérénissime.* — The Modern Charlemagne. — The Viceroy. — The Princesse Elisa. — The Princesse Pauline. — A Chilling Reception. — The Third Coalition. — Trafalgar and Austerlitz. — A Batch of New Kings. — "King Franconi." — Madame Mère. — A Revival.

THE ceremonial of the coronation, after long and heated discussion, was at length definitively, if not to all parties quite satisfactorily, arranged. There had been terrible heartburnings when the length and amplitude of the imperial mantles of state, and the proportion of ermine and embroidery the several princes and princesses might justly lay claim to, came under consideration. Court costume generally had been a difficult subject to settle; and it had been found necessary to smooth down the ruffled vanity of the newly created princesses on being appointed trainbearers to the empress, by changing the phrase *porter la queue* to *soutenir le manteau*.

The Pope's arrival was now anxiously awaited. He travelled slowly, and a whole retinue of Italian priests accompanied him. The season was inclement; the roads, too, were bad, and Pius VII. was an aged man. However, on the 25th of November, Napoleon, as if to meet his holiness by chance, arranged a hunting party, and rode out by the way the venerable visitor was expected to arrive. The meeting took place on the road to Nemours. Napoleon alighted. Embraces and benedictions followed,— the emperor and the Pope then proceeding together to the imperial palace of Fontainebleau, which had been refurnished, and with great magnificence, for the occasion. There Pius VII. remained a few days to recover from the fatigue of his long journey.

Meanwhile, it was urged by those who still clung to the republic, as gradually its every vestige was wrested from them, that the emperor should be installed (they refused to say crowned) in that revolutionary arena, the Champ de Mars. "This," said Napoleon, "would be to awaken reminiscences of the *Fête* of the Federation. The times are greatly changed, and his holiness cannot be expected to repeat the *rôle* then assumed by the Bishop of Autun. The Church of Les Invalides has also been proposed, and glorious recollections are doubtless associated with it. But greater ones, that appeal more forcibly to the imagination, are associated with Notre-Dame, and will impart a more august and solemn character to the ceremony."*

On the day preceding the coronation, Napoleon's uncle, lately the Abbé Fesch but now a cardinal, performed the marriage ceremony between Napoleon and Joséphine; having been authorised to do so by the Pope. An attestation to that effect, and in proper form, was given to Joséphine by the cardinal, who strongly advised her not to part with it. He in after years, also, openly asserted that she had been duly married. Two of Napoleon's aides-de-camp, one of whom was under age, witnessed the civil marriage of 1796. But the signature of the curé of the parish was wanting. Advantage was afterwards taken of those informalities to annul a union consecrated by the sanction of a Pope and the benediction of a cardinal. However, the not very scrupulous conscience of the Emperor Francis II. was satisfied when, by and by, it suited his views to propose his daughter for a wife to Napoleon.

The morning of the 2d of December was cold, damp, and unpromising. Yet before daylight Paris was up and in full activity; a large number of its inhabitants were at that early hour also in full dress. Many others had not been to bed at all. Ladies, who formed part of the *cortège* of

* Pelet de la Lozère, "*Mémoires Militaires.*"

the empress, were in several instances — so busy were the court *coiffeurs* — compelled to have their hair dressed on the previous evening, or in the course of the night. The fashionable *coiffure* being then very elaborate, the poor ladies were propped upright in chairs, lest, when taking an hour's rest before completing their *toilette*, they should damage their head-dresses, if they could not drive sleep from their eyes.

The official programme, arranged by the Vicomte de Ségur, grand master of the ceremonies, announced that the imperial *cortège* would leave the Tuileries at nine o'clock; and the emperor's known punctuality made similar exactness obligatory on others. As that hour approached, the clouds began to disperse, the weather brightened, and every window along the line of procession was filled with eager spectators. Extravagant sums had been paid for these windows. For Paris was so full of provincial families and foreign visitors that it was impossible to issue tickets of admission to Notre-Dame to half the number that applied for them. And in spite of the weather, what a display of *toilettes* at these windows! — light, bright, and beautiful, a souvenir of May in December.

This great event revealed also the pleasant fact that France was not so poor as she was supposed to be. It was evident she had hoarded her money, as she has done on more than one occasion since.

Cardinal Fesch.
Photo-etching after the engraving by **Wm. Read.**

What a good time — as American cousins say — it must have been for the florists, the jewellers, the *modistes*, the tailors, and many other providers of the needs of fashion; for a fabulous sum — considering what had occurred in past years — is said to have then been put into circulation.

The pontifical *cortège* preceded that of the emperor. But Pius VII., although a man of venerable and dignified appearance, was not received with much show of respect, nor did he create the impression expected. His *entourage* of dingy priests displeased the people, and the donkey or mule ridden by a priest carrying the cross, and which, according to the Roman custom, preceded his carriage, gave occasion for much profane mirth. But when he entered the cathedral, and the assembled clergy — as he took his seat on the throne prepared for him near the grand altar — intoned the canticle "*Tu es Petrus*," the effect was grand and imposing.

For the rest, it was a spectacle of dazzling magnificence, astonishing to many foreigners of distinction, who visited Paris expressly to witness it. Seated on his throne with Joséphine beside him, Napoleon was anointed by the Pope on the forehead and hands. Prayer followed. He then removed the gold laurel wreath he wore on entering the church, and, taking from the Pope's hands the crown of Charlemagne that had stood on the altar, and had been brought from Aix-la-Chapelle for this ceremony, he placed it on his head himself. At this moment he is said to have glanced rapidly around him, with a sort of triumphant expression in his eyes, and his countenance became singularly animated. Well, indeed, it might.

What an astonishing, what an unparalleled career! How striking a contrast this brilliant scene presents with that frantic one in the orangery of St. Cloud just five years ago! How strangely these shouts of "*Vive l'empereur!*" — echoed from one end of Paris to the other — sound in the ears of those who remember the vehement cries of "Down with the traitor!" "Down with the despot!" "He is outlawed; down with the tyrant!" Even he was confused, and, pallid as death, was hurried away by his partisans. And but for the energy of Lucien — an exile from this imposing scene — the Directory would have triumphed and sent him a prisoner to Cayenne. For it is remarkable how little Bonaparte did to ensure success on the 18th Brumaire. He did little more than take advantage of the energetic efforts of his brothers; whom now he loads with wealth, but jealously excludes from a share of the power which they too had aimed at.

But the Empress Joséphine has yet to be crowned, and the brilliant throng that now fills the ancient edifice is deeply interested in her. She is looking her very best, and playing her part in this grand drama with much dignity and true royal bearing. She descends from the throne and advances towards the altar. Her train is borne by the four princesses, — Elisa, Caroline, Julie, and Hortense. The ladies of the palace follow. Napoleon's eyes, as they rest upon her, seem to speak the admiration he feels, as she kneels before him with clasped hands, and tearful eyes that evince her deep emotion. The small open crown with its cross is handed to him from the altar. He first places it on his own head, then carefully arranges it within the glittering diadem that encircles her brow.

Hand in hand they return to the throne. Then the full choir bursts forth with the triumphant shout of the *Vivat*, which, as it resounds through the cathedral, is responded to by a salvo of artillery from without, — sending a thrill through every breast, and creating much general and genuine emotion. The ceremony should have ended with the administration of the holy communion to the newly crowned emperor and empress. But, after due consultation, it was decided to dispense with it. For among the Pope's retinue of gloomy priests there smouldered strong revengeful feelings towards France and her ruler; and the preparation of the bread and wine for the eucharist would afford an opportunity for vengeance that some of their number — it was suspected — would be unable to resist.

Grand banquets, illuminations, and the usual joyous demonstrations, prevailed throughout France. On the morrow a grand review took place in the Champ de Mars, followed by the presentation of eagles to the several regiments assembled there from different parts of the kingdom to receive them. The soaring eagle had become the emblem of the empire, and displaced the goddess of liberty on the great seal of state. Again, *fêtes* and rejoicings. Concerts and theatres open gratis to all. There were fountains running over with wine instead of water, — a miracle that called forth an expressive shrug of the shoulders and the *jeu de mots,* "*C'est en vin (en vain) que cet César veut se faire aimer,*" from the irreconcilable M. Langlès.

Nevertheless, the people were pleased with these public festivities, which were continued for fifteen days. For the same space an uninterrupted succession of balls, banquets, grand receptions, solemn audiences, court theatricals, dress parades, and other ceremonials or gaieties took place at the Hôtel de Ville, or at the imperial palaces of the Tuileries and St. Cloud. Both had been refurnished with extraordinary splendour, and orders were issued to the numerous grand chamberlains and ladies and gentlemen generally, composing the imperial household, as well as all who were invited to these *fêtes*, that they were to appear in the costume worn at the ceremony of the coronation. Napoleon was resplendent in violet and gold. The black stock had disappeared, and the

Louis Quinze cravat of rich lace had taken its place. The famous diamond, the "Regent," glittered conspicuously in the hilt of his sword.

Some persons professed to regret the familiar epithets — citizen and citizeness — long since abolished in society, and now destined to disappear officially. Servants and shopkeepers, it was thought, might still be thus addressed. But they were of a different opinion. They had gloried in them when shared in common with "aristocrats;" but the times had changed, and manners also, and they would now be Monsieur and Madame as well as the best of them. At the request of the Pope the restoration of the Gregorian calendar was promised. But, as the people said, "Madame Decadi had in reality long since married Monsieur Dimanche." But the revolutionary term is abolished when the decade of the empire begins, — a decade of years during which Napoleon is to overrun Europe and partly subdue it.

The grand cross of the Legion of Honour was forwarded to those European sovereigns who recognised "Napoleon I., Emperor of the French," and sent ambassadors to congratulate him on his accession. In return, he received the Black Eagle of Prussia, and the Spanish Order of the Golden Fleece. The latter had, in former years, been conferred on Monsieur, now known as Comte de Lille, and sometimes Louis XVIII. As soon as he heard that Charles IV. had sent this order to

Napoleon, he immediately returned the insignia in his own possession. "He could not consent," he said, "to hold anything in common with the military usurper then seated on the throne of his fathers."

In this he imitated Gustavus IV. of Sweden, who returned the Black Eagle to the King of Prussia, on learning that he had sent it to Napoleon, and that both he and the Duke of Brunswick had accepted from him the Legion of Honour. The hatred of Gustavus towards Napoleon was almost fanatical, and his attempt, single-handed, and with an inadequate force, to prevail against him at Stralsund, was attributed to mental aberration. There was, however, something chivalrous in it, which the craven kings of Europe dared not imitate, or Napoleon might have been compelled to restrain his ambitious views within narrower limits.

To the imperial crown of Charlemagne was soon to be added the iron crown of Lombardy — iron then only in name, its modern successor being a crown of purest gold. He, indeed, offered to bestow it on Joseph, as a sort of vassal-king. But he refused it indignantly, — mortified that he was cut off from his right of succession to the imperial throne. With Louis he had no better success. He was to govern Lombardy, but in his son's name. Enraged at the vehemence with which this proposal was rejected, Napoleon suddenly seized his brother by the waist, and threw him out of the room. And his violence was almost pardonable. What a family of harpies surrounded him — all wanting to be kings and queens, he, too, quite willing to provide them with kingdoms; while they, discontented with that portion of Europe he offered to each, fixed their minds on what he had resolved on disposing of elsewhere. Well might he say of his sisters: "Of what do they complain? One would suppose I had deprived these ladies of some portion of the heritage of the late king, our father."

Early in the spring of 1805 Napoleon left *son peuple, et très fidèles sujets* (grating epithets the French people were not readily reconciled to), and, accompanied by Joséphine, set out for Milan, to be crowned King of Italy; stopping at Lyons and Turin to receive the felicitations and addresses of the authorities of those cities. The imperial family, left in Paris, were ordered to be gay in the absence of their majesties. And with gaiety there must be magnificence also, — everything about them sumptuous. "Mesdames," he said to the wives of his officers, "I expect you to open your *salons*, not once only, but twice, thrice, in the week, and to entertain in a style that shall do credit to the empire."

Madame de Genlis had recommended that luxury and magnificence should walk hand in hand with glory, each deriving lustre from the other. Therefore, the ladies of the court were reminded that, before all things, they must be *grandes dames;* that there must be no niggardliness in their expenses; no English muslins worn, or at most only as *peignoirs* or morning wrappers. They must wear rich silks, velvets, and satins for winter, and taffetas for summer; that the manufacturers of Lyons might again become flourishing.

Junot, with his young wife, kept open house in grand style. Promoted from Commandant to Governor of Paris, he did the honours of the capital with great *éclat*. The most splendid equipages seen in Paris belonged to Général Junot; also the finest stud of high-bred horses. His liveries were sumptuous, and as nearly resembling the emperor's as was permissible. His hôtel in Paris, his Château de Raincy (formerly belonging to the Duc d'Orléans), were furnished with princely magnificence; and the service in every department of these establishments was kept up in the same style. The finest wines were in his cellars, and especially those of his native province of Burgundy. Better still, he possessed a very fine library, containing many of Didot's choicest editions, and other valuable works,—also a collection of pictures and objects of art of great rarity. It was his fancy that his household should consist exclusively of Burgundians, who too frequently, it is said, rewarded his preference of them by frauds and robbery to a considerable extent.

Another establishment, magnificently mounted also, but where a certain air of quiet grandeur reigned, with more gravity and strict observance of etiquette than prevailed at Junot's, was that of the arch-chancellor of the empire — after the emperor, the person of highest authority in the state. Cambacérès was a man peculiarly suited for the office he held. He was one of the "lawyers of the Directory," as Napoleon once disdainfully termed them, and, of course, one of the stern and stanch republicans who had voted for the death of Louis XVI. when condemned by the revolutionary tribunal.

"He now wears ermine and velvet, and is a man of such noble presence that he wears it with exceeding dignity. His aspect is not severe, but it is solemn. He walks with leisurely and measured step; and he and his subordinates of the arch-chancery are always in full dress." "It was advisable," he said to Napoleon, "to habituate the younger men to it, that they might acquire with it ease and grace."

Cambacérès was about fifty when, from Second Consul, he was transformed into arch-chancellor. Together with the former title he then cast off the brown cloth coat, black stockings, and breeches, plain buckled shoes, and round hat, he had been accustomed to wear. These, with his new dignity, were replaced by silk, velvet, and embroidery, with fine point lace — of which he had four kinds, adapted to the four seasons — white silk stockings, diamond buckles, dress sword, and three-cornered hat. Carefully curled and powdered he had always been — even at the risk of losing his head. During the Consulate he piqued himself on his dinners. He had then a first-rate "citizen-cook" — a gentleman who now styled himself *artiste culinaire*, — and with reason: he had a so much wider field for the display of his talent; and the difference in the company, whose refined tastes he now strove to gratify, and succeeded in doing so, called for artistic combinations in the preparation of his *plats* that might well entitle him to be named an *artiste*.

Twice in the week these dinners were given. And punctually at six the guests were expected to sit down, — the formal invitation each received naming ten minutes before the hour as the time of their arrival. For the arch-chancellor waited for no man. A lady of great distinction he would allow five minutes' grace, which, in fact, was a quarter of an hour. But, unless she had some very satisfactory reason for availing herself of this concession, there would be a slight suppression of the customary graciousness in his grand manner of receiving ladies. Full dress was the rule at those grand repasts, and it was a rule to which he permitted no exceptions. The ladies must wear velvets and diamonds in winter; silks and satins, flowers or feathers, in summer. If any unfortunate lady, however elegantly dressed, sinned against this rule, he would smilingly reprove her by saying very pointedly, "Madame, your *négligé* is charming."

This excess of ceremony and etiquette was partly ordered by the emperor, and appeared to him by no means ridiculous. Perhaps it was less so in Cambacérès than when attempted by some other of the grand dignitaries of the empire. For his manner was naturally grave, and he was always disposed to exact order and regularity in his household. Napoleon said he was the only one among his grand officers who fully comprehended his position. Nevertheless, Cambacérès could unbend, and was accustomed to tell anecdotes and stories connected with the revolutionary days with great effect.

Nor did he avoid referring to the fatal 21st of January; for he affirmed, and many others affirmed and believed it too, that his vote was given with a view of saving the king. How they explained it does not appear, for he is said to have voted against the appeal to the people, which alone could have possibly saved him. Cambacérès was not married, and was deaf to the emperor's recommendation to take a wife. He urged him to buy a country house, and Cambacérès then bought an hôtel in the adjacent suburb of Monceaux. He never took any journeys or followed the *beau monde* to the baths, or to their provincial châteaux. When the emperor was absent, Cambacérès reigned in Paris, and the court of the Tuileries was transferred to the *salons* of the arch-chancery. Personally, Napoleon did not greatly like him; but he had the firmest trust in his good sense, his circumspection, and his honesty.

M. de Talleyrand was, in manner at least, a far more genial host. The basis of his society was the *corps diplomatique*, which, with the exception of the Batavian minister, had been entirely changed on the accession of Napoleon as emperor. The new ministers had but recently presented their letters of credence, and, with their wives, formed a new social circle. They may be said to have been chiefly of his own nomination, as he employed his influence with foreign courts to secure the appointment of men whose principles he was acquainted with, and whom he could dominate. Added to these were the official personages who, either from the duties of their position, or their friendly intimacy with the Minister for Foreign Affairs, frequented the *salon* of the Rue d'Anjou. The amnesty had also increased the number of his guests, and as he continued his suppers in the old French style, his *réunions* were considered the most agreeable in Paris, and his hôtel the only one where returned exiles were reminded of the France of other days, which, with them, meant Versailles and Paris.

To accommodate this enlarged *cercle intime* a

gallery, in the form of a conservatory, adorned with choice plants, light drapery, and statuary, had been added to the perfumed *salon* of the hôtel Talleyrand. There, reclined on a luxuriously cushioned couch, his flowing curls powdered and scented, he would listen with an air of nonchalance, and in a kind of cat's sleep, to the lively chit-chat of the ladies grouped around him. The *belles amies* of M. de Talleyrand were numerous, and their persistent attentions and devotion to him naturally tended to disturb the serenity of Madame Grandt, his *belle amie par excellence*, and soon to become Madame Talleyrand and Princesse de Benevento. It was a marriage that excited much indignation among these ladies, which amused M. de Talleyrand. But Madame then assumed very grand airs, and made her would-be rivals feel that she was now, as she loved to style herself, *une altesse sérénissime*.

From his habitual silence and habit of nearly closing his eyes — a habit that grew upon him as he advanced in years — he must have seemed but an inattentive and uninterested listener to the prattle of these fair dames. But when, half rising from his couch and slightly changing his position, he lifted his drooping eyelids, and, with a glance full of malice and a smile hovering on his lips, uttered some piquant remark or amusing *bon mot*, which he may have been meditating, he gave, in a few words, a concentrated reply, as it were, to the whole conversation. And these rare utterances were so pithy, so epigrammatic and full of meaning, that they took root in the memory; and have gained for one who from policy was a silent man, and, except on special occasions when it served his purpose to appear otherwise, reticent in the extreme, the reputation of a brilliant conversationalist.

On the Minister for Foreign Affairs, the arch-chancellor, and the Governor of Paris, it chiefly devolved then to do the honours of the capital in the absence of the imperial court of the Tuileries. Prince Joseph, at Mortfontaine — though his *salon* had latterly become a shade more political than during the Consulate — entertained especially the world of art and letters. The emperor's injunctions to the ladies left in Paris, to dress and to dance and receive, and to keep up a constant succession of pleasures, were but very partially obeyed.

The "*haute société*" were rather weary of being always in court costume, and were glad to take the opportunity of the emperor's and empress's departure to visit their estates — many confiscated domains which had remained unsold having been restored by Napoleon to their owners. Others followed him to Milan. In the ancient cathedral of that city the modern Charlemagne was crowned, or, more correctly, crowned himself, — exclaiming, as he placed the crown on his head, "God hath given it me; woe to him that toucheth it!" Joséphine did not participate in this new honour. She merely graced the scene by her presence, and, surrounded by her ladies, was one of its most gratified spectators — but chiefly for Eugène's sake. Cardinal Caprara officiated. The Pope refused. He had expected that for his condescension in making the journey to Paris to crown the emperor in his capital, restitution would have been made of some portion of the territory of which the Holy See had been deprived.

Assuming for himself the title of king, after that of emperor, Napoleon named Eugène de Beauharnais viceroy, — having first given him the rank of an imperial prince, and conferred on him the post of arch-chancellor of state. Murat was also elevated to the same high dignity. He was also named grand-admiral, the only appointment then unfilled that gave the rank of a grand official of the empire. Both of these new grandees received the Order of the Iron Crown, which Napoleon instituted on the occasion of his coronation. A grand review was held next day on the battle-field of Marengo — the manœuvres directed by Maréchal Lannes, afterwards Duc de Montebello. Napoleon sent to Paris for the hat and coat he wore on the day of that memorable battle. The moths, it appears, had not spared the coat. The hat, too, was quite out of shape, and its shape out of date, and only to be tolerated, says Baron de

Méneval, because of the souvenirs connected with them. But Napoleon wore them.

Genoa also sought and obtained the honour of being incorporated with the empire, and evinced her gratitude by *fêtes* far outdoing in splendour and ingenious conception those of Milan.

The little independent state of Lucca, fearing to be overlooked and excluded from sharing in the benefits of this new arrangement of the Italian republics, the gonfalonier, or chief authority of the state, waited on the emperor and king, and pleaded that Lucca might be taken under his protection. The Princesse Elisa — Madame Bacciochi, afterwards Grand Duchess of Tuscany — had then just been named sovereign princess of the little principality of Piombino. Lucca was united to it and placed under her rule. She condescended to accept the gift, but thought it a miserable appanage for an imperial princess. Her husband, who occupied the position of a prince consort, was named commander of the detachment of troops that formed the army and the guard of honour of the princess. The prince, who changed his name from Pascal to Felix on becoming a royal personage, in no way interfered in affairs of state. He passed his time in drilling his army, playing the violin, and attending his wife as *chevalier d'honneur*.

The principality of Guastalla was not given to Pauline until the following year. "*Peu de chose,*" she said. But she had not the same ambition as her sisters. She was content to be a "real princess," and to be worshipped for her beauty. She did not follow the court to Milan, or obey orders to receive and be gay; but retired to Trianon, lay on her couch all day, and played the interesting invalid, while inventing new dresses to excite the envy of the absentees on their return.

This creation of princes and princesses was but a preliminary to the setting up of new kings and queens after Napoleon's next victory. Already he was looking forward to it; for though affecting to seek peace, he did not ensue it, but was preparing for war. The return from Turin to Fontainebleau was made without stopping on the road. And he travelled with so much rapidity that the escort, which was divided into detachments stationed at short intervals throughout the journey, could not keep up with his carriage and six.

Joséphine accompanied him. He would have had her travel more leisurely. But whispers of his infidelity were already rife in her gossiping court; and in the midst of triumphs, in which she then fully shared, the word "divorce" often rang, as the knell of joy, in her ears. She preferred then, for the sake of not being separated from him, to bear the temporary fatigue and privation incidental to the galloping speed with which he traversed the country, — in haste to lay down his imperial sceptre and take up the sword of the general. Fontainebleau was reached on the 15th of July.

The principal authorities awaited his arrival, eager to offer their felicitations to the emperor and king. Loaded with honours, satiated with the adulation of which so lately he had been the object, he gave but a chilling reception to this obsequious deputation. To the officers of his household, many of whom had been on terms of intimacy with him, his manner was equally frigid. A stricter etiquette was observed, and he seemed desirous of impressing on them that the distance between him and them was now a wide one, and at that distance they must henceforth keep. "No graciousness of manner, no sign of kindly feeling, tempered this austerity, so greatly did the emperor seem to dread the awakening of any reminiscence of the days of their friendly equality." *

From Fontainebleau he repaired to Paris, and in a secret council informed the Senate of the "third coalition," or alliance between Russia, England, and Austria, and of his own warlike intentions, — his determination, in fact, to crush that perfidious House of Hapsburg, which forced him to make war when he so longed for peace. A decree of the Senate authorised a levy of 80,000 conscripts, and the reorganisation of the National Guard in the provinces, where necessary. The army of England was then ordered to turn its

* *Mémoires du Comte Miot de Melito.*

back on the White Cliffs and the ocean, and march towards the Danube. At midnight, on the 24th of September, he set out from Paris to join the army. Joséphine was with him. After many entreaties, he at last had consented that she should bear him company as far as Strasburg. But her preparations must be made within an hour, and one *femme de chambre* only accompany her. At Strasburg they parted,—she returning with a numerous escort, he proceeding with his troops towards Vienna; which was occupied on the 13th of November. On the 2d of December, the first anniversary of his coronation, the decisive battle of Austerlitz was fought, and was followed by the peace of Presbourg.

"Marengo sanctioned the Consulate; Austerlitz established the empire." Nelson's victory of Trafalgar, which occurred on the 21st of October, and annihilated the combined French and Spanish navies, was not mentioned in the *Moniteur*. Admiral Villeneuve was taken prisoner, and the details of the battle were but imperfectly known at the time; while, the French being dazzled by the successes of the army, the naval defeat received but a passing notice. Napoleon was indeed fully aware of its importance, and bitterly regretted a loss that, during his reign, no efforts could repair. It put an end to his projects for the invasion of England. All reference to it was therefore strictly prohibited.

To the hero of Austerlitz a grateful country awarded the title of "Napoléon le Grand," and the Senate decreed him a triumphal monument. The colours taken during the campaign were conveyed to Notre-Dame amidst the enthusiastic acclamations of the people, and preceded and followed by a grand procession — civil, military, and religious. It was headed by the Archbishop of Paris — the famous Abbé, now Cardinal, Maury. Napoleon had met him in Italy, and induced him not only to return to Paris, but to accept the archbishopric, contrary to the Pope's commands. The hero himself did not immediately return to gladden the eyes and the hearts of his faithful subjects.

Joséphine and her court had left for Munich, whither Napoleon, on leaving Shœnbrunn, proposed to repair in order to be present at the marriage of his adopted son, Eugène, with the Princess Augusta of Bavaria. This was one of the few happy marriages that took place at his order. The Electors of Bavaria and Wurtemberg were then raised to the dignity of kings as a reward for allying themselves with France. Many other similar promotions were made at this time. Ferdinand of Naples, having taken up arms against France during the Austrian campaign, was driven from his kingdom, and Joseph Bonaparte reigned in his stead. That unhappy couple, Louis and Hortense, were sent to reign over the republic of Holland, as king and queen.

Berthier.

Photo-etching after the Painting by Bosio.

Joachim Murat and his wife became Grand Duke and Duchess of Berg. Murat, "the intrepid," who always leads on his troops to the attack, brandishing a riding whip, with his magnificent plumes, embroidered mantles, and costume of Francis I., and familiarly called "King Franconi," is soon to be King of Naples, *vice* Joseph, promoted to the throne of Spain. The minor promotions are Général Berthier, to be Prince of Neufchatel, and M. de Talleyrand, Prince de Benevento. Twelve other towns became duchies, to be distributed among the marshals of the empire.

The court returned to Paris at the end of January. The empress, it was remarked, was looking very bright and happy. She was pleased with the advantageous marriage and prospects of Eugène, and with the charming young princess, his wife. She hoped, too, though the result did not realise her hopes, that the lot of poor Hortense might be rendered less intolerable when her tyrannical husband had the cares of a kingdom on his shoulders. In the course of the same year, her niece, the Princesse Stéphanie de Beauharnais, was married to the hereditary Prince of Baden.

As for the emperor, short though his absence had been, he had become considerably stouter. But his health was good, and his activity as great as ever. He was even more animated than usual, and, in referring to the recent campaign, and the peace he had wrung from Austria, seemed satisfied with his victory, and with having so large a portion of the continent under his heel, to crush whenever it pleased him.

Madame Mère had not yet been created a princess. She was fond of Lucien, and would defend him when Napoleon spoke against him. It was to punish her, then, that she continued to be simply Madame Lætitia, when her sons and daughters were emperors, kings, queens, and princesses. But at length her household was formed, — the result to her being only discomfort and restraint. Her natural reserve and timidity were increased by the *entourage* of a court. Yet she possessed dignity of manner, and the remains of great beauty, and was always appropriately dressed. Her knowledge of French was so limited that she rather guessed at, than understood what was said to her; her replies were therefore confused. She appears to have been a very worthy woman, greatly misunderstood, because in a false position, as she sometimes very painfully felt, and was ungenerously made to feel. She had no faith in the stability of the empire. And if she economised a portion of her large income, it was that she might be able to assist those thoughtlessly extravagant sons and daughters in the hour of need, which she fully believed would some day overtake them.

Madame Mère gave away large sums to the poor, and she revived the Order of Sisters of Mercy.

CHAPTER XXI.

The Divorce Again on the *Tapis*. — Establishing the Dynasty.
— The Imperial Mausoleum. — Following the Headquarters.
— Queen Louise at Jena. — Marriage of Jérôme. — A Fresh
Crop of Laurels. — Wanted, a Rich Heiress. — Comte Louis
dé Narbonne. — The Exiles of Coppet. — A Courtier of the
Old School. — A Mysterious Story. — Reinforcing the *Noblesse*. — "If Anything Should Happen." — Convention of
Cintra. — Count Metternich. — The Blockade. — Plots, Intrigues; Europe Arming. — A New Campaign. — The Archduchess Maria Louisa. — Prayers for the Emperor. — The
Peace of Vienna.

URING the short time that Napoleon, before entering on another campaign, devoted to affairs of state, and to the various alterations and improvements for the embellishment of the capital, he doubtless began also seriously to entertain the idea of repudiating Joséphine. His head was turned by the flattery and ready obedience to his will that met him on every side. The servile homage of the Belgians convinced him, he said, that to attain his ends no divorce was needed. Then he was but First Consul; now he is the crowned and consecrated Emperor of the French; and as conquest every year extends the limits of the empire, his views and intentions undergo a change.

He had married his adopted son and daughter into princely and sovereign houses, and declared the former his heir. But one born to the throne, and brought up with the expectation of wielding the mighty sceptre swayed by himself, was alone capable, he now thought, of worthily succeeding him. Eugène, excellent and honourable as doubtless he was, never, till recently, had dreamed of such a position. Of his brother's descendants, the only one he had been inclined to adopt had lately died. Why not, then, marry into a royal house himself, and thus invest the heir that would probably be born to him, and would be reared under his own eye, with the *prestige* of birth? Such considerations were continually thrust upon Napoleon by those who hoped, no doubt, more firmly to secure their own interests should he succeed in establishing his dynasty by a matrimonial alliance with one of the European Powers.

He had thoughts, at this time, of restoring the neglected and dilapidated palace of Versailles, and of residing there. It was to be decorated and furnished in a style of splendour far surpassing that of the Louis Quatorze period. The much-talked-of wonders of the Château de Marly — so wantonly destroyed by the fanatics of the Revolution — would even then have paled, it was believed, when compared with the magnificence of the imperial court, as displayed in the recent redecoration and refurnishing of Fontainebleau, Compiègne, St.

Cloud, and the Tuileries. The Cathedral of St. Denis was already restored, and the mausoleum of the Bonapartes erected in that ancient place of sepulture of the kings of France. The first-born of Hortense and Louis lay buried there.

But all these minor projects, together with that project of divorce — against which he so long struggled, for his affections doubtless were with Joséphine — must, for the present, be laid aside. For again the clarion of war is sounded, and Napoleon must away to the battle.* The fourth coalition has been formed, and that peace-loving monarch, Frederick William III. of Prussia, almost as weak and irresolute as Louis XVI., has ventured to join Russia and England, and to require that some detachments of French troops, which have taken up their quarters in Prussian territory, be withdrawn within a specified time. There is a menace of war in the tone of this demand, and Napoleon proposes to administer due chastisement.

The empress and her court have become so accustomed to these short and successful campaigns, that they have begun to regard them more in the light of reviews on a grand scale, to end with balls, *fêtes*, and illuminations, grand crosses, and a new batch of dukes and princes. Defeat is

---

* It has been computed that during the ten years of Napoleon's reign little more than two and a half years were spent by him in Paris.

never dreamed of. The troops are full of enthusiasm, and the officers set out for the seat of war as though they were going to a ball. Sometimes, to break the monotony of court life, the empress follows the headquarters of the army with her ladies, forming a sort of ambulatory party of pleasure. Then all is life and gaiety, — the whizzing of bullets, the trumpet calls, the impatient neighing of the war-horse, and other cries of battle near at hand, adding wonderful piquancy to the revels; disturbed only when the name either of husband, brother, or son, appears on the list of killed and wounded.

But the court does not follow on this occasion. The ladies stay at home and amuse themselves, while Napoleon and his troops overrun Prussia, enter her capital, and annihilate her army at Auerstadt and Jena. In some accounts of the battle of Jena, the beautiful Queen Louise is represented as having harangued the troops, and, in uniform, placed herself at the head of a regiment. It is entirely an error. She did neither. Though she possessed courage, she had also too much womanly feeling, and was too refined, to play the part of an Amazon. She was at Jena with her husband, to whom she was devotedly attached, and she rightly urged him to resist his oppressor. On the approach of the French, the Duke of Brunswick, who held a chief command in the Prussian army, recommended that she should leave, and accordingly she was conducted to a place of safety, and in the midst of a regiment — a strong escort being necessary. The country was laid waste by the French; the people impoverished; the king and his family driven from place to place; often sheltered in a single room in some mean dwelling.

The campaign ended with the defeat of the Russian army, the occupation of Poland, and the Peace of Tilsit, by which the king was deprived of half of his dominions. Out of them was carved a kingdom for Jérôme, who, after abandoning Miss Patterson, was restored to the good graces of Napoleon, and married to a princess of Wurtemburg, — a noble-minded woman, who deserved a better fate. The infamous libels inserted in the *Moniteur*, having reference to the Queen of Prussia, were disgraceful to Napoleon, — though he might well have pointed to the equally groundless and contemptible inventions that appeared in the English papers, respecting his mother and other members of his family, as no less disgraceful to their authors. It was a pitiful sort of warfare.

The kind-hearted Joséphine was much grieved by these attacks on the reputation of an amiable woman, who in her domestic relations was irreproachable, and who was esteemed for the virtues of her private life as much as she was renowned for her beauty. To Joséphine's reproaches, Napoleon replied that he loved women of sweet and gentle temper like her own, and by informing her that, at the entreaties of Madame Hatzfeld, he had spared the life of her husband, whose intercepted correspondence revealed his treasonable communications, as he termed it, with the Prussian headquarters.

On visiting the tomb of the great Frederick at Potzdam, Napoleon took possession of that warrior's sword, his riband of the Black Eagle, and general's sash. These, together with the colours borne by the Prussian guard in the Seven Years' War, were despatched to Paris to be placed in the Hôtel des Invalides. He returned to his capital in the following July, and was received with the usual enthusiasm. The French were pleased with the fresh crop of laurels he brought them to heap on the altar of the *grande nation*, though they began to perceive that a high price must be paid for them; for to the announcement of a peace was added that of a new conscription. Nevertheless, trade was brisk, prosperity general, and money plentiful in spite of the war; for the war paid its own expenses and something more.

Paris was gradually absorbing the faubourgs; and the improvements planned within the barriers were being rapidly carried out. Old roads were put into good order, and new communications opened with the principal towns of distant departments; all of which had their due part, either begun or designed, in the general restoration, and their share of the good things of that well-supplied horn of plenty which was then being poured out over France. The years 1807 to 1809 were perhaps the most brilliant of the imperial court. No other in Europe equalled it in luxury and magnificence. Its graceful empress, with her dignified air and gracious manners, was fit to sit on any throne; while the ladies of her court were for the most part youthful, beautiful, and elegant.

The younger officers, many of whom were men of education and honourable family, had generally obeyed the injunctions of the emperor and married rich wives, the daughters of wealthy financiers. M. de Talleyrand was annoyed at this. He had not taken a wealthy bride for himself when he married Madame Grandt; but he wanted one for his nephew. He was unable to marry that nephew satisfactorily, he afterward told the Emperor Alexander, when the interview at Erfurth took place, — Napoleon having taken all the great heiresses for his generals. He therefore begged the emperor — in return for his betrayal of the secrets of Napoleon — to use his influence in obtaining the hand of the young Duchess of Courland for this nephew, M. de Périgord. Alexander thought his treachery merited this concession. The marriage took place soon after.

Napoleon's system of fusion, too, though it may not have accomplished all he expected from it, yet brought to his court a very considerable sprinkling of the old *noblesse*. From some of them, and especially from Comte Louis de Narbonne, valuable hints were gathered of the usages of the old court of the monarchy at grand receptions and grand court balls. M. de Talleyrand, at the request of the count, presented him to the emperor. He had returned to France when, on the proclamation of the empire, a general amnesty was announced, and he was not unwilling to hold office under the new chief of the state. His former *liaison* with Madame de Staël, though long since ended, at first prejudiced Napoleon against him; and the more so as that lady had but recently, after the death of her father, returned to France, with the idea of figuring in the arena of politics, and repeating the noisy part she had played under the Directory.

But the moment was not a propitious one for the success of her projects; she was ordered to retire to a distance of forty leagues from Paris, and as she could not be quiet there, to leave France. Joseph Bonaparte and Général Junot interceded for her, but her former *ami intime*, M. de Talleyrand, rather ungratefully refrained from adding his voice to theirs. It would have been of no more avail probably, for Napoleon intensely disliked her. "I cannot endure this woman," he said; "and mainly because I have an aversion to women who fling themselves at my head. God knows she has done this persistently enough by her flattery." Madame was therefore compelled to withdraw, and, with the train of needy *literati* she gathered around her, to take refuge at Coppet.

There Schlegel wrote the chief part of her book on Germany, of which country she herself knew but little, but where she was exceedingly disliked for the insolence and arrogance with which she repaid the friendly welcome and distinguished reception she met with when she visited it. At Coppet the chief amusement was the rehearsal and performance of plays, — Madame de Staël, of course, in the principal parts; sentimental ones in which she could talk of the love for which with little delicacy she proclaimed herself languishing, but which, alas, she never inspired. Indeed, one can scarcely imagine a more unlovable woman, in spite of Dr. Stevens's panegyric. Her disregard of the *convénances* had often put her needy lovers to the blush. Madame d'Arblay had frequently noticed the secret vexation of this same Comte Louis de Narbonne, when an exile in England, at the little restraint she put on herself.

But whatever their relations then were, they must have entirely ceased when he made the Austrian campaign with Napoleon, who gave him an appointment as officer of ordnance, and placed so much confidence in him that he entrusted him with a political mission. He was no less favoured by the empress and ladies of the court. Many errors of etiquette were rectified at his suggestion, for he was a perfect courtier of the old school. He was then about fifty, and although at that age even a man is perhaps a little *passé*, he was distinguished for his good looks, as well as for politeness and gallantry and great amiability of character.

A mysterious story was current in society concerning his birth. It was, however, never alluded to but in so low a whisper that it may be called an undercurrent. No words were necessary to explain it to those who had seen any good portrait of Louis XV. When standing in the *Grand Salon* of St. Cloud, or other of the imperial palaces, and — as then strictly required — in the full dress of the Louis Quinze period, if some elderly member of the court society of forty years back chanced then to enter, he or she might be observed to be momentarily startled, as though the apparition of the "Well-beloved" had revisited his former abode. And the resemblance was the more striking to such persons, because the count was then of about the same age as was the monarch at the time to which their recollection of him carried them back.

But again the divorce is on the *tapis*. It is the chief subject of gossip in the court, so many private interests being connected with it. Joséphine is *triste*. She strives to conceal it under forced gaiety, but is often surprised in tears. The emperor is cold, distant, gloomy, and rarely deigns to pull the ears, or pinch the nose, either of the empress or his favourites. When those impressive marks of his favour are sparingly bestowed, or cease altogether, it is a sign that there is mischief in the air, that a storm is brewing. The court being now for a short time at Fontainebleau, he rides out with only one attendant, for hours together in the forest, to meditate on the course he shall pursue. Until the death of Louis Bonaparte's son, he perhaps, had wavered, but the question has now become serious, and must be settled.

As a preliminary to the founding of a dynasty, he not only confers titles, but makes them and the domains attached to them, hereditary; sending, he says, a reinforcement of *noblesse* into the *salons* of the Faubourg St. Germain. But the Faubourg St. Germain, though it gives no cordial welcome to this new *noblesse*, these *parvenus* barons, dukes, and princes, and places them far, far beneath its own viscounts and marquises, — titles that Napoleon did not venture to create, — is yet annoyed that its ranks should be reinforced by this plebeian host. "Why should these nobles be annoyed at our elevation?" said Junot. "They boast of their ancestors; should not we rather boast of being ourselves ancestors?"

Napoleon had named Général Junot his ambassador to the court of Lisbon. Junot was unwilling to accept the post, and complained to Cambacérès of its unsuitableness. "You must now obey his majesty, you know," replied the arch-chancellor, with a slight tinge of irony in his smile. "As to your want of diplomatic ability, be frank and truthful. It is the most able diplomacy." But Junot lingered on. He was in the toils of the intriguing Caroline Murat, who was anxious that she and her husband should sit on the imperial throne, if a spent ball or other missile perchance created a vacancy. Junot was very popular with the Parisians, and as governor of the city his jurisdiction extended as far as Tours, and he had a detachment of 60,000 troops under his command.

"If anything should happen," said Caroline, "would not her dear friend Junot proclaim Joachim emperor? The capital and surrounding districts secured, the rest of France would follow." The susceptible Junot would not promise. The idea of his adored emperor's death was too terrible a one to be complacently entertained by him; yet he continued to bask in the smiles of the Grand Duchess of Berg, until scandal began to raise her voice. Then Junot received his marching orders, and took with him 30,000 men, — the army of observation assembled at Bayonne. Napoleon had declared that the House of Braganza had ceased to reign; and Junot played the part of viceroy when the royal family of Portugal fled to the Brazils. Madame Junot followed her husband to Lisbon. "His heart," she said, "was always with her and his family, though the ladies did sometimes lead him astray." Perhaps she was right. We all know that ever since our mother Eve inveigled Adam, artless man is prone to fall into the toils of artful woman. Junot took the town of Abrantès, which procured him his title, and afterwards signed with Lord Wellington the Convention of Cintra; he and his troops marching out with the honours of war. A sad blow it was to Napoleon, with whom all that was not victory was defeat. Poor Junot! His wounds, his fatigues, and his ardent temperament, ended in mental alienation and self-destruction in 1813.

After Junot left Paris, Napoleon, suspicious of the intentions of Austria, visited his Italian states. He had also a kingdom to dispose of, with which he proposed to tempt Lucien to attach himself again to his fortunes. It was Poland. Murat greatly coveted it,—the ancient Polish costume became him so well, and would allow him so much latitude for the indulgence of his taste for feathers and jewels, velvets and gold embroidery. As King of Poland he would be the most superbly dressed monarch in Europe. But Napoleon had other views.

He and Lucien met secretly at Mantua. Their interview was without result. The sacrifice of his domestic affections and political independence was required of him, and Lucien, to his credit, would not, could not, yield so far to that spirit of conquest, violence, and oppression, which increased with every succeeding year of Napoleon's reign. * It was also proposed to Lucien to give his eldest daughter in marriage to the prince of the Asturias, who had solicited the honour of being permitted to ally himself to the Bonaparte family. But this scheme, like the former, was not carried out.

During his absence the gallantries of Count Metternich formed a lively theme for court gossip. Though about thirty-five years of age, his fair complexion and flaxen hair gave him so youthful an appearance that he wore an unusual quantity of powder to bleach his flax, and make him look older. At first Pauline's beauty captivated him, and he paid assiduous court to her. But she received such homage as due to her as a matter of course, and evinced no gratitude for it. He next discovered that there was sympathy of tastes between him and Hortense, — musical tastes, that gave opportunity for tender glances, as well as words of sweet consolation when she looked sad. It was on her return to France after the death of the heir to the empire. His death was long mourned, and perhaps she found a solace in music. The "*Partant pour la Syrie,*" "*En soupirant j'ai vu naître l'aurore,*" "*Le bon Chevalier,*" etc., were composed at that time.

But a more wily lady was lying in wait to entrap

* *Mémoires du Baron de Méneval.*

him — Caroline Murat. Politics were a forbidden subject to the ladies of Napoleon's court, and so much secrecy was observed respecting the affairs of the government that they in fact were generally in ignorance concerning them. They had been informed of the continental blockade, and knew that they were rigidly to abstain from the use of every article manufactured by England or produced by her colonies; that they were to drink chicory coffee, Swiss tea, and sweeten them with raisins and beet-root. But Caroline Bonaparte had political views of her own, and M. Metternich was so much under the spell of her fascinations that had Murat behaved differently he might probably have secured him his kingdom of Naples. She was the most bitter of all the Bonaparte family in her hatred of Joséphine, of Hortense, and Eugène; and M. Metternich was able and willing to aid her schemes for placing another on the throne of France.

After the grand doings at Erfurth, where Napoleon and Alexander swore an eternal friendship, and while the former was engaged in arranging the affairs of Spain, her king having abdicated in his favour, Austria was silently arming. A rising also took place in Tyrol. King Jérôme, who indulged in very unseemly revels, and played at royalty as though his palace were the cockpit of a man-of-war, was driven from his capital by the Westphalians. Italy was wavering in her allegiance. The Pope fulminated against the mighty potentate with a bull of excommunication, and poor Prussia was doing her best to reassemble and equip a small army, ready to take advantage of any opportunity of freeing herself from the bondage to France.

Joséphine had received orders from Napoleon to follow him to Bayonne to do the honours of France to the deposed Charles IV. and Maria Louisa of Spain. On her way thither she was to make a halt at Bordeaux, and to be amiable and gracious to the Bordelais, — by way of compensating them for the losses they had suffered, and the injury done to the land and the crops, by the passage of troops for the Spanish war. And Joséphine was so amiable and gracious, as it was her habit and her nature to be, that the Bordelais were charmed with her, and expressed much regret at her departure.

But no sooner does Napoleon hear of the warlike preparations of Austria, than, leaving Spain, he traverses the country with the speed of an arrow, leaving his escort far behind. Arrived in Paris, the 23d January, 1809, he demands of M. Metternich the meaning of those armaments. His replies being evasive, a new conscription is ordered, and rapidly the emperor prepares for another campaign. The Austrians now take the initiative, pass the Inn on the 9th of April, and invade Bavaria. On the 17th Napoleon joins his army. Joséphine very earnestly entreats that, as in his former campaign, she may accompany him on his journey. He yields, and, her preparations as hastily made as before, and with one attendant, they set out for Strasburg, travelling with a swiftness, relays being in readiness, that raised astonishment in those days.

On the 20th he gains the battle of Tann; on the 21st, Abensberg; the 22d, Eckmühl; the 23d, Ratisbon; and on the 24th is successful in the two skirmishes of Peyssing and Landshutt, having taken, in these four days, 100 pieces of cannon, 40 standards, and 50,000 prisoners. On the 27th the Austrians evacuated Bavaria and the Palatinate. On the 3d of May they were defeated in an engagement at Ellersberg; on the 9th Napoleon and his victorious host were under the walls of Vienna. On the 11th the city opened her gates to him, and on the 13th he for the third time entered the Austrian capital as a conqueror.

The Austrian royal family were compelled during this war to fly from town to town. When the French entered Vienna they took refuge in Hungary. False news continually reached them of the success of the Austrian arms, and under the impression that a victory had been gained, the Archduchess Maria Louisa, on the 25th of April, thus writes to her father:

"We have heard with great pleasure that the Emperor Napoleon was himself present when he lost this battle. I hope he will also lose his head. The people hereabouts prophesy many things concerning him. They have learned from the Apocalypse that in 1809 he will die at Cologne from eating red crabs at a tavern. Though one cannot put faith in such prophecies, yet I should be heartily glad if it turned out true.

"I this moment learn that you have again won a brilliant victory. My head is quite turned with delight."

The Austrians had fought valiantly at Eckmühl and Landshutt, but were defeated on the 23d under the Archduke Charles. Better informed on the 28th, the archduchess again writes to her father:

"I cannot bring myself to believe that this news is true. I think I must have been in a dream, and that it is impossible so great a misfortune has really happened to us. Yet again I cannot doubt that God will bless your arms, and put an end to the Emperor Napoleon's iniquitous conduct.

"Constantly I am fancying that I hear the Schloss gates being opened, and I listen with hope for the arrival of good news. Often we are told of victories gained by the Viennese; but even while exulting over them, there comes, unfortunately, intelligence of the falsehood of these reports, and we sink into deeper sorrow and distress of mind.

"But we may expect all things from the goodness of God. In His mercy He has never forsaken us, and will not forsake us now. The advantage will surely turn to our armies, and the moment at last arrive when this usurper shall be humbled."*

But with the entry into Vienna the campaign was not ended. The battles of Essling on the

* From Von Helfert's "Maria Louisa."

21st of May, in which Générals Lannes and Lasalle were killed, and of Enzerodorff and Wagram, fought on the 4th and 7th of July, when from twelve to fifteen thousand men lay dead on the field, occurred before a suspension of arms took place. The conqueror then took up his residence at Schœnbrunn, where he narrowly escaped falling a victim to the knife of an assassin. The Peace of Vienna, — a peace whose conditions humbled Austria to the dust, as Tilsit had humbled Prussia, — was signed on the 14th of October.

CHAPTER XXII.

The Zenith of Glory.— The Hour of Trial.— The Guide of Napoleon's Actions.— Poor Joséphine.— La Malmaison.— The Austrian Marriage.— A Dutiful Daughter.— The Imperial Nuptials.— The New Empress.— " From Gay to Grave." — The Old Love and the New.— The King of Rome.— General Count Neipperg.— The Russian Campaign.— Consolation.— His Majesty of Rome.— Death of Joséphine.— Return of Louis XVIII.— Saint Helena.

THE great soldier is now arrived at the zenith of his glory, the emperor at the apogee of his fortunes. His empire, consisting of one hundred and thirty-three departments, extends from the coast of Brittany to the shores of Greece, and from the Tagus to the Elbe. His power has reached a height, his prosperity a degree of splendour, to which, in the world's history, fortune has rarely elevated any man. A short halt is made on the summit of this glory and grandeur, then, rapidly as he climbed it, more rapidly still he is destined to descend.

The long-menaced divorce — from different motives, the thought uppermost in the hearts of all who surround him — is at length finally determined upon. Poor Joséphine! The evil day is not come suddenly upon her; yet she has gone on hoping that it might be averted, and fully resolved that the initiative step, "*le parti noble*," as Fouché urged, should never be taken by her. And Napoleon seems to shrink from taking it, so long has he been nerving himself to speak the fatal word. But at last it is uttered, and the prelude is: "Joséphine, *ma bonne* Joséphine; you know how I have loved you."

It was the evening of the 30th of November. The guests who had dined with them, chiefly his vassal kings and grand dukes, — Paris being thronged with these German grandees, — had taken their departure. They were alone; Napoleon for some moments was apparently buried in thought; she, sorrowful and silent. For "I knew," she said, when she afterwards spoke of this scene, "that the hour of my trial had arrived. I read in his countenance the struggle that was passing in his soul. "Joséphine," he repeated, taking her hand and pressing it to his heart, "my destiny is more powerful than my will. My dearest affections must be sacrificed to the interests of France."

"Say no more," she exclaimed. "I understand, I expected it." Disregarding her sobs and tears, he continued, "I suffer perhaps even more than you. But the wants, the interests, of my people have ever guided my actions. They ask of me a guarantee of the stability of that throne on which they and Providence have placed me — Joséphine, we must separate."

Joséphine was carried insensible to her chamber. On recovering consciousness she became aware that the hand that clasped hers was her daughter's. Corvisart, the emperor's physician, was seated beside her, and at the foot of her couch, anxiously gazing upon her, stood Napoleon. Their eyes met, but Joséphine's eyelids drooped under his fixed and earnest look. When she again ventured to raise them he was gone. "I thought she was dead," he afterwards said to Duroc.

Not until a fortnight after, the 15th of December, was the official part of the drama played out — she being compelled in the interval to attend a *Te Deum* at Notre-Dame, and a grand *fête* in celebration of the Peace of Vienna. A family council, attended by the arch-chancellor of the empire, Cambacérès, and the secretaries of state, then assembled at the Tuileries. The Queen of Naples, Caroline Murat, had come to Paris expressly for the pleasure of assisting at this council. Eugène, too, was summoned from his vice-regal duties to perform the painful one which now devolved upon him as arch-chancellor of state. Hortense accompanied her mother. Both were dressed in black satin, and wore no jewels. Poor Joséphine's voice faltered, her eyes filled with tears, and courage wholly failed her after reading a few sentences of the statement concocted for her. It expressed her conviction that the sacrifice she was about to make, in separating herself from her dear husband — whose praises filled a long paragraph — was necessary for the welfare and happiness of France.

Having got thus far, the paper dropped from her hands. Eugène picked it up and read it to the end. (It appears in the *Moniteur* as spoken by her.) Napoleon then retired to Trianon, Joséphine to La Malmaison, while the brilliant Queen of Naples did the honours of the Tuileries to the distinguished visitors who this winter thronged to the court of the empire. A *Sénatus-Consulte* declared the civil marriage dissolved. It had taken place in the presence of Barras, who was then the head of the government, and was of course as valid as any other marriage of the same period. The religious tie was annulled, "after some explanations," by the clerical officials of the chancery of the archbishopric of Paris.

When, after the divorce, Joséphine retired to La Malmaison, that residence became of peculiar interest to the French people. Notwithstanding that her divorce was represented as required by the nation, the sympathy of the nation was with her. Popular feeling in Paris was also strong in her favour, and many a tear had responded in France to the words uttered by Prince Eugène at the time of the separation. He lost something of his popularity by consenting to utter them. But Joséphine may have preferred his aid on so painful an occasion — for Eugène felt deeply for her — to that of one who was unconnected with and indifferent to her great humiliation.

Napoleon shut himself up at Trianon for a week's sorrowing widowhood. When he returned to the world, he is said to have been struck by the air of loneliness that Joséphine's absence produced at the Tuileries. However, all the continental potentates who had daughters or nieces to marry were anxious to enable him to fill the void in his palace. The indirect offer of the Russian Grand Duchess Anne, a mere child, was probably not made in sincerity. But Austria was intriguing on all sides to turn his thoughts towards her archduchess. Singular that there should have been any disposition on the part of the Emperor Francis to give France another "Autrichienne," and as a wife to the man who had three times entered Vienna as a conqueror, and compelled him to renounce his title of Emperor of Germany.

But German princesses, and indeed, princesses generally, were born but to be disposed of as best suited the political views of the sovereigns whose property they were.

Napoleon was beset with stratagems devised by M. Metternich and the agents he employed in order to bring about the Austrian marriage. It was even mysteriously whispered in his ear by an unknown individual, at one of the Princesse Borghèse's receptions, that Maria Lousia was at his service.* The mysterious personage was a Comte Laborde, a returned emigrant, who was to be disowned by the Austrian government should his communication be ill received; for both Russian and Saxon offers were then under the great man's consideration. The untruth of the account given in the Metternich memoirs, of the part Joséphine, Eugène, and Hortense are said to have played in this matrimonial arrangement, must strike every one most forcibly. It is so utterly at variance with every other statement, whether favourable or otherwise to Joséphine, and so entirely opposed to what is well known of her character and feelings, that on reading it one is reminded of what M. de Talleyrand said of Count Metternich — "*Il ment toujours, mais ne trompe jamais.*" The political agent, Gentz, wrote something to the same effect, in February, 1810, and with reference to this marriage.

The marriage of a daughter of the Cæsars with a *parvenu* potentate was an exceptional event; but for other reasons, in this case, than his want of royal quarterings, Maria Louisa's feeling on the subject was casually asked. She replied, like a dutiful German maiden, that her father's will was hers. Maréchal Berthier, Prince of Neufchatel and Wagram, made the formal demand of the hand of the archduchess. He had with him the portrait of Napoleon set in diamonds. This was presented

* See "*Mémoires et Anecdotes,*" *par* Lombard de Langres.

to Maria Louisa, who, glancing at it, said, "*qu'il n'etait pas mal.*" The imperial bride left Vienna on the 13th of March, 1810 — having been married by proxy on the 11th — the Archduke Charles representing Napoleon. On the 27th she arrived at Compiègne to meet, as her husband, the "usurper," whose humiliation she had prayed for but a few months before, and whose death she had expressed her desire to hear of.

At St. Cloud on the 1st of April the civil marriage took place. On the following day the benediction was pronounced by Cardinal Fesch, in the chapel of the Louvre, and with all possible pomp and magnificence, both of the Roman Catholic Church, and the *cortège* of the imperial bride and bridegroom. The same bridal presents were made by Napoleon to his new empress as were given by Louis XV. to Marie Antoinette. The same illuminations and festivities, public and private, followed the inauspicious event. And chance carried out the parallel so far that they terminated in that fearful calamity, the fire which destroyed the ball-room at Prince Schwartzenberg's *fête*, by which his wife lost her life and many persons were seriously injured. It was regarded as an ill omen, bringing back the memory of that similar catastrophe with which the nuptial *fêtes* of Louis XVI. and the unfortunate Marie Antoinette concluded.

The court of the empire may be said to have

ended with the repudiation of the Empress Joséphine. Maria Louisa was incapable of replacing her; Joséphine was so thoroughly French, so perfectly a woman of the world, and of the society she lived in. Everything was new to Maria Louisa. Even the splendours with which Napoleon surrounded her she was so entirely unused to that her natural timidity, stiffness, and reserve were increased on finding herself in a court so unlike the staid, homely one with which she had any acquaintance. She formed no intimacy with any lady at the court except Général Lannes's widow, the Duchesse de Montebello.

German phlegm and French gaiety could not assimilate. The *dames du palais* wearied of their occupation: there was no longer any lively badinage, as in the days of Joséphine; no breakfasts for the *cercle intime*, including a favourite cavalier or two; no *spirituelle causerie*, or occasionally a little whispered scandal. Maria Louisa understood none of these things. Napoleon surrounded her with the youngest and gayest at the court; but the younger and gayer they were, the more they held aloof from her, — her gravity of manner and attachment to the etiquette and formal restraint of the court she was brought up in casting a damp on the spirits of the liveliest.

Maria Louisa was then eighteen, but beautiful only with what the French term "*la beauté du diable*," or the freshness of youth. Her face was plain, the Kalmuck expression with the Hapsburg mouth. She was of the middle height. Her complexion was fresh rather than fair, and she had a high colour, blue eyes, very light golden hair, and an abundance of it. Her bust and shoulders were more fully developed than is usual at her age, being quite *à la* Rubens. Yet her arms were thin and small, and out of proportion. And in the *tout ensemble* of her person there was something inharmonious, which a total want of grace made more conspicuous.

As soon as possible after her arrival, she was put into the hands of court milliners and dressmakers; for French fashions travelled slowly then to the German courts, and were even then very partially adopted. Music, drawing, and dancing masters were also engaged, the aid of the latter being especially needed. M. Metternich urged her not to attempt to dance at court balls until she could dance with ease and grace. Writing to his wife respecting the new empress, he says (at least in his memoirs there is a letter to that effect, though one would suppose his wife was as well informed on the subject as himself): "She is rather ugly than pretty (*plutôt laide que jolie*); but she has a good figure, and when she is better dressed, and has had a few dancing lessons, she will do very well, as she goes with a desire to please."

And she, at least, pleased Napoleon in some respects. Yet he did not find in her the consoling friend to whom, when domestic or other vexations troubled or thwarted him, he could turn, as he frequently did to Joséphine, and confide a part of them to her. Advice he looked not for; but ready sympathy that soothed his mind he was always sure of. With Maria Louisa he feared to appear *triste*. She might reveal his perplexities to her father, and the Austrian court would have the satisfaction of knowing that the tide of his prosperity was on the turn. For in the Spanish and Portuguese war — in which the French were so vigorously resisted — his best troops were being slain by tens of thousands, and the levying of the conscription was thinning the agricultural population and carrying sorrow and mourning into many once happy peasant homes.

On the 20th of March, 1811, a salute of twenty-one guns proclaimed the birth of an heir to the empire. He received at his birth the title of King of Rome, — the Pope having been deprived of his temporal power and detained prisoner in France. *Fêtes*, exceeding in expensiveness, if not outrivalling in magnificence, all that hitherto have been given, celebrate the birth of this poor infant. In the midst of these noisy demonstrations — for of real joy there is little — a note of warning comes from the North. Alexander abandons the continental blockade, and renews his relations with England; preparations on both sides are made for war. "Fate is urging on the Russians!" exclaims

Napoleon, arrogantly. "Let, then, their destiny be accomplished!"

On the 9th of May, 1812, the emperor and empress set out for Dresden, the rendezvous of the confederate kings and princes of the Rhine. Maria Louisa meets her family there. There, too, she meets for the first time General Count Neipperg, who is in the suite of the Emperor of Austria, and to whom she addresses some gracious words in acknowledgment of his attentions to her. During the visit she made with her family to Prague — when Napoleon, leaving Dresden, set out on his ill-fated Russian expedition — Count Neipperg was appointed to attend on her. Thus began that intimacy by which — favoured by subsequent events — he obtained unbounded influence over her, and eventually became her husband.

All was mirth and gaiety at this conference of sovereign princes, the allies of the despot, but even then preparing to unite their forces and form a hostile alliance against him. An army of 500,000 men surrounded the charming capital of Saxony, waiting the return of Comte Louis de Narbonne's mission to Wilna to confer with the Emperor Alexander. *En attendant, fête* succeeded *fête*. The *troupe* of the Théâtre Français was summoned to Dresden, and Napoleon there fulfilled his promise to Talma and Mdlle. Mars, that they should perform before a *parterre* of kings.

The great tragic actress, Mdlle. Georges, had

Battle of Friedland.

Photo-etching after the Painting by Horace Vernet.

been carried off from the scene of her triumphs some fews years before, by a Russian prince, to St. Petersburg, where she lived in a style of such magnificence that her equipages rivalled in splendour those of the imperial family. But she proved herself a true Frenchwoman, when, after the defeat of Napoleon, she refused to obey the general order to illuminate. The emperor's command was alike unavailing, and her hôtel remained dark, — representing a house of mourning amidst the national rejoicing.

On the return of Comte Louis from his fruitless mission, the confederate princes dispersed, and Napoleon and his army began their march towards Moscow. The horrors, the sufferings, of that terrible campaign are surely unparalleled in military history. Comte de Ségur's narrative of the retreat of the remnant of that host, composed of the flower of the nation, is one of the most harrowing tales of human misery, despair, fortitude, acts of frightful cruelty, rare humanity, and desperate courage, that ever was penned. A whole nation is plunged into deepest sorrow; black seems the national colour; for where, from one end of France to the other, is there a household that mourns not the miserable death of husband, brother, or son, amidst the snows and frosts of the barren steppes or in the icy streams of Russia?

And this fearful calamity is the result of one

man's overweening spirit of domination and military ambition. But the nation has its consolation. He is not dead, as has been reported. And not only has he survived when all around were perishing, — becoming "demoralised," for, as he said, "he had seen his bravest generals weep like children from utter helplessness under the physical suffering and mental anguish they were enduring," — but he assures his people that "his health is excellent."

It was during the Russian campaign, when no tidings of the army were allowed to reach Paris, and fears of the worst agitated every breast, that Maria Louisa failed most to comprehend the duties of her position. She evinced no sympathy with the families of the absent generals. Her feeling towards them, as an Austrian, was antipathetic, and strict German etiquette widened the distance between them. It was from the true empress, Joséphine, that messages of sympathy and consolation came to them. Private letters were intercepted, and every precaution taken to prevent a true account of the reverses, and dismal prospects of the grand army reaching the capital. But the friendship of the Comte de Ségur for Joséphine led him to take advantage of every opportunity of transmitting intelligence, — sad intelligence, indeed, yet sometimes softened by a ray of hope — which Joséphine hastens to impart to her afflicted friends.

Poor Maria Louisa was but little concerned with the troubles of the nation. She took her daily music lesson, worked calmly enough at her tapestry-frame, and went out for an hour's ride on a jog-trot pony. Sometimes she saw her child; but showed but little affection for him, and she is said to have worn so enormous a plume of feathers — in imitation probably of Marie Antoinette — that his majesty of Rome was frightened at her, and clung firmly to his *gouvernante*, Madame de Montebello.

But the emperor returns to his people. He has not yet had enough of war. Conciliation is with him out of the question. Europe rises in arms against him. The campaigns of 1813-14 follow. Victory clings to him, but forsakes his generals. His orders to those he has left at the head of affairs in Paris are disobeyed. M. de Talleyrand chooses to stay there, to play a part he conceives to be more advantageous to his interests. He welcomes the allied sovereigns, and plays the host to the invaders of France. To do this so effectually he is greatly indebted to one of his fair friends,* and by stratagem is *forcibly* prevented from leaving the city.

The abdication follows. The emperor is allowed, temporarily, to retire to Elba, where he arrives on the 3d of May, 1814. On the 2d of June, Joséphine, who had consented to see Lord Cathcart on

* See *Mémoires de la Duchesse d'Abrantès*.

that morning, died suddenly. She was walking with the Duchesse d'Abrantès in the gardens of La Malmaison on the previous day. The duchess was to have presented Lord Cathcart, who, with some officers of his staff, was quartered in her hôtel. Extreme concern for the fate of Napoleon, and intense indignation at the publication in the papers of infamous libels on Hortense, had so much excited her that the duchess advised her to seek calmness of mind in rest and the quietude of her chamber. And rest she found there, but it was rest in the sleep of death.

The Bourbons were again inflicted on France. But King Tartuffe did not quite realise the expectations of M. de Talleyrand, — active though he had been in bringing him back to a people who had no wish that he should reign over them. Louis XVIII. had disposed of, to his partisans who were with him in exile, all the places and posts in the government, even before he had any sure hope of returning to France as its sovereign. It was thus he kept them about him. There was money in abundance, too, in the vaults of the Louvre to divide amongst his family and followers; yet M. de Talleyrand declared, soon after Louis's return, that he had not yet been able to obtain a prefecture even for the Remusats, * to whom he was so greatly indebted for his forced detention in Paris.

* *Mémoires du Baron de Méneval.*

But what a scuffle ensues amongst these people when it is anounced that the exile of Elba has landed in France! How soon the Congress is dissolved! Paris is so far herself again that she resounds with cries of " *Vive l'Empereur!* " But short and fleeting is this revival of the empire; Waterloo is fought; the great drama played out, and its hero spends the remnant of his days on that rock in the midst of a wide waste of waters — the dreary rock of Saint Helena!

THE END.

INDEX

Adélaïde, Madame, influence of, I., 21, at Bellevue, 44, cupidity of, 63.
Alexander makes warlike preparations, II., 379.
Amiens, treaty with, II., 279.
Amnesty, proclamation of, II., 59, revocation of, *ib.*
Amusements of the court, I., 101.
Arnauld, Sophie, musical talent of, I., 78.
Arras, camp at, II., 314.
Assembly of Notables, convocation of, I., 353.
Auerstadt, victory at, II., 354.
Augereau, Général, in Paris, II., 203, promotion of, 204.
Austerlitz, battle of, II., 347.
Balsamo, Joseph, sketch of, I., 336, trial of, 337, exile of, 340; practices of, II., 73.
Barnave, his friendly attitude toward Marie Antoinette, II., 136.
Barras, Général de, appointment of, II., 181, manners of, 192, influence of Madame de Staël upon, 203, character of, 210, his intimacy with Madame Tallien, 211, his life at the Luxembourg, 213, cupidity of, 247, retirement of, 248.
Bastille, storming of the, II., 42, demolition of the, 46.
Beauharnais, Eugène de, appointment of, II., 343, marriage of, 348, his sentiments on marriage of Joséphine, 373.
Beaumarchais, his influence over Louis XVI., I., 175, enterprises of, 177, literary productions of, 304, condemnation of play of, 306, personal appearance of, 308, ability of, 309, complications in presenting a play of, 312, anecdote of, 314, triumph of, 318, arrest of, 322, release and second triumph of, 323, enmity of Mirabeau against, 325.
Beaumont, Monsieur de, fanaticism of, I., 149.

Beauvais, Abbé de, sermon of, I., 2.
Bellevue, château de, description of the, I., 43.
Bernadotte, Général, embassy of, II., 203.
Besenval, Baron de, his interview with Marie Antoinette, I., 165; command bestowed upon, II., 37.
Boëhmer, concern in diamond necklace of, I., 330.
Bonaparte, Caroline, becomes Grande Duchesse of Berg, II., 349, intrigues of, 365.
Bonaparte, Elisa, kingdoms bestowed upon, II., 344.
Bonaparte Family, banishment of the, II., 165, fortunes of the, 184, their dislike of Joséphine, 205, ambition of the, 244.
Bonaparte, Joseph, his advice to Napoleon, II., 313, declines crown of Lombardy, 334, made King of Naples, 348.
Bonaparte, Louis, marriage of, II., 286, made King of Holland, 348.
Bonaparte, Lucien, departs to Italy, II., 314, his interview with Napoleon, 363.
Bonaparte, Madame Mère, sketch of, II., 350.
Bonaparte, Napoleon, at Brienne, I., 300; his criticism of Louis XVI., II., 141, at Ajaccio, 165, at Toulon, *ib.*, meets Duroc and Junot, 167, arrest of, 170, declines appointment, 172, personal appearance of, 174, his friendship with Junot, 176, at the Tuileries, 183, made commander-in-chief, *ib.*, change in fortune of, 186, meets Joséphine, 187, marriage of, 190, early successes of, 193, his address to army, 195, his conquests in Italy, *ib.*, arrogance of, 196, reported conversation of, 198, portrait of, 201, signs treaty of Campo-Formio, 204, at Turin, 206, received by Directory, 223, goes to Egypt, 229, victories in Egypt, 245, returns to France, 246, his coldness toward Joséphine, 250, his installation at Tuileries, 255, installation banquet of, 259, his negotiations with England, 265, his victories in Austria, 266, superstition of, 267, triumphal entry into Paris of, 269, favors emigrants, 271, his presentation of swords and pistols to soldiers, 272, promotes Junot, 274, his policy toward Rome, 277, signs Peace of Lunéville, 279, made First Consul for life, 283, projects of, 290, at St. Cloud, 291, at La Malmaison, *ib.*, home life of, 293, his trouble with England, 304, visits Normandy and Belgium, 305, at the theatre, 310, plans for coronation of,

311, his grief at execution of Duc d'Enghien, 318, receives proposal of being made emperor, *ib.*, distributes crosses, 319, receives Pope, 326, consecration of marriage of, 327, coronation of, 329, coronation at Milan, 342, various appointments by, 343, receives Lucca and Genoa, 344, returns to Paris, 346, battle of Austerlitz, 347, new honors bestowed upon, 348, bestows kingdoms upon family, *ib.*, victories of Auerstadt and Jena, 354, result of campaign in Prussia, 355, visits tomb of Frederick the Great, 356, returns to Paris, *ib.*, titles conferred by, 361, his interview with Lucien, 363, perplexities of, 366, new victories of, 367, meets Maria Louisa, *ib.*, at Schoenbrunn, 369, at zenith of glory, 370, proposes divorce, 372, retires to Trianon, 373, projects for new marriage of, 376, second marriage of, 376, birth of King of Rome, 379, begins Russian campaign, 381, receives allied sovereigns, 383, abdication of, *ib.*

Boucher, paintings of, I., 57.

Bouilly, operetta of, II., 241.

Bréteuil, Monsieur de, characterisation of, I., 341; influence of, II., 68.

Broglie, at the beginning of revolution, II., 37.

Cadoudal, Georges, conspiracy of, II., 317.

Cagliostro, see Joseph Balsamo.

Calendar, promulgation of new, II., 151.

Calonne, M. de, declining days of ministry of, I., 350, anecdote of, 352, resignation of, 353.

Cambacérès, appointment of, II., 337, habits of, 340.

Campan, Madame, authenticity of history by, I., 329; latter days of, II., 192.

Carnival of 1775, description of the, I., 105, of 1776–77, 154.

Carnot, dissatisfaction of, II., 280.

Cazotte, prophecies of, II., 72, fate of, 75.

Chartres, Duc de, his attitude toward Louis XVI., I., 100, his enmity toward Marie Antoinette, 113, conduct of, 259.

Chartres, Duchesse de, anecdote of, I., 83, vanity of, 100.

Chenier, Joseph, play written by, II., 111.

Choiseul, Duc de, attempts at reinstallation of, I., 24, suspicions against, 26, at Chanteloup, 27, his return to court, 28, his interview with Marie Antoinette, 127.

Clotilde, Madame, marriage festivities of, I., 109, affectionate disposition of, 131.
Compiègne, ball at, I., 129.
Concordat, proclamation of the, II., 279.
Condorcet, Madame de, *salon* of, I., 145.
Contat, Louise, *début* of, I., 217; brilliancy of, II., 243.
Convention, tactics of the, II., 181.
Corday, Charlotte, deed of, II., 152, death of, 153.
Corn, monopoly of, I., 107.
Coronation of Louis XVI., proposals concerning, I., 115, description of, 122, *fêtes* after, 128.
Court, French, condition of during reign of Louis XV., I., 2; reverses created by revolution in, II., 66, extravagances of, 300.
Crown, description of the, I., 121.
D'Aiguillon, Duc, concessions made by, I., 22, resignation of, 65.
D'Angoulême, Duc, birth of, I., 133.
Danton, execution of, II., 160.
D'Artois, Comte, his attitude toward Louis XVI., I., 97; influence of, II., 12.
D'Artois, Comtesse, joy at birth of son of, I., 133.
David, paintings by, II., 109.
Dazincourt, reputation of, I., 328.
Deffand, Marquise du, *salon* of, I., 136.
D'Enghien, Duc, execution of, II., 318.
D'Éon, sketch of, I., 232, adventures of, 236.
Desmoulins, Camille, first appearance of, II., 33, wife of, 146, cowardice of, 148, execution of, 161.
Diamond necklace, complications of the, I., 328.
Diderot, at the *salons*, I., 139.
Du Barry, Madame, retirement of, I., 4, *bon mot* of, 75, at the theatre, 218, visited by Emperor Joseph, 219.
Dumas, Général Alexandre, order sent to, II., 181.
Dumouriez, Général, defection of, II., 152.
Duroc, meets Napoleon, II., 167.
Elisabeth, Madame, at Versailles, I., 132; execution of, II., 160.
Emigrants, return of the, II., 180.
Emigration of the nobles, II., 49, of the king's aunts, 134.
Fersen, Count, his infatuation for Marie Antoinette, I., 270,

reception at court, 272, his return to France, 348; his influence over Marie Antoinette, II., 68.

Fesch, Abbé, performs marriage ceremony of Napoleon and Joséphine, II., 327.

Fêtes, after coronation of Louis XVI., I., 128, on farewell to Joseph, 227, on birth of dauphin, 282; on anniversary of taking of the Bastille, II., 124.

Fouché, ability of, II., 262, his friendship for Joséphine, 263.

Franklin, Benjamin, his visit to Paris, I., 178, anecdote of, 181, his regard for Voltaire, 249.

French Revolution, horrors of the, II., 2, first effects of the, 26, progress of the, 60, fashions of the, 99, sacrifices caused by the, 101, its influence upon art, 108, reaction upon the nation of the, 178.

Genlis, Madame de, reputation of, I., 214, appointment of, 294; famous brooch of, II., 102, anecdote of, 218.

Geoffrin, Madame, *salon* of, I., 134.

Georges, Mdlle., dramatic talent of, II., 294, patriotism of, 381.

Gérard, sketch of, II., 4.

Girodet, artistic ability of, II., 110.

Gironde, rise of the, II., 138, guillotining of members of the, 158.

Gluck, operas of, I., 72, negotiations with, 75, in Paris, 77, triumph of, 82, jealousy of, 89, return from Germany of, 243.

Goldoni, position of, I., 132.

Grammont, Duchesse de, ambition of, I., 27.

Grétry, talent of, I., 73, 74, popularity of, 92.

Guéménée, Princesse de, appointment of, I., 266, misfortunes of, 289.

Guillotin, Doctor, invention of, II., 117.

Guimard, Mademoiselle, anecdote of, I., 223.

Hatzfeld, Madame, Napoleon's opinion of, II., 356.

Head-dress, introduced by Marie Antoinette, I., 40, curious anecdote of, 258.

Hoche, Général, sketch of life of, II., 168.

Jacobin Club, rise of the, II., 62.

Jena, victory of, II., 354.

Jesuits, their sentiments towards Louis XVI., I., 24.

Joseph, Emperor, his visit to Paris, I., 192, his sentiments toward the royal family, 195, personal appearance of, 200, characterisation of, 202, suspicions against, 208, proposed visit to America of, 210, visits Madame du Barry, 219, effect of visit of, 228, his advice to Marie Antoinette, 230, claims of, 240; death of, II., 100.

Joséphine de Beauharnais, personal appearance of, II., 188, suitors of, 190, marriage to Napoleon of, *ib.*, children of, 191, her popularity in Italy, 200, in Paris, 208, beauty of, 226, social eminence attained by, 231, receptions given by, 238, celebrities entertained by, 239, coldness of Napoleon toward, 250, at the Tuileries, 256, her life at La Malmaison, 292, accomplishments of, *ib.*, visited by Pauline Bonaparte, 300, receptions at St. Cloud by, 307, religious marriage of, 327, coronation of, 330, accompanies Napoleon to Milan, 335, goes to Munich, 348, to Bayonne, 366, divorce proposed to, 372, retires to La Malmaison, 373, her interest in Napoleon's welfare, 382, death of, 384.

Junot, Général, his first meeting with Napoleon, II., 167, early life of, 171, his infatuation for Pauline Bonaparte, 175, made commandant of Paris, 273, marriage of, 277, reform instigated by, 315, new appointment of, 336, sent to Lisbon, 361, scandal concerning, 362, takes Abrantès, 363, unhappy end of life of, *ib.*

Jussieu, M. Laurent de, at Versailles, I., 65.

La Fayette, Marquis de, his visit to Versailles, I., 238, prophecy of, 326; at the National Assembly, II., 25, receives key of Bastille, 46, dislike incurred by, 93, at Versailles, 95, oath taken by, 130, efforts of, 139, Marie Antoinette's dislike of, 142, release from imprisonment of, 205.

Lamballe, Princesse de, position bestowed upon, I., 147, jealousy of, 157, ambitious hopes of, 293; at the Tuileries, II., 106, death of, 148.

Langlès, Monsieur, anecdote of, II., 321.

Larivée, in opera, I., 79.

Launay, Marquis de, at the attack of the Bastille, II., 44, death of, 45.

Lebrun, Madame, anecdote of, I., 350.

Le Clerc, Général, effect of his death upon France, II., 296.

Legion of Honor, distribution of crosses of the, II., 319.

Legislative Assembly, first session of the, II., 136.

Léonard, his skill as hairdresser, I., 120, favor bestowed upon, 205.
Loménie, de Brienne, ambition of, I., 356, appointment of, 357, becomes cardinal, 359.
Louis XV., illness of, I., 3, death of, 4, dignity of, 15.
Louis XVI., receives news of death of Louis XV., I., 7, at Marly, 9, tastes of, 12, entrance into Paris of, 14, characterisation of, 16, presents the Petit Trianon to Marie Antoinette, 30, his hatred of Abbé Vermond, 36, new code of, 50, his lack of appreciation of art, 58, examines papers of Louis XV., 61, appoints new cabinet, 66, recalls old Parliament, 68, family quarrels of, 95, his action regarding corn monopoly, 107, preparations for coronation of, 115, his journey to Rheims, 122, description of coronation of, 123, receives Order of Saint Esprit, 126, dismisses Turgot, 152, famous "*bon mot*" of, 157, friendly assistance rendered to Americans by, 175, his gifts to his brothers, 185, signs treaty with United States, 239, his attitude toward Voltaire, 246, receives the Duc de Chartres, 261, statue in Philadelphia of, 273, his prejudices against Austria, 280, his delight at birth of dauphin, 281, his criticism of Beaumarchais, 306, resentment toward Beaumarchais of, 321, anecdote of, 345, assembles Notables, 353; at the States General, II., 8, perplexities of, 20, interview granted by, 22, concessions made by, 29, indignation against, on Necker's dismissal, 36, after the attack of the Bastille, 48, fatal mistake of, 50, receives tricoloured cockade, 53, fears of, 72, his fondness for the chase, 82, interviews women at Versailles, 92, leaves Versailles, 97, at the Tuileries, 105, at *fête* of anniversary of taking of the Bastille, 129, flight and arrest of, 135, dismisses Girondin ministry, 138, shameful concessions of, 140, condemnation and execution of, 152.
Louis, Comte de Narbonne, anecdote of, II., 359.
Louise, Sister, her indignation against Louis XVI., I., 69, her life at the convent, 132.
Luxembourg, life at the palace of the, II., 214.
Machault, M. de, Louis's sentiments toward, I., 19.
Maillard, Stanislaus, heads attack on Versailles, II., 88, 91.
Mailly, Duchesse de, resignation of, I., 169.

Malesherbes, M. Lamoignon de, appointment of, I., 66, influence over Louis XVI. of, 115.

Malmaison, La, home life of Napoleon at, II., 293.

Marat, at beginning of the revolution, II., 40, death of, 152.

Maria Louisa, marriage of, II., 376, characterisation of, 377, birth of son of, 379, meets Count Neipperg, 380, stolidity of, 382.

Maria Theresa, political intrigues of, I., 23, motherly counsels of, 40, desires the coronation of Marie Antoinette, 118, political advice of, 211, demands made upon Louis by, 240, her disappointment at birth of daughter of Marie Antoinette, 265, death of, 277, characterisation of, 278.

Marie Antoinette, her influence over Louis XVI., I., 21, folly of, 22, delight with Petit Trianon, 30, influence of Abbé Vermond upon, 35, personal appearance of, 38, at La Muette, 45, dress of, 46, her disregard of etiquette, 48, her extravagance, 64, influence at court of, 66, at the opera, 79, domestic quarrels of, 95, scandals against, 98, amusements of, 102, charges brought against, 106, receives Maximilian at court, 111, irritates Duc de Chartres, 113, preparations for attending coronation, 119, her journey to Rheims, 122, her interview with M. de Choiseul, 127, at Compiègne, 129, her enmity against M. Turgot, 147, introduces sledging into Paris, 154, imprudence of, 164, her interview with Besenval, 166, interview held with Comte de Périgord, 171, gambling propensities of, 186, political influence of, 212, her dislike of Madame du Barry, 218, in amateur theatricals, 226, effect of Joseph's visit upon, 228, advice given her by Joseph, 230, reproved by Maria Theresa, 240, her sentiments toward Voltaire, 248, her aversion for the Duc de Chartres, 262, birth of her daughter, 264, imprudence of, 268, baptism of Madame Royale, 269, her sentiments toward Count Fersen, 271, receives news of death of Maria Theresa, 277, birth of son of, 281, luxurious appointments of, 297, birth of second son of, 327, complications of diamond necklace, 328, effect of affair of necklace upon her reputation, 329, her intimacy with Count Fersen, 347, power of, 356, unpopularity of, 360; on 5th of May, II., 5, death of dauphin, 17, assurance of, 29, makes preparations for flight, 49, influenced by Count Fersen, 68, at a famous banquet, 84, various plans for her flight, 85, her terror at the attack of Versailles, 93, leaves Versailles, 97, her interview with Mirabeau, 119, at *fête* of the Federation, 132, flight and arrest of, 135, her correspondence with Count Fersen, 137, her dislike of La Fayette, 142, obstinacy of, 143, at the attack upon the Tuileries, 145, in the conciergerie, 154, trial of, 155, execution of, 157.

Marmontel, talents of, I., 75, his estimation of Gluck, 87, anecdote of, 130.

Maupeou, policy of, I., 67.

Maurepas, Comte de, recalled to court, I., 21, characterisation of, 51, his influence over Louis XVI., 54, anecdote of, 58, counsels of, 65, policy of, 70, his attitude toward M. Necker, 153, death of, 275.

Maximilian, his visit to Versailles, I., 109.

Melito, M. de, Napoleon's fondness for, II., 199.

Meromesnil, M. de, reinstallation of, I., 69.

Mesmer, practices of, II., 73.

Metternich, Count, scandals against, II., 364, his description of Maria Louisa, 378.

Mirabeau, anecdote of, I., 325; personal appearance of, II., 8, 121, private life of, 80, his interview with Marie Antoinette, 119, suspicions against, 123, death of, 134.

Montesson, M. de, sketch of life of, II., 289.

Moreau, ambitious schemes of, II., 317.

Motte, Comtesse de la, see Jeanne Saint-Rémy.

Mozart, reception in Paris of, I., 203.

Murat, appointment of, II., 343, receives Berg, 349.

Music in Paris, state of, I., 72.

Muy, Comte de, appointment of, I., 66.

National Assembly, convocation of the, II., 16, members of the, 23, decrees of the, 60, demands of the, 85, debates of the, 117, announcement of the, 135.

National Convention, act of the, II., 150.

Navy, French, victory of, I., 257, second engagement of, 259.

Necker, Madame, *salon* of, I., 138, receives Franklin, 181.

Necker, Monsieur, pamphlet issued by, I., 108, characterisation of, 141, his attacks on M. Turgot, 146, entrance into power of, 152, resignation of, 275, marriage of daughter of, 349, recalled to France, 360; advice of, II., 5, at the assembly, 11, sentiments of, 19, resignation of, 24, dismissal of, 29, recall of, 55, proclaims amnesty, 59, final resignation and flight of, 133.

Neipperg, Count, meets Maria Louisa, II., 380.

Nelson, victory of, II., 347.

Noailles, Madame de, anecdote of, I., 102.

Orléans, Duc d', in England, I., 103; arrest and execution of, II., 159.

Pamphlets against Marie Antoinette, I., 99.

Paoli, Général, in Corsica, II., 164.

Paris, disturbances in, I., 107; at beginning of revolution, II., 27, excitement in, on Necker's dismissal, 35, insurrection at, 39, confusion at, 65, tumultuous scenes in, 71, its life and manners under the directorate, 216.

Parliament, reinstatement of, I., 67.

Peace of Lunéville, II., 279.

Peace of Tilsit, II., 355.

Peace of Vienna, II., 368.

Périgord, Comte de, his interview with Marie Antoinette, I., 171.

Permon, Madame de, receives Bonaparte, II., 173.

Pétion, appointment of, II., 139.

Piccini, operas of, I., 72, triumph of, 91, generous conduct of, 245.

Pichegru, Général, suspicions against, II., 317.

Polignac, Comtesse Jules de, anecdote of, I., 168, influence of, 285, appointment of, 290, her intimacy with M. de Vaudreuil, 291.

Pope Pius VII., entrance into France of, II., 326.

Provence, Comte de, his enmity toward Marie Antoinette, I., 49, perfidy of, 62, characterisation of, 93, extravagance of, 99; envious policy of, II., 50.

Récamier, Madame, beauty of, II., 249.

Rheims, preparations for coronation at, I., 115.

Robespierre, at the National Assembly, II., 118, his denouncement of Girondins, 152, prominence of, 159, attempted assassination of, 161, execution of, 163.

Robespierre, Maximilian, characterisation of, II., 168.

Roederer, Monsieur, at the attack of the Tuileries, II., 145.

Rohan, Cardinal de, arrest of, I., 328, trial of, 338, exile of, 340.
Roland, Madame, execution of, II., 159.
Rome, King of, birth of, II., 379.
Rousseau, his opinion of Gluck, I., 76, anecdote of, 86, death of, 255.
Royal Academy of Music in Paris, I., 72.
Saint-Germain, Comte de, reforms introduced by, I., 161.
Saint-Rémy Valois, Jeanne, her complicity in affair of diamond necklace, I., 332, arrest and punishment of, 338.
Sainval, Madame, anecdote of, II., 79.
Salons, celebrity of the, I., 134.
Senatus Consulte, decree of, II., 373.
Sicard, Abbé, release of, II., 241.
Sieyès, Abbé, influence of, II., 19, prediction by, 64, resignation of, 262.
Soissons, gateway of, I., 120.
Staël, Madame de, her admiration for her father, II., 57, fearlessness of, 94, attempts to leave Paris, 148, intrigues of, 203, sketch of, 236, Napoleon's dislike of, 358, at Coppet, 359.
States General, assembly of the, II., 6.
Talleyrand-Périgord, Charles Maurice de, character of, I., 150, his sentiments toward Voltaire, 248; his hatred of the directory, II., 203, his reception of Napoleon, 220, establishment of, 233, new position of, 262, entertainments by, 340.
Tallien, Madame, vanity of, II., 211, anecdote of, 225.
Talma, art of, II., 113.
Tencin, Madame de, *salon* of, I., 134.
Tennis Court, oath of the, II., 21.
Terray, Abbé, as financier, I., 65.
Théâtre Français, condition of, I., 216.
Tiers État, at the assembly, II., 13, demands of the, 16.
Trafalgar, victory of, II., 347.
Treaty of Campo-Formio, II., 204.
Trianon, Petit, description of, I., 32.
Tuileries, royalty at the, II., 105, attack on the, 144, Napoleon at the, 183.
Turgot, appointment of, I., 65, his advice on corn monopoly, 107, influence of, 115, reforms instigated by, 116, M. Necker's

attacks upon, 146, enmity of royal family against, 147, dismissal of, 152.
Vaudreuil, Comte de, manners of, I., 213, his intimacy with the Duchesse de Polignac, 291.
Vauguyon, Duc de, his hatred of Abbé Vermond, I., 35.
Vergennes, Madame de, ball given by, I., 350.
Vergennes, Monsieur de, recalled to France, I., 66, diplomacy of, 241, responsibility resting upon, 276, death of, 354.
Vermond, Abbé, influence of, I., 33, his attitude toward Voltaire, 248, jealousy of, 291, deference paid to, 357; hatred of people for, II., 51, flight of, 52.
Versailles, attack at, I., 107, gaieties at, 108, description of, 163, Joseph's impressions of, 197; on the 5th of May, 1789, II., 4, during early part of revolution, 72, march of women upon, 87, 94.
Villeneuve, Admiral, taken prisoner, II., 347.
Vincent, artistic powers of, II., 110.
Voltaire, return to France of, I., 245, reception of, 247, popularity of, 249, ovation in honor of, 252, death of, 254.
Vrillière, Duc de, appointment of, I., 66.
Whitworth, Lord, characterisation of, II., 303.

www.ingramcontent.com/pod-product-compliance
Lightning Source LLC
Chambersburg PA
CBHW030212170426
43201CB00006B/67